TEN ZEN OXEN

BOOK COVER SYMBOLISM
Sky Blue • Inner Truth/Inner Peace/Freedom
Emerald Green • Vitality/Harmony/Compassion
Sea Blue • Depth/Trust/Spiritual Realization
White • Purity/Simplicity/Spaciousness

By The Author

LAO TZU'S *TAO TE CHING*
Psychotherapeutic Commentaries
A Wayfaring Counselor's Rendering
of The Tao Virtuosity Experience
[Regent Press, 2016]

CHUANG TZU'S *NEI P'IEN*
Psychotherapeutic Commentaries
A Wayfaring Counselor's Rendering
of The Seven Interior Records
[Regent Press, 2017]

LIEH TZU'S *HSING SHIH SHENG*
Psychotherapeutic Commentaries
A Wayfaring Counselor's Rendering
of The Nature of Real Living
[Regent Press, 2017]

LAO TZU'S TAO TE CHING
Soul Journeying Commentaries
A Sojourning Pilgrim's Rendering
of 81 Spirit Soul Passages
[Regent Press, 2018]

TEN ZEN OXEN
A Way-Showing Path of Enlightenment

Psychospiritual Commentaries

Raymond Bart Vespe

REGENT PRESS
Berkeley, California

Copyright © 2024 by Ray Vespe

Paperback
ISBN 13: 978-1-58790-675-6
ISBN 10: 1-58790-675-9

E-book:
ISBN 13: 978-1-58790-676-3
ISBN 10: 1-58790-676-7

Library of Congress Control Number: 2023946997

Manufactured in the United States of America
REGENT PRESS
www.regentpress.net
regentpress@mindspring.com

Contents

Dedication and Acknowledgement ... 1
Opening Caveat and Wisdom ... 3
Foreword ... 7
General Introduction ... 13
The Buddha and Buddhism ... 19
Ch'an Buddhism, Zen Buddhism and Zen ... 33
Ten Zen Oxen Introduction ... 47
10 Way-Stations of the Path of Enlightenment ... 55

The Awakening / Pre-Enlightenment ... 69

    1. Seeking the Ox – Way-Station One ... 70
        Recognizing and Acknowledging ... 72
        Original Illustration and Text ... 73
        Way-Showing Synoptic Comments ... 74
        Psychospiritual Commentary ... 77

    2. Tracking the Ox – Way-Station Two ... 84
        Exploring and Learning ... 86
        Original Illustration and Text ... 87
        Way-Showing Synoptic Comments ... 88
        Psychospiritual Commentary ... 89

    3. Glimpsing the Ox – Way-Station Three ... 94
        Illuminating and Experiencing ... 96
        Original Illustration and Text ... 97
        Way-Showing Synoptic Comments ... 98
        Psychospiritual Commentary ... 100

4. CATCHING THE OX – WAY-STATION FOUR ... 108
    Realizing and Understanding ... 110
    Original Illustration and Text ... 111
    Way-Showing Synoptic Comments ... 112
    Psychospiritual Commentary ... 113

THE TRANSFORMING / MID-ENLIGHTENMENT ... 119

5. TAMING THE OX – WAY-STATION FIVE ... 120
    Identifying and Cultivating ... 122
    Original Illustration and Text ... 123
    Way-Showing Synoptic Comments ... 124
    Psychospiritual Commentary ... 126

6. RIDING THE OX – WAY-STATION SIX ... 136
    Integrating and Practicing ... 138
    Original Illustration and Text ... 139
    Way-Showing Synoptic Comments ... 140
    Psychospiritual Commentary ... 141

THE LIBERATING / POST-ENLIGHTENMENT ... 149

7. FORGETTING THE OX – WAY-STATION SEVEN ... 150
    Assimilating and Emptying ... 152
    Original Illustration and Text ... 153
    Way-Showing Synoptic Comments ... 154
    Psychospiritual Commentary ... 155

8. FORGETTING THE SELF – WAY-STATION EIGHT ... 162
    Forgetting and Transcending ... 164
    Original Illustration and Text ... 165
    Way-Showing Synoptic Comments ... 166
    Psychospiritual Commentary ... 168

A WAY-SHOWING PATH OF ENLIGHTENMENT

9. RETURNING TO THE ORIGIN – WAY-STATION NINE...176
   Returning and Sourcing...178
   Original Illustration and Text...179
   Way-Showing Synoptic Comments...180
   Psychospiritual Commentary...182

10. BEING IN THE WORLD – WAY-STATION TEN...190
    Actualizing and Transmitting...192
    Original Illustration and Text...193
    Way-Showing Synoptic Comments...194
    Psychospiritual Commentary...196

CONCLUSION...207
TO BE PRESENT AS I-AM CHARACTERS...218
AFTERWORD...219
THIS-IS-IT / I-AM-THIS CHARACTERS...225
APPENDIXES
   ONE   TEN ZEN OXEN CHARACTERS...227
   TWO   WAY-STATION SUMMARIES...228
   THREE   THE PATH AND PLAY OUTLINED...232
   FOUR   CLASSIC OX-HERDING VERSIONS...236
   FIVE   A COMPARISON OF TEN STAGES...239
   SIX   CORRELATIONS OF TEN STAGES – 1...244
   SEVEN   CORRELATIONS OF TEN STAGES – 2...245
   EIGHT   TEN MENTAL ABIDINGS...246
   NINE   EGO-SELF'S PATH TO TRUE NATURE...248
   TEN   SOME ISSUES AND FEELINGS...251
I-AM AND JUST-THIS CHARACTERS...258
NOTES...259
A KOAN...264
TRUE NATURE CHARACTERS...265
EGO-SELF AND TRUE NATURE...266

Postscript ... 267
References ... 269
About the Author ... 273
Encore ... 276

Sanjen
The Three Origins

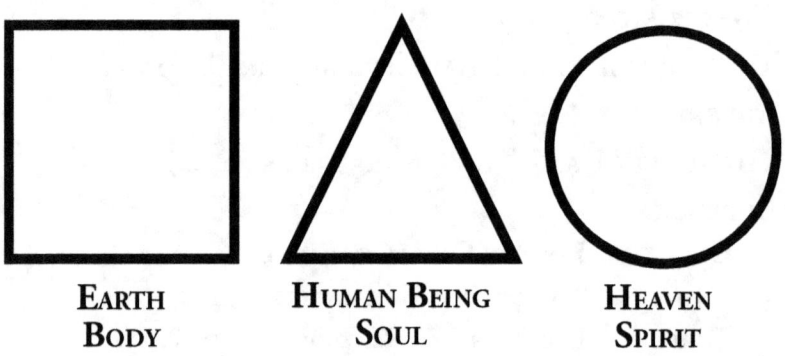

Earth / Body   Human Being / Soul   Heaven / Spirit

Dedicated to

My eight grandchildren. You hold the future of our society, world, civilization, species and planet in your caring hearts, open minds and capable hands. Make the very best of it and of yourselves in the time that you have, in the life that you live and in the Way that you journey.

Acknowledging of

My gratitude for the blessed bestowal of precious human life and the splendid gift of conscious human awareness.

Hindu, Taoist, Buddhist and Zen teachers, colleagues and friends; Haridas and Bina Chaudhuri, Alan Watts, Al Chung-liang Huang, Gia-fu Feng, Bishop Nippo Syaku, Shunryu Suzuki Roshi and Deng Ming-Dao.

California Institute of Integral Studies and John F. Kennedy University former graduate students and now friends; Roger and Susan, Bob, Ted, Art, Barry, Richard and Richard and Helen. Thank you for staying in touch and for your continuing love and support.

Daughters and sons-in-law, Cheryl and Shachar and Arianna and Ashley for just being who you are; for including me in your lives and for your ongoing acceptance, love, caring, patience, kindness, support and assistance.

Mark Weiman of Regent Press for creatively and proficiently formatting this book and for effectively and efficiently publishing it.

Thank you each and all for significantly, meaningfully and immeasurably contributing to my personal growth, professional development, waking up, ego-transformations, soul-journeying, spiritual evolving, creative expression and occasionally being True Nature.[1]

'Cogito ergo sum'.
'I think, therefore I am'.
RENE DESCARTES (1596-1650 CE).

'I am, therefore I think.'
EXISTENTIAL PHILOSOPHERS (20th C. CE).

"'I' am 'not', therefore 'I' think 'not'".
ANONYMOUS ZEN MASTER (Now CE).

PESSIMIST – *'The glass is half empty'.*

OPTIMIST – *'The glass is half-full'.*

ANONYMOUS ZEN STUDENT –
'The glass is half-empty'.
'The glass is half-full'.
'The glass is both half-empty and half-full'.
'The glass is neither half-empty and half-full'.

ANONYMOUS ZEN MASTER –
'There is no 'glass''.

Dear Reader –
Sit
Breathe
Relax
Enjoy
– Dear Author

Opening Caveat and Wisdom

From **Lao Tzu's** (6th Century BCE)
Tao Te Ching.
[Tr. this author]

Tao spoken of is not eternal Tao.
[Passage 1]

Those who speak may not know.
Those who know may not speak.
[Passage 56]

True words are not always beautiful.
Beautiful words are not always true.
[Passage 81]

From **The Buddha's** (563-483BCE)
Eightfold Path Perfections

Right speech — true, kind, timely words
without gossip, slander.

From **Chuang Tzu's** (365-286 BCE)
The Chuang Tzu
[Tr. Burton Watson]

Great words are clear and limpid.
Little words are shrill and quarrelsome.
Words have something to say.
Speech has no constancy.
[Chapter 2]

Do not transmit words of exaggeration.
[Chapter 4]

Lofty words make no impression on the minds of the crowd.
Superior ones gain no hearing. Vulgar ones are the majority.
[Chapter 12]

The words of the sages...chaff and dregs of the men of old.
[Chapter 13]

Those who know don't speak. Those who speak don't know.
The sage practices the teaching that has no words.
Truly great words; complete, universal, all-inclusive...
point to a single reality.
[Chapter 22}

I have heard of the speech and the debate that are not spoken...
words come to rest at the place of no-understanding...
applying names is inviting trouble.
[Chapter 24]

Community words are general terms or concepts that subsume
a number of differing particulars bringing things together
to attain general acceptance...share a common groundwork.
[Chapter 25]

Imputed words...are for the purpose of exposition...repeated
words...are to put an end to argument...goblet words...
harmonize all things in Heavenly Equality...we must have
no-words...words that are no-words.
[Chapter 27]

Goblet words...pour out endless changes, repeated words
give a ring of truth and imputed words impart greater depth.
[Chapter 33]

Words exist because of meaning. Once you've gotten the
meaning, you can forget the words.
Where can I find human beings who have forgotten words
so that I can have a word with them?.
[Chapter 26]

A WAY-SHOWING PATH OF ENLIGHTENMENT

From **Seng-t'san's** (d. 606 CE?)
Faith in the Heart Verses.
[Tr. Richard Clarke]

To come directly into harmony with this reality
(the world of suchness and neither self nor other-than-self)
just say 'Not-two'...nothing is separate, nothing is excluded,
enlightenment is entering this truth.
[Verse 13]

Words! The Way is beyond language, for in it
there is no yesterday, no tomorrow, no today.
[Verse 16]

This book contains a great number of words throughout which have been thoughtfully considered and carefully employed in the real spirit of true language.

Words are not just cultural nominalizations, lexical signifiers, conceptual abstractions and linguistic artifacts or proverbial fingers pointing to the bright, radiant moon and reflections mirrored in calm, clear water.

Words stand alone as real entities of, in and as themselves so and are not simply symbolic representations, identifying labels and verbal or written expressions of the realities and phenomena which they indicate, name, define and describe.

Words and language come from the natural, evolutionary and developmental needs, desires, intentions and abilities to recognize, identify, organize, name and communicate realities. They inherently contain that original reality and order and comprise an interconnected and interwoven lattice-like structured network of meaning.

Words are alive and vibrate sounds and images at various auditory and visual frequencies, e.g., lower-dense-gross in the words of the perverse ('screw you...$@&%#!') and higher-clear-subtle in the sound of the universe ('AaaUuuMmm aka OM').

Our body, chakras, mind, consciousness, soul and Spirit resonate with the energies, vibrational frequencies and Hz levels of music, songs, chants and hymns and is why they are so integrating, balancing, harmonizing, calming, healing, inspirational and uplifting. Such sounds and their images are a surrounding energy field and aura that preserve the original space of absolute darkness, silence and emptiness from which they issue and come to light and sound and to which they return or from which they never have departed.

As such, words intrinsically embody (or 'en-word'), immediately convey and directly transmit the original vitality, energies, veracity, meaning and power of the source from which they originate and of the phenomena that they form and 'name' for use in spoken and written communicating.

Words can be meditatively 'reverse engineered' in conscious awareness, enabling listeners and readers to return to and to veridically experience the original reality and vibrancy of particular phenomena and also to intuit and feel the intentionality and vitality of speakers and writers when they originally spoke and wrote them.

From simple collective primitive gestures, vocalizations, utterances and expressions to more complex illuminating sacred texts, mantras, chants and hymns; language is a splendid gift, faculty, resource, opportunity and conveyance of and for our blessed bestowal and precious treasure of conscious human incarnation, awareness and relatedness.

Words spoken and written by human beings in the real spirit of true words simultaneously contain, preserve and reveal the darkness of, in and as Light; the silence of, in and as Sound, the emptiness of, in and as Form and the beautifully radiant spectrum and flowing streaming between them. Like now?.........Yes, like right now!......... See?

Foreword

After having explored Existential-Phenomenological Philosophy and Humanistic-Transpersonal Psychology, my consciousness naturally dovetailed with spiritual traditions of 'The East'. Attending a San Francisco presentation by Alan Watts in the late 1960s, I became aware of the California Institute of Asian Studies (CIAS), later named the California Institute of Integral Studies (CIIS), and became a faculty member, doctoral student and counseling supervisor in 1972. (No 'conflicts of interest' in those days, particularly at an educational institution professing 'integralism'.)

When teaching a graduate psychology course entitled 'Eastern Sutras and Integral Counseling', I included *The Ten Ox-Herding Pictures* in course materials. Students found them extremely useful as a way of becoming and being more conscious about 'stages' of the path to awakened, enlightened and liberated human being and living.

I cautioned students not to necessarily understand the ten 'stages' as discrete, linear, sequential and hierarchical and, given the multidimensionality and simultaneity of our consciousness, to rather consider them: 1) as co-existing, co-equal, circular, spiraling, overlapping and interwoven focuses of entering and abiding in the whole continuum of the path of enlightenment and 2) as dependent upon what particular interconnected aspect of conscious awareness is being focused on and worked with, e.g., ontological/being, mental/thinking, emotional/feeling, volitional/acting or relational/interacting.

Nevertheless, there still is a progressively developing direction and continuum overall. The 'stages' can be considered as guideposts, guidelines and guideways (defined as 'signs, indicators, channels or tracks for controlling or directing the line of motion of something'), i.e., as Way-markers, Way-guides and Way-stations along the path of enlightenment.

I also reminded students that *The Ten Ox-Herding Pictures* and 'stages' probably depicted the best 'concepts', (along with salvation, deliverance, resurrection and reincarnation) that our ego-self could 'think up', i.e., the existence, awareness, realization, attainment and actualization of enlightenment; and that 'knowing' the concepts was, of course, not 'having' or 'being' the experience. But, like 'menus are not the meals' and 'maps are not the territories', the conceptualized 'stages' are useful for making nourishing choices and orienting intended journeys.

During the 1970s; through taking courses and tutorials, studying sutras and texts, attending presentations, participating in workshops and retreats and practicing meditations, both at CIAS/CIIS and in the Greater SF Bay Area; I became familiar with the teachings and practices of the spiritual traditions of Hinduism; Vedanta; Yoga; Tantra; Kashmir Shaivism; Sufism; Theravada, Mahayana, Vajrayana, Ekayana, Ch'an and Zen Buddhism and Taoism.

Fortunately, most of these spiritual traditions were the native ones of many CIAS/CIIS faculty members and I was blessed with the incredible opportunity and benefits of establishing and enjoying both a teacher-student and a collegial relationship with them.

My interests in Eastern spiritual traditions were primarily those of ancient Chinese Taoism and Ch'an/Zen Buddhism. Meetings, meditations and T'ai-Chi practices with Alan Watts, Al Chung-liang Huang, Gia-fu Feng, Bishop Nippo Syaku and Shunryu Suzuki Roshi helped to experientially solidify, integrate and actualize those interests as a Way of being and living that was meaningful, illuminating, awakening, self-transforming, liberating and life-changing.

During the 1980s, I participated in shamanic healing circles. Experiencing the oneness, pure consciousness, egolessness, openness and spaciousness induced by a variety of 'plant medicines' and natural psychotropic substances was valuable in validating, corroborating, reinforcing and expanding meditatively-facilitated spiritual experiences and was equally as meaningful, illuminating, awakening, self-transforming, liberating and life-changing.

Since retiring from teaching, training and supervising in 1992 and clinical directorships and private counseling practice in 2006; I authored four books integrating the wisdom of Lao Tzu's *Tao Te Ching*, *The Chuang Tzu* and *The Lieh Tzu* with psychotherapeutic practice, soul-journeying and spiritual development that were published between 2016 and 2018.[2]

Recently, I was reflecting upon the extensive amount and quality of human consciousness, commitment, effort, realization and enlightenment that have historically gone into awakening to, teaching, recording, translating and transmitting the spiritual knowledge, truths, wisdom, meditations and practices contained in the ancient scriptures, sutras and texts of India, China, Tibet and Japan.

I became aware of how much I valued and appreciated *The Ten Ox-Herding Pictures* during my own spiritual path-making and Wayfaring journey. So, I decided to create a book that included the two most popular sets of original pictures, text renditions, related *Tao Te Ching* quotes, Way-showing synoptic comments and psychospiritually-oriented commentaries.

I titled this book '*Ten Zen Oxen*' instead of the usual titles of '*The Ten Ox-Herding or Ox-Tending Pictures*'. I deleted the 'herding' or 'tending' designations in the main title; since seeking, tracking, glimpsing, catching and taming the Ox end with Picture Five; the Ox is united with and ridden home with the Ox-herder in Picture Six and is absent, assimilated and 'forgotten' by the Ox-herder in Picture Seven.

However, I realize that 'herding' and 'tending' are the cultivating and practicing; of even a realized, internalized, embodied, assimilated and 'forgotten' enlightened True Nature; that never really end and are ongoing in new, transformed, deeper and more expanded and complete ways; since our living naturally, continually and endlessly presents us with ample opportunities to refine, reconstitute, embody and actualize True Nature.

This is respectively shown in Pictures Eight, Nine and Ten; where the Ox-herder transcends ego-self and 'forgets' True Nature, returns to the Source and Origin and enters the world; naturally, wisely, compassionately and generously vitalizing, energizing, assisting, benefiting and often awakening, enlightening and liberating fellow human beings.

The classic *Ten Ox-herding Pictures* are here considered as Way-stations or as Way-marking guideposts and Way-showing guidelines along a Way-making path toward and to becoming and being an awakened, enlightened and liberated human being that have come to fruition in the spiritual tradition of Zen Buddhism. Accordingly, this book is titled and subtitled '*Ten Zen Oxen: A Way-Showing Path of Enlightenment*'.

It has been a wonderful reflecting, affirming, integrating and consummating experience; further refining, clearing, emptying and opening my consciousness and allowing the book, for the most part, to 'write itself' and for me to 'receive' and to 'record' what 'came to mind'. I am grateful for the opportunity to have 'collaborated' in its writing and to share it with you.[3]

Most importantly; from the center of my heart, the depth of my soul and the vast spaciousness of Spirit, pure consciousness, True Nature and 'I-Am'; I am grateful for and appreciative of you, its readers.

I hope that you find the book of some value and meaning, inspiration and encouragement and use and benefit for and in your own spiritual Wayfaring journey toward becoming and being awakened, illuminated, realized, enlightened, transformed and liberated One, Original, Absolute, Ultimate, Essential, Inborn True Nature.

A WAY-SHOWING PATH OF ENLIGHTENMENT

We all are sacred, valid and precious human beings, spiritual kinfolk, soul-journeying companions, Wayfaring friends and sojourning pilgrims in This 'Now-Here' ('no-where') present moment of synchronous time and current abode of coterminous space.

As such; we critically, urgently and courageously need: 1) to equally, empathically and intimately respect, include and understand one another; 2) to generously, wisely and compassionately engage, join and cooperate with each other; 3) to whole-heartedly inspire, support and encourage one another and 4) to beneficially assist, guide and reinforce each other in realizing and actualizing the reality, light, truth, unity, dignity and beauty of enlightened True Nature and its openness, spaciousness, peacefulness, freeness, happiness, playfulness and joyfulness. Many thanks and blessings to you!

<blockquote>
The Pathway of True Nature is the goal.
The Journey of True Nature is the destination.
The Wayfarer *as* True Nature is the arrival.
</blockquote>

Raymond Bart Vespe
Scotts Valley, California
Winter Solstice 2023

INITIAL QUESTIONS OF OUR EGO-SELF

Pre-Enlightenment/Awakening
1. Can I become and be enlightened True Nature?
2. Can I find a pathway to enlightened True Nature?
3. Can I glimpse the reality of enlightened True Nature?
4. Can I hold the reality of enlightened True Nature?

Mid-Enlightenment/Transforming
5. Can I continue cultivating enlightened True Nature?
6. Can I continue practicing enlightened True Nature?

Post-Enlightenment/Liberating
7. Can I forget enlightened True Nature as a 'thing'?
8. Can I forget my ego-self as a 'object-being'?
9. Can I return to the original Source of everything?
10. Can I enter the world, actualize and transmit enlightened True Nature and enliven, benefit and possibly awaken fellow human beings?

General Introduction

As human beings, we create our own 'reality'. True reality is 'in here' and relative reality is 'out there' in the material, physical world of things, objects, events and affairs. Also, we 'are' whatever we think. Energy follows our thought, form follows our energy and form is our experienced objective 'reality' with which we typically identify as our ego-self in our ego-mind. Positive experiences follow positive thinking and energy and negative experiences follow negative thinking and energy. What and how we are thinking creates, determines, constitutes, manifests and expresses what and how we experience.

Zen is the fruition of the spiritual tradition of Buddhism. It teaches that: 1) Ultimate Reality, Tao, the Buddha, Buddha-Nature, Buddha-Dharma, Buddha-Mind, Buddha-Eye; 2) our One, Original, Absolute, Ultimate, Essential, Inborn True Nature and 3) spiritual awakening, illumination, realization, enlightenment, transformation, liberation and actualization are all 'realities' that are created by and are present to, in and *as* our consciousness.

Objects, events and affairs; ourselves and other human beings; our thoughts, feelings and actions; the ordinary experiences of our everyday living, etc. are also 'things' that occur as the 'objective' phenomena and mental concepts of our 'subjective' conscious awareness. Both outwardly and inwardly, we also 'are' what we see, are aware of and experience and to whom and to what we relate, etc..

Who we are is what we identify with as it arises and appears in our awareness (and we need go no further than words that begin with the letter 'a') e.g.,

1. What we are aware of, alert to, attend to, acknowledge, appreciate and admire.
2. What we accept, approve of, agree with, affirm,

allow, associate and affiliate with.
3. What we adjust, accomodate, adapt and accede to; align and accord with and assimilate.
4. What we assume, allege, avow, attest to, adopt, advocate for, aspire to and aim for.
5. What we ask for, anticipate, assert, achieve, accomplish, attain, acquire and actualize.

Also, we are that which we seek. Apropos of the classic *Ten Ox-Herding Pictures;* the Ox of awakening, enlightenment and liberation is our One, Original, Inborn True-Nature which, essentially and ultimately, is not a 'lost object' either to be sought after as a 'goal' or to be found as an 'attainment'. One Zen Master characterizes the search for enlightenment as 'Riding the Ox of enlightenment looking for the Ox of enlightenment'.

However, we do not ordinarily experience our naturally being spiritually awakened, enlightened and liberated due to being exclusively and completely identified with our socially conditioned, separated, illusional, fictitious, collectively and consensually deluded, ignoring, obscuring and obstructing ego-mind and ego-self.

The classic *Ten Ox-Herding Pictures* have, for over one-thousand years, been used by masters and teachers in supporting, assisting, reinforcing, guiding and monitoring disciples and students on their path and in their practice and process toward becoming and being an awakened, enlightened and liberated human being.

Seeking answers to questions, solutions to problems, settlements of issues, resolutions of conflicts and the uniting of dualistic separations, divisions, dichotomies, antitheses and oppositions; usually focus on an 'outside' source via requests, entreaties, supplications, prayers, etc.. However, these 'askings' are fundamentally acknowledgements and affirmations of desires for some kind of 'positive' effect, result or change to occur.

There are differences between 1) our asking an external source for something desired, 2) our clearly and fully acknowledging what it is that we really inwardly desire and 3) our affirming that, at a deeper level, we already are or have it but are not or may not be aware of it, e.g.,

1. **Asking** – Dear 'other' x (or X), e.g., please let me be, know, do, have, etc. some y.
2. **Acknowledging** – 'I', as x, e.g., truly and deeply want to be, know, do, have, etc. some y.
3. **Affirming** – 'I', as x, e.g., already am or may be being, knowing, doing, having, etc. some y.

Asking for what is needed or wanted; relinquishes, abdicates, externalizes and projects our personal inner creative power in the 'nots, won'ts, don'ts, can'ts and didn'ts' of an impossible past and the 'musts, oughts, coulds, mights and maybes' of a possible future.

Acknowledging clearly identifies, energizes, intensifies and potentiates what is needed or wanted by bringing the personal inner creative power of our consciousness into the 'cans and wills' of an immediate future.

Affirming is contacting, owning, solidifying, activating and being our personal creative power and to have, at a deeper level and without realizing it, already actualized what is needed or wanted in the 'ams, ises, ares, yess and ahas' of an actual present reality.

We need to be exactly aware of what it is that we are, in effect, really thinking and affirming. For example, covertly hidden within 'positive' thinking and affirming can be an underlying fear that has a stronger 'negative' energy charge and thus becomes the more dominant created 'reality', overriding, displacing or blocking the overtly intended positive desire, thought or affirmation.

Along with our precious human incarnation, human being and human life; our consciousness is a blessed bestowal that carries with it the innate and intrinsic power to create, transform and heal our reality and experience. This has been evidenced, for example, in the visualizing, acknowledging and 'befriending' of cancer cells; fearlessly affirming a cancer-free body and the resultant remission of cancerous conditions.

Also, what happens with 'pain'? Pain naturally and immediately directs our consciousness to, and focuses our awareness on; an affected part, area, state, or condition of our body for the purposes of transforming and healing. Pain is like an automobile's dashboard 'warning light', alerting us to a deeper and more systemic issue. The awareness of pain can be a 'wakeup call' or a transforming, healing and curative event in itself that results in an amelioration of symptoms and/or the complete cessation of the condition that it signals.

One of the unfortunate results of being unaware of; or of ignoring and denying; the intrinsic creative, healing, corrective, transformative and restorative power of consciousness; is the pharmacological 'treatment' of symptoms only rather than deeper underlying systemic causes.

So-called 'Big Pharma' is another for-profit business enterprise and quasi-medical establishment that is an unwanted 'by-product' and unwelcome 'side-effect' of the historical American and industrial revolutions and their legacy of colonialism, capitalism, corporatism, collectivism, commercialism and consumerism.

The producing, packaging, promoting, purveying, marketing, prescribing and overpricing of drugs is, to quote another Zen Master, like 'selling water by the river'; instead of educating, encouraging, supporting and guiding human beings to discover and partake of the naturally occurring nourishing, sustaining and healing riverwater right in front of them. The negative side-effects and harmful interactions of many prescribed drugs are as bad as, if not worse than, the conditions they are purported to treat and their 'benefits' may not, in all reality and truth, outweigh their 'risks', as the 'authoritative' liturgy goes.

Zen cultivating and practicing, as a Way of human being and living, is the spirit of the Buddha's life and Buddha-Dharma teachings and the soul of the Buddhist tradition and Buddha-Dharma transmission that is 'straight from the heart'; concretely, directly and immediately whereby and wherein True/Buddha-Nature can be realized in momentary kenshos of an awakened and illuminated 'seeing into' it and as more extended satoris of the enlightened and liberated 'being' of it.

The Buddha's teachings reportedly were suited to the particular perceived nature, kind, quality, degree, level, extent and characteristics of the consciousness, development, understandings, abilities and 'readiness' of particular disciples and students. The same 'ethic' appears to be carried forward in the contemporary dissemination and practical usefulness of the wide array of available practices; whereby, for example, yoga, meditation, T'ai-Chi and Ch'i-Kung are advertised, promoted, marketed and taught as 'stress reduction', 'physical fitness', 'health-restoring', etc.; the beneficial need for which we all can appreciate.

When we open, direct and commit our consciousness to learning, healing and enlightening; everyone and everything in our experience naturally educates, transforms and liberates us. When we are at the place of being adequately prepared and sufficiently 'ready' on our spiritual Wayfaring path of discovery, transformation and enlightenment; synchronistically; a master or teacher may often 'appear' who is present and available to acknowledge, inspire, encourage, support, assist, reinforce, guide, monitor and confirm it.

Essentially, we all are; and have always been; pure and empty consciousness, clear and open awareness and the same One, Original, Inborn True Nature. While being that which we are seeking, i.e.; awakened, enlightened and liberated True Nature;

we are not usually aware of ourselves as such due to being completely and exclusively identified with our conditioned, separate, divided, dualistic, deluded, obscuring and obstructing ego-self and ego-mind and mistaking them for the True Nature and I-Am who we really, essentially and truly are.

At some point in our lives, and for a variety of unique reasons, this case of mistaken identity and the limitations of our fabricated, insubstantial, artificial, illusional, fictitious and suffering ego-self come to light; are often painfully revealed and initiate a search for a more awakened, enlightened and liberated way of being and living and one that brings with it more lasting peacefulness, freeness and happiness.

The Ten Ox-Herding Pictures portray the path leading from non-consciously, exclusively and completely identifying with our conditioned, finite, limited, unawakened, unenlightened and unliberated ego-self to consciously, inclusively and fully *being* unconditioned, infinite, limitless, awakened, enlightened and liberated True Nature.

<blockquote>
True Nature is all that is as it is.
Feelings, thoughts and actions,
questions, problems and conflicts,
enlightenment and liberation
are just different names
for its different forms.
</blockquote>

The Buddha and Buddhism[4]

Buddhism begins with Siddhartha Gautama who, after his awakening and enlightenment, becomes known as Sakyamuni, the Buddha, the Awakened and Enlightened One. He is born near the border of India and Nepal and lives, teaches and dies in India between 563 and 483 BCE. As his story goes; he is born a prince prophesied to succeed either in being a royal monarch or an enlightened Buddha. He lives a life of opulence in a royal castle; marries at the age of 16; has a son at the age of 29, at which time; he leaves his parents, wife and newborn son to see what life is like in the world outside of the palace.

Siddhartha observes four signs of a sick human being, an aged human being, a dead human being and a meditating human being and is struck by the suffering and sorrowing of human beings; the transiency of human life and the possibility of finding some peacefulness and freedom through world-renunciation, self-contemplation and attaining Nirvana; the complete 'blowing out' of the flames of desiring and the ending of the samsaric cycling of birth, death and rebirth.

Siddhartha embarks on a spiritual journey, as a wandering monk, searching for the ultimate truth of the self and reality of life. For the next six years or so, he learns from various teachers, experiences a variety of teachings and ascetic practices, but all of which fail to provide the spiritual illuminations and realizations that he is seeking.

At around the age of 35 years, Siddhartha becomes a solitary forest-dweller. He finds a fig tree (which came to be called the Bodhi Tree of Awakening located in Bodh Gaya, the spiritual center of Buddhism) under which he sits meditating for some forty days vowing to understand the nature of suffering.

During this time Siddhartha: 1) confronts and defeats Mara;

the personification of obscuring, threatening, seductive and obstructing worldy fears, passions, desires and temptations and 2) undergoes strict aceticism and endures extreme self-mortification, which he later abandons as being only physically emaciating and ultimately spiritually futile. He then accepts much needed nourishing food given him by a young girl.

Siddhartha emerges as a fully awakened and perfectly enlightened human being who has realized spiritual realities and truths and who has discovered a 'Middle Way' between the extremes of sensual indulgence and austere abstinence. He renounces his royal family lineage for the ancient lineage of Buddhas and identifies as Sakyamuni, the sage of the Sakya clan, the Buddha, the Awakened and Enlightened One.

As the Buddha, he vows to begin a path of teaching his spiritual insights and spreading the Dharma, the Law and wisdom, throughout India; which he fulfills for approximately forty-five years of giving sermons, performing miracles, generating monasteries, ordaining male and female disciples and lay-persons, bestowing arhatship and establishing spiritual communities/sanghas until his final journey of dying/parinirvana at the age of 80 years.

The Buddha reportedly realizes that the essence and truth of his enlightenment cannot be fully communicated or understood by the majority of human beings and suits the fundamentals of his learnings and teachings to fit the prevailing abilities of disciples, students and laypersons. He thus judiciously avoids discoursing and answering inquiries concerning the nature of metaphysical realities and, reportedly, maintains 'a noble silence' regarding them.

In the Buddha's final moments; he encourages followers: 1) to work on themselves and toward their own enlightenment with and through their own diligent effort, 2) to practice living the Dharma and Dharma teachings as the highest and finest homage to him, 3) to distribute his cremation ashes and 'relics' equally to the several communities present at his parinirvana and 4) to memorialize the several places where he is born, attains enlightenment and accepts nourishment, delivers his first sermon and where he is dying.

The Buddha's inner life is the history of the journey of the mind, heart and self of human being on the Dharma path of awakening, illumination, enlightenment, transformation and liberation from the characteristics, activities and limitations of the conditioned ego-self that lead to suffering in samsara; the wheel and unending cycling of birth, death and rebirth.

The basics of the Buddha's teaching have to do with: 1) renouncing worldly concerns, pursuits and pleasures; 2) not seeking name, status, fame, wealth and power; 3) not desiring, pursuing, acquiring, possessing, amassing and being attached to material goods and 4) the insubstantiality of 'I', the ego-self, the impermanence of phenomena and the pervasiveness of suffering.

The 'basics' also include: 1) cultivating a clear, empty and open mind free of illusions, ignorance, defilements, afflictions, fetters, deluded thoughts, misleading concepts, outer-directedness and external forms; 2) discovering and achieving insight into the dependent origination, mutually arising and interconnectedness of all beings and things; 3) realizing the inner treasure of one's own One Original Inborn True Nature; 4) finding refuge in the triple jewels of the Buddha, Dharma/Truth and Sangha/Spiritual Community and 5) steadfastly walking the path and earnestly living the reality and truth of Dharma, the cosmic law, behavioral norms and the phenomena of the human mind and the world.

Buddha-Dharma is the truth, law and teachings of the historical Buddha based upon his awakening and enlightenment and of the path leading to their attainment through teachings and meditation. It is generally synonymous with the basis of everything, Buddhism in general as a spiritual tradition and as True/Buddha-Nature. In Zen Buddhism, Buddha-Dharma can be directly transmitted and immediately realized as one's own enlightenment experience and not through exclusively rational and conceptual explanation and understanding.

True/Buddha-Nature or Buddhahood is the one, original, absolute, ultimate, essential, immanent and inborn nature of all beings that is immutable, infinite and eternal. It is our birthright by virtue of being human beings and is our highest end that can be awakened to, reached and realized in and as enlightenment. In Zen Buddhism, every human already is True/Buddha-Nature that is not an object to have or a goal to attain but is only a reality and truth that is awakened to and realized spontaneously and immediately through direct transmission and enlightened cultivating and practicing.

Dharmata is the nature of the dharmas, the basis of everything and is synonymous with Buddha-Nature/Tathata, the such-coming, such-being and such-going of the Buddha. Tathagata is the thus-come, thus-gone, thus-perfected title of the Buddha and Tathagata-Garbha is the 'germ' of the Tathagata that is the unconditioned, ultimate and essential reality dwelling in all sentient beings. Dharmadhatu is the 'realm' of Dharma, True/Buddha-Nature/Tathata and Dharmata is the empty/shunyata, all-pervading, all-encompassing open space/akasha and the totality in which all things and phenomena arise, dwell and pass away.

Some of the Buddha's principal teachings are the following:
Conditioned arising/pratitya-samutpada; which is the doctrine that all phenomena of human existence are interdependent, mutually condition each other and are involved in entangling human beings in suffering: 1) the relativity, unreality and emptiness of existence and 2) samsara, the endless cycling of birth, death and rebirth. Understanding this doctrine is fundamental to realizing buddhahood.

The twelve-fold chain of causation/origination comprising conditioned arising:

1) ignorance/avidya, 2) mental formations/samskara, 3) consciousness/vijnana, 4) name and form/namarupa, 5) the six sense organs/shadayatana, 6) contact with their environment/sparsha, 7) sensation/vedana, 8) craving/trishna, 9) clinging/upadana, 10) becoming/bhava, 11) birth/jati and 12) old age and death/jara-maranam, which relate to past, present and future temporal life.

The five aggregates/skandhas of: 1) bodily form/rupa, 2) sensation/vedana, 3) perception/ samjna, 4) mental constructs/samskara and 5) consciousness/vijnana, all of which constitute the illusional ego and personality and which involve desires and attachments that bring about human suffering. The characteristics of skandhas are birth, old age, death, duration and change and are without essence, impermanent, empty and ridden with suffering.

The three conditions or characteristics of human existence:

1. Anicca/anitya – all phenomena are conditioned, impermanent, transient, ephemeral, not fixed and constantly changing. All beings and things arise, persist for a time and pass away.

2. Anatta/anatman – the 'I'/self/personality is unreal, insubstantial and only the aggregates of body, feelings, perceptions, thoughts and consciousness.

3. Dukkha/duhka – all is suffering, unsatisfactoriness, disease and sorrow: 1) due to partial, limited, false, ignorant, erroneous and deluded mental views and separations, divisions, dualities, contraries, oppositions, desires and attachments and 2) due to being lost and aimlessly wandering in samsara, craving and clinging to impermanent things.

The Four Noble Truths/*arya satya*:

1. Dukkha – life is the suffering and sorrow of impermanence and transiency.
2. Samodaya – the origin and cause of suffering is attachment and being bound to desiring, craving and thirsting/tanha/trishna, grasping and clinging.
3. Nirodha – the cessation, elimination and end of suffering is through non-attachment and nirvanic liberation from desiring, craving and thirsting, grasping and clinging.
4. Magga – the 8-fold path; the way and means of attaining liberation and leading to the cessation, elimination and end of suffering.

The 8-Fold Path/*asthangika-marga*:

1. Samma-Ditthi – right views, outlooks, ideas, understandings. Pure vision of the 4 Noble Truths, the non-individuality of existence/anatman and the suffering nature of human existence.
2. Samma-Sankappa– right thought, aspiration, purpose, intention, determination, resolve. To stay on the path of renunciation, non-harming and perfection.
3. Samma-Vacha – right speech; kind, true and timely words without gossip and slander.
4. Samma-Kammanta – right action and behavior. Work as an offering of love and devotion.
5. Samma-Ajiva – right livelihood and vocation. Not evil and harmful but good and helpful.
6. Samma-Vayama – right effort. Cultivating the karmically wholesome and not the unwholesome.
7. Samma-Sati – right mindfulness, remembrance, watchfulness, attentiveness, alertness, self-knowledge. Watchfulness and mindfulness of feeling, thinking, the path and in life.
8. Samma-Samadhi – right relationship, concentration, contemplation, self-transcendence. Blissful union and communion embracing both the physical and spiritual dimensions

(The 'Middle Way'). The highest state of consciousness wherein mind, self and objects are completely one. Full awakening, deep meditative absorption and pure consciousness of peace and joy. Joy disappears. Consciousness of 'I'-sense disappears. Samadhi itself and nirvana disappear. No consciousness, experience or objects. Perfect void. No coming-going, rising-falling, standing-moving, etc..

The Ten Transcendent Perfections or Virtues/Paramitas that reach the other shore:

1) generosity, 2) discipline, 3) patience, 4) energy or effort, 5) meditation, 6) wisdom, 7) right means, 8) vow, 9) manifesting the ten powers/dashabala (see Appendix Six) and 10) knowing the true definition of all dharmas. Anusati is contemplation of the Buddha, Dharma and Sangha, discipline, generosity, human beings, the body, death, the breath and peace.

Succinctly put, Buddha's principal teachings are:

1) liberation from suffering due to the belief in an ego-self and permanence, 2) the cessation of ignorance and false views, craving and attachment, pride, greed, fear, hatred and anger; and 3) the ending of the samsaric cycling of births, deaths and rebirths; i.e., of the kleshas which are the defilements, passions, afflictions, fetters and the unwholesome roots of desire, hatred and delusion of the ego-self that obscure the mind, bind one to samsara and obstruct the enlightened realizing of nibbana/nirvana, the complete departure from samsara and the consequent entry into the awareness of one's limitless identity with the absolute without distinction between samsara and nirvana.

Also:

1) practicing 'mindfulness' meditation/vipassana/vipashyana and 2) freedom from accruing and inheriting more 'bad' karma by purifying the mind, doing good and right works and

living the ten perfections which result in entering the streaming of the reality and the truth of Dharma and finding peace, fulfillment and happiness within one's own heart-mind and living one's own illuminated, radiant and True/Buddha-Nature in one's lifetime in the midst of the world.

During the Buddha's life, his Dharma teachings spread throughout India and, following his death, bodhisattvas and disciples promulgate and carry forward the Dharma and numerous sutras, scriptures and texts are written, shared and brought to neighboring Asian countries.

The voluminous wealth of wisdom and comprehensive understanding of the nature and truths of human being and experiencing; the extensive, profound and deeply-penetrating analyses of how the mind is constituted and the way it works and what enlightenment is and how it can be attained are unparalleled in the historical spiritual, religious, philosophical and psychological literatures of humankind.

Three major Buddhist traditions that develop are those of: 1) Theravada/The Doctrine of the Elders or Hinayana/The 'Lesser' Vehicle, primarily in India, Burma/Myanmar, Sri Lanka, Thailand, Cambodia and Laos; 2) Mahayana/The 'Greater' Vehicle, primarily in India, China, Taiwan, Singapore, Japan, South Korea and Viet Nam and 3) Vajrayana/The Diamond or Thunderbolt Vehicle, primarily in Tibet, Nepal, Bhutan and Mongolia.

Other branches and schools of Mahayana Buddhism in China and Japan are, e.g., Ekayana/One Vehicle, Pure Land, Yogacara, Nichiren, Kegon and Tendai and of Vajrayana Buddhism, e.g., Shingon in Japan. Ch'an/ch'an-na Buddhism originates in China as a syncretic development of Indian Mahayana Buddhism, Yogacara Buddhism and Chinese Taoism and becomes Zen/zenna Buddhism, primarily in Japan and South Korea.

1) The Buddha and Theravada/Hinayana Buddhism are the seed-planting and rooting of Buddhism; its source and origin, its establishing and instituting and its ground, foundation and body.

2) Mahayana and Vajrayana Buddhism are the cultivated-growing and blossoming of Buddhism; its refining and furthering, its evolving and expanding and its flowering, flourishing and heart.

3) Ch'an and Zen Buddhism are the ripened-fruiting and nourishing of Buddhism, its culminating and perfecting, its realizing and accomplishing and its sustaining, supporting and soul.

4) 'Zen' (where the '-ism' of 'Buddhism', the '-ology' of 'Buddhology' and even 'the Buddha' as 'concepts', 'objects', 'entities' and 'things' fall away) is the Spirit and Way of concrete practice, direct transmission and immediately seeing into/kensho and being/satori; One Original Inborn True Nature free of historical, scriptural, ideological, dogmatic, institutional, sectarian and orthodox conventional 'Buddhism'.

Toward the end of his life, the Buddha reportedly gathers together numerous bodhisattvas for the purpose of selecting a Dharma heir and delivers what has come to be called 'The Flower Sermon'. At one point, the Buddha silently holds up a flower to the gathered learned bodhisattvas, the gestural act of which is smilingly acknowledged by only Mahakashyapa; who immediately understands it as the reality, truth, beauty and simplicity of the Dharma and is chosen as the Buddha's succeeding patriarch.

Some authorities surmise that this concrete, simple and direct transmission of the Dharma is the early beginning of Ch'an and Zen Buddhist teachings and practices with regard to how awakening, illumination, enlightenment, realization, transformation and liberation can spontaneously occur beyond sutras, teachings and words.

Buddhism and Buddhist teachings, in general, are characterized by the following; although there are some relative differences of emphasis between Theravada, Mahayana, Vajrayana, Ch'an and Zen Buddhist schools:

Veneration of the Buddha as a fully self-awakened, enlightened, realized, transformed and liberated human being and not as a supreme being.

The Three Bodies/trikaya of the Buddha:
   1. Dharma-Kaya – The Law Body, the transcendent ultimate reality, perfectly enlightened and true oneness nature of the Buddha and buddhas.
- in Vajrayana – the intermediate bardo state at the moment of dying.
- in Zen – cosmic consciousness, oneness of existence beyond all concepts.

   2. Sambhoga-Kaya – The Bliss Body, the enlightened enjoyment of samadhi and the embodied truth of the Buddha and buddhas.
- in Vajrayana – the intermediate bardo state of Supreme Reality.
- in Zen – the ecstasy of enlightenment, the Dharma-Mind of the Buddha.

   3. Nirmana-Kaya – The Transformation Body, the earthly emanation body of the Buddha and buddhas present in the world appearing to all to teach and guide.
- in Vajrayana – the intermediate bardo state of becoming reincarnated.
- in Zen – transformed, radiant Buddha-Body personified by the Buddha.

The Five Deadly Sins:
   1) killing a father, 2) killing a mother, 3) killing an arhat (the ideal human being in Theravada Buddhism who reaches nirvana and liberation from samsara), 4) shedding the blood of a buddha and 5) destroying the harmony of a sangha.

The Ten Evil Deeds:
   1) killing, 2) stealing, 3) committing adultery, 4) lying, 5) using immoral language, 6) gossiping, 7) slandering, 8) coveting, 9) venting anger and 10) holding wrong views.

The Ten Cardinal Precepts:
   1) not take life, 2) not steal, 3) not misuse sexuality, 4) not lie, 5) not indulge in drugs and alcohol, 6) not speak of the shortcomings of others, 7) not praise oneself and revile others, 8) not withold material and spiritual aid from others, 9) not indulge in anger and 10) not disparage the Three Treasures of the Buddha, Dharma and Sangha.

The Seven False Appetites:
   1) lust, 2) greed, 3) envy, 4) pride, 5) sloth, 6) wrath and 7) gluttony that result in a separation of spirit and body and are causes of death.

The Ten Fetters:
   1) belief in ego and individuality, 2) ignorance and delusion, 3) doubt and skepticism, 4) clinging to rules and rites, 5) desire and craving, 6) desires for corporeality and being, 7) desires for incorporeality and aversion to being, 8) hatred and anger, 9) pride and conceit, 10) resentment and excitability that hinder the mind, obstruct insight and prevent samadhi.

The Five Hindrances:
   1) desire, 2) ill will, 3) sloth, 4) doubt and 5) restlessness.

The Seven Latent Passions:
   1) sensual desire, 2) ignorance; believing that the illusions of the phenomenal world are the only reality, failing to recognize the true nature of the world as emptiness, obscuring True/Buddha-Nature by the conventional 'reality' of ego-self and the

creating of illusional appearances, 3) skepticism, 4) recalcitrance, 5) craving for existence, 6) arrogance and 7) false view; a belief in individual identity, the repudiation of karma, a belief in either eternalism or nihilism and doubting the truths of Buddhism.

The Three Unwholesome Roots:
   1) greed, 2) hatred and 3) delusion respectively overcome by 1) generosity, 2) kindness and 3) insight.

The Three Unenlightened Worlds:
   1) desire, 2) form and 3) no-form.

The Four Stages of the Supramundane Path:
   1) Stream-enterer, 2) Once-returner, 3) Never-returner and 4) Arhat, the ideal human being of Theravada Buddhism who attains nirvana.

The Four Pledges:
   1) to give oneself wholly to, and to take refuge in, the Three Treasures of Buddhism, 2) to keep the ten cardinal precepts, 3) to avoid evil and to practice goodness and 4) to strive toward the liberation of all sentient beings.

The Four Vows:
   1) to liberate the innumerable sentient beings, 2) to uproot the inexhaustible blind passions, 3) to enter the immeasurable Dharma gates and 4) to actualize the incomparable and unsurpassable True Way of the Buddha.

The Six Contemplations:
   1) the Buddha, 2) the Dharma, 3) the Sangha, 4) discipline, 5) generosity and 6) heavenly beings.

The Meditative Practices/bhavana of:
1) mindfulness/satipatthana observation of breath, body, feeling, mind, mental objects, 2) dwelling in tranquility/shamatha, 3) clear seeing/vipashyana, 4) contemplation/samapati, 5) concentration/samadhi and 6) absorption/dhyana.

The Three Liberations:
1) realization of emptiness, formlessness and passionlessness, 2) recognizing that self-nature, ego-self and dharmas are empty, and 3) recognizing that existence is unworthy of desiring due to its suffering.

The Four Realms of Enlightened Being:
1) Shravakas – arhats attaining by hearing and gaining insight into Buddha-teachings, 2) Pratyeka-buddhas – solitary attaining without a teacher and teaching, 3) Bodhisattvas – ideal earthly and transcendent beings in Mahayana Buddhism who, with wisdom and compassion, forsake their own nirvana to enlighten and liberate human beings, and 4) Buddhas who are fully awakened, enlightened, realized, transformed and liberated human beings.

And:
True/Buddha-Nature, Buddha-Mind and Buddha-Eye as: 1) essentially One, nondual and empty/shunyata state of pure consciousness devoid of an ego-self identifying with and attaching to conceptual thoughts, emotional desires, volitional habits and relational separations and 2) open and clear awareness of all of the 'things', beings, phenomena, taos and dharmas of human experience; just as they uniquely are in and of themselves and just as they are presencing themselves as the state of suchness/tathata of consciousness.

1) Theravada Buddhism tends more toward doctrinal teachings and meditative practices, 2) Mahayana Buddhism tends more toward the pureness, oneness, negation and emptiness of

consciousness, and 3) Vajrayana Buddhism; which is a Tantric or esoteric Buddhism; uses visualizations, mandalas, mudras, mantras and chanting in esoteric and exoteric practice. There are teachings about six realms of existence, i.e., 1) Hell, 2) Hungry Ghosts, 3) Beasts, 4) Fighting Demons, 5) Human Beings and 6) Heavenly Beings; any of which realm human beings are karmically presently living, have lived in previous incarnations or may live in future reincarnations.

Ch'an and Zen Buddhism regard Buddhist doctrines, teachings, meditations and practices as valuable foundations for awakening, enlightenment and liberation. However, zazen sitting meditation and koan problem solving are the main vehicles employed to concretely see into/kensho, fully experience and to completely be/satori One, Original, Absolute, Ultimate, Essential, Inborn True/Buddha-Nature. This occurs through a direct transmission from teacher to student, rather than through understanding traditional teachings and practicing conventional meditations.

As human beings, we all are potentially 'Buddhas'. A Buddha is an enlightened human being and a human being is an unenlightened Buddha. To become and be enlightened, we have to awaken to, realize and actualize One, Original, Ultimate, Essential and Inborn True/Buddha-Nature through sincere intention, great doubt, devoted faith, dedicated effort, determined cultivation and diligent practice.

The Buddhist Way of being a true human Buddha-Being who is living a true human Buddha-Life is fundamentally and essentially characterized by the qualities of acceptance and inclusion, equality and empathy, compassion and loving-kindness, wisdom and skill, availabilty and assistance and generosity and altruism; the unselfish commitment to the awakening, illuminating, enlightening and liberating of fellow human beings and to their benefit, well-being, peacefulness, happiness, freedom and joyfulness.

CH'AN BUDDHISM, ZEN BUDDHISM AND ZEN

Bodhidharma/Daruma (?-532 CE), the 28th and last Indian Buddhist patriarch, is historically identified as the first Chinese Ch'an/Zen patriarch and legendarily as originating Ch'an/Chan (an abbreviation of 'ch'an-na', the Chinese rendering and 'zenna', the Japanese rendering of the Sanskrit, 'dhyana'/meditation/absorption) Buddhism in 520 CE by bringing Mahayana scriptures, sutras and texts from India (most notably the Lankavatara Sutra) into China and introducing the reality of sunyata and the opening of the Buddha-Eye.

Bodhidharma, and/or his disciples, espouse four characteristics of Ch'an/Zen teachings and practice as: 1) a special transmission outside of scriptures, 2) no reliance upon words and letters, 3) a direct pointing to Buddha-Nature/Fo-hsing, and 4) seeing into that One, Original, Inborn True Nature and attaining Buddhahood.

Ch'an/Zen Buddhism rapidly develops and spreads as a compatible, interweaving, integrating and mutual influencing of the teachings of Mahayana, Madhyamika/Middle Way and Yoga Cara Buddhism and Chinese Taoism; the latter having numerous ideological and practical similarities, e.g., Ultimate Reality and One Origin/Tao; the truth and virtue of inner Tao-Nature/te; nondual bipolar unity/yin-yang; non-doing/wu-wei; non-being/wu, nothingness, and emptiness; egolessness; non-conceptualizing, desiring and attaching; simplifying and returning and the wise/sheng-jen, true/chen-jen and real/shih-jen sage.[5]

The Third patriarch in the Ch'an/Zen patriarchal lineage is Seng-T'san/Sosan (? – 606 CE) best known for his *Faith in the Heart-Mind Verses/Hsin-Hsin-Ming*, a highly valued and influential composition on 'the perfect Way', 'not-two', 'the oneness of the void', 'letting things be as the one suchness/tathata that they are' and an 'absolute faith in the timeless trusting heart-mind beyond external conditions and words'.

Hui-Neng/Eno, (638-713 CE), the Sixth Ch'an/Zen patriarch, authors *The Platform Sutra on the Treasure of the Law* and is instrumental in developing and disseminating Ch'an/Zen Buddhism. He is considered by some authorities to be the first 'real' Chinese founder of Ch'an/Zen Buddhism, free of both an idealistic and metaphysical imported Indian heritage and the superstitious and magical aspects of popular Chinese Taoism.

Hui-Neng rejects meditating and contemplating solely as ways to achieve liberation or salvation. He advocates a more direct, concrete and sudden satori awakening and realizing characteristic of a 'Southern' School: 1) seeing one's 'original face' before birth, 2) seeing into one's birthless and timeless True Nature, 3) not looking to or for externals, 4) realizing enlightenment non-conceptually in one's inner consciousness and 5) simplicity with 'nothing hidden'.

Hui-Neng emphasizes: 1) the reality that everything is a manifestation of Buddha-Nature which is neither defiled in passions and afflictions nor purified in awakening and enlightenment, 2) the unconditioned, absolute and nondual truth of emptiness, 3) the actuality of non-doing, 4) the goodness of human nature and 5) the instantaneous intuitive realizing of the united substance, form, function and purpose of enlightenment in the midst of being, living, relating and working in the world.

This is contrasted with the more intellectual, continuous and gradually unfolding process of attaining enlightenment through sitting quietly in meditative concentration characteristic of a 'Northern' School advocated by Shen-Hsiu/Jin Shu (? -706 CE). However, the dhyana/ meditation practice of the North can be considered as the 'body' of prajna/wisdom and the prajna/wisdom practice of the South as the 'use' of dhyana/meditation.

After Shen-Hsiu and Hui-Neng, the lineages of their contradictory approaches are furthered by disciples throughout the T'ang/Tang Dynasty (618-907 CE) and Sung/Song Dynasty (960-1280 CE). They are later reflected in 1) the tradition of Soto Zen Buddhism, primarily using zazen/tso-ch'an/sitting meditation, originated by T'sao/Cao Shan/Sozan (840-901 CE) and Tung/Dong Shan/Tozan (910-990 CE); (So-To, combining the first two letters of their names) and 2) the tradition of Rinzai Zen Buddhism, primarily using koans/kung-an/public notices, originated by Lin-Chi/Rinzai Gigen (?- 866 CE), a Dharma successor of Ch'an/Zen Master Huang-Po Xi-Yun/Obaku Kiun (d. 850 CE).

The Rinzai Zen Buddhist tradition is introduced in Japan in 1191 CE by Myoan Eisai (1141-1215 CE) emphasizing intuitive wisdom/prajna, sudden awakening/tongo and seeing into True Nature, which is Buddha-Mind. After a period of decline from the 1400s, the Rinzai tradition is revitalized by Zen Master Hakuin Zenji/Hakuin Ekaku (1686-1769 CE), who integrates koan and zazen practices and is, historically, considered to be the 'father' of modern Rinzai Zen Buddhism.

The Soto Zen Buddhist tradition is introduced in Japan in the 1200s CE by Dogen Kigen (1200-1253 CE) emphasizing 'just sitting'/shikantaza meditation practice/dhyana, gradual awakening/zengo and, also, seeing into True Nature and Buddha-Mind. These two traditions are the principal ones of present day Zen practice in Japan.

Both traditions essentially agree that all human beings: 1) have One, Original, Ultimate, Essential, Inborn True/Buddha-Nature; 2) are potentially the Buddha and 3) are able to discover and realize True/Buddha-Nature for themselves through cultivating, practicing and becoming awakened, enlightened and liberated in the same Way that the Buddha originally did and taught and that later evolves in Mahayana, Vajrayana, Ch'an and Zen Buddhist teachings and practices.

There is fundamental agreement in Rinzai and Soto Zen Buddhist traditions that Ultimate Reality is void and empty and can be realized by going beyond conceptual thinking and words to an awakened 'seeing into' One, Original, Inborn True Nature/kensho and to an enlightened '*being*' True Nature/satori; often through a direct Mind to Mind transmission from a master or teacher to a disciple or student.

Kensho is, in itself, a transient moment of experiencing 'seeing into' One, Original, Inborn True Nature that naturally follows (however, involving considerable concentration, discipline, time and effort) during Zen Buddhist meditative practices of either 'sitting' zazen or of 'solving' koans. Satori is a deeper and more ongoing '*being*' of kensho that is the awakened, enlightened, realized and liberated True Nature and pure, empty, illuminated and radiant consciousness.

Soto zazen 'sitting' involves wakeful attention; suspending all directed, discriminating, evaluating and judgmental thinking and allowing and observing contents, images, thoughts, feelings, etc. to enter, pass through and out of the streaming of conscious awareness without dwelling upon or attaching to them. Meditation alone, 'just sitting'/shikantaza; absorption with no contents, objects, concepts, words or goals in awareness; calms and opens awareness to a deep inner tranquility and a clear realization of One, Original, Inborn True Nature.

Rinzai koans are puzzling questions and conundrums that are used to snare, challenge, expose and ultimately defeat rational-logical thinking. Koans cannot be 'answered' or 'solved' by using discursive intellect and logical reasoning and; in the process of attempting, striving, struggling and failing to do so; can result in a momentary kensho awakening to True Nature. Question and answer dialogues/mondo between teacher and student are also used for the same purpose and with the same result.

The characteristics of the Soto and Rinzai Zen Buddhist traditions in their strictly orthodox forms, respectively speak to two

A WAY-SHOWING PATH OF ENLIGHTENMENT

general co-existing aspects of human being, the intellectual and the intuitive. The former focuses more on reason in the zendo and is more abstract, concentrative, contemplative and gradual and the latter focuses more on conduct in the world and is more concrete, insightful, practical and sudden.

In the former, e.g., practicing morality/sila, meditation/dhyana and wisdom/prajna lead to enlightenment and in the latter, enlightenment leads to living morality, meditation and wisdom. However, hard and fast distinctions between these two 'ways' and their relative emphases cannot be made.

The two apparently divergent Zen Buddhist traditions of Soto and Rinzai are often non-dualistically united in actual 'integral Zen' practice, since the original and pure Buddha-Dharma is the same Buddha-Dharma (and No-Buddha-Dharma!) in both traditions and there is no 'gradual' or 'sudden' dualistic distinction and contradiction in the Buddha-Dharma.

The 'eureka', 'aha', 'This is It' experience of awakening and enlightenment occurs spontaneously through both practices of 'sitting' zazen and 'solving' koans; when One, Original, Inborn True Nature is purely and clearly seen and realized either by a gradual wiping clean of the dust-covered mirror of the mind or an abrupt blowing away of the drifting obscuring clouds of the mind.

Ch'an/Zen Buddhism is a Way of human being and living and of awakening, illuminating and liberating the conditioned ego-self and its obscured, defiled and deluded mind; desiring, afflicted and attached heart; fettered, obstructed and erroneous will and separated, divided and dualistic being.

Zen Buddhism, in common with its historically preceding Indian and early Chinese Ch'an Buddhist teachings; holds that: 1) samadhi is a heightened nondual state of the deeply peaceful absorption of Mind in itself; 2) one-pointedness is intense but effortless centering concentration; and 3) nirvana is an unconditioned state of the extinction of ignorance and craving, liberation from the relative and changing world and the karmic cycle of endless death and birth/samsara and awakening to inner peace, freedom and happiness.

Emptiness/sunyata is the reality, form, substance, function and purpose of True/Buddha-Nature; pure objectless consciousness, the empty void and open matrix of the pure potentiality and constant originating and presencing of the suchness/tathata of all phenomena and their unique manifestations.

Emptiness is, thus, both no-'thing'ness and all-inclusive reality. The Buddha is the 'Thus-coming/Thus-being/Thus-going'/Tathagata of the emptiness/sunyata and the suchness/tathata of the reality and truth of human being that is possible for all human beings and actual for only some few.

'Radical' ('to the root') Zen masters, teachers, disciples, students and practitioners typically do not dwell upon concepts of the '-ism' of Buddhism, the '-ology' of Buddhology, the '-ist' of Buddhist or even of 'the Buddha'; all of which are foundational but ultimately found to be unnecessary for the concrete cultivating, useful practicing, direct transmitting and actual realizing of awakened and enlightened True Nature. Zen is the who, what, how and 'This' of the Way of real, true and actual human being, ordinary experiencing and everyday living.

Four common Zen principles are:

1) the unreality and insubstantiality of the ego-self/'I', 2) the dependent origination, mutual arising, interconnectedness and interdependence of everything, 3) recognition that mental discriminations and delusions and emotional desires and attachments are the source of human suffering, and 4) realization that human perception and cognition are erroneous and misleading and obscure and obstruct directly and concretely experiencing an awakening to, and a realizing of, enlightened consciousness; the awareness and being of One, Original, Inborn True/Buddha-Nature/busso and True/Dharma-Nature/hosso.

A WAY-SHOWING PATH OF ENLIGHTENMENT

Four common Zen vows are:

1) to save all living beings, 2) to eliminate ignorant delusions and attached passions, 3) to learn, but ultimately not be attached to, teachings and 4) to embody and fulfill the Buddha-Dharma and Way of the Buddha and buddhas.

Zen and Zen practice are synonymous with Nature, Tao/Way, the Buddha, being itself, living itself, everyday life itself and ordinary experience itself. Being a real and true human being is: 1) not being separate from Nature, human nature and life just as they are, and 2) being one with fellow human beings, creatures, the environment, world, planet and universe.

As previously noted, Zen is, as first expounded by Bodhidharma and/or his disciples:

1. A direct transmission of Buddha-Nature outside of traditional sutras and teachings.
2. No founding or dependence upon words or concepts, e.g., doctrines, creeds, dogmas.
3. Direct pointing to One, Original, Absolute, Ultimate, Essential, Inborn True Nature.
4. Seeing into/kensho and being/satori True Nature and reaching Buddhahood.

The Three Pillars of Zen are:

1) great faith, 2) great doubt, and 3) great determination, resolve or perseverance.

Ten Zen Precepts are:

1) no killing, 2) no stealing, 3) no misuse of sex, 4) no lying, 5) no drugs, 6) no speaking of the faults of others, 7) no praising of self while abusing others, 8) no sparing of Dharma assets, 9) no indulgence in anger and 10) no slandering of the three treasures of the Buddha, Dharma and Sangha.

Five Types of Zen are for:

1) improving the body and health, 2) following along with teachings outside of Buddhism, 3) attaining one's own inner peace, 4) self-realizing and actualizing of enlightenment in daily living, and 5) realizing True/Buddha-Nature in everyone and everything.

Five Degrees of Enlightenment are:

1) realizing 'hen'/the relative and phenomenal, attributes and differences of ego-self in the midst of 'sho'/the absolute and fundamental, emptiness and oneness of True Nature, 2) realizing sho in the midst of hen, 3) seeing the oneness and emptiness coming out of sho and hen; 4) entering the in-betweenness and suchness of sho and hen and 5) arriving in the in-betweenness and suchness of sho and hen and the interpenetration and identity of emptiness and form in its highest uniqueness.

In Zen practice; there is a direct pointing to, and transmitting of, the reality and truth of teachings independent of scriptures, sutras and texts; spontaneously, immediately and completely, in tutelage and practice; resulting in now-here (nowhere) epiphanic, eureka, 'aha' moments of awakening, illumination, realization, transformation and liberation, i.e., enlightenment/bodhi/bodai and enlightened Mind/bodhichitta.

The Zen teacher/sensai or master/roshi wisely, creatively, intuitively, uniquely, empathically, compassionately, directly and with skillful means/upaya; does anything necessary to awaken Zen students to that enlightening moment of experiencing the reality of One, Original, Inborn True Nature and of discovering who it really and truly is that is grappling with koan questions, uncomfortably sitting on zafus, being shouted at or struck with a stick. Zen teachers also have periodic individual private meetings/dokusan with students to review progress and assist with practicing.

A WAY-SHOWING PATH OF ENLIGHTENMENT

Zen is the inner life of the Buddha; the spirit, innermost essence and experience of Buddhism and the opening of the Buddha-Eye. It is spiritual awakening and enlightenment and the realizing of the absolute oneness, emptiness, suchness and primordial perfection of all reality, beings and things; reality itself, being itself and life itself.

Enlightenment is:
1) freeing ego-mind from exclusively and completely identifying with the conditioned ego-self's sense of 'I-ness', 2) the turning inward of consciousness of, in and as itself so, 3) unobscured, unobstructed and unbound pure, empty, clear and open consciousness, 4) liberation from ignorance, delusion, concepts, defilements, afflictions, attachments, fetters and errors and 5) realizing the nondual oneness, emptiness, suchness, uniqueness and wholeness of everyone and everything just as they are.

Zen is the reality, truth and actuality of One, Original, Inborn True Nature and its 'practice' becomes a natural Way of being, living, relating and working in the everyday world of ordinary experience and not only struggling with challenging koans and sitting in concentrated meditation in zendos.

Zen practice continually culminates itself in the One-Mind of nondual consciousness, the No-Mind of empty consciousness/sunyata and the All-Mind of full manifestation/tathata.

Zen practicing is:
1) liberation from the ego-self's and ego-mind's clutter, filler, baggage, busyness and splits of ignorance and delusions, desires and attachments, habits and errors and separations and divisions, 2) living a simple 'Middle Way' (of No-Middle!) between extremes and 3) acknowledging, accepting, attuning to and according with the Way beings and 'things' are just *as* they *are*.

Zen is:

1) 'Just This'; 2) the present here-now moment; 3) Buddha-Nature, Buddha-Dharma, Buddha-Mind, Buddha-Eye; 4) Tao/Way; 5) one's own True Nature; 6) sunyata/negation-emptiness and tathata/affirmation-suchness and 7) awakening/bodhi and enlightenment/satori. Zen is a complete transformation and a new birth or renaissance of one's whole being and a realization and actualization of the precious treasure of human being and human life and its ineffable, indescribable and unspeakable peacefulness, freedom and happiness.

The reality and truth of Zen is experiencing Nature, True Nature, human nature and everyday living and ordinary experience and accepting them as just what, how and as they are, i.e., without evaluative judgments, devised schemes, contrived strategies and without being influenced, manipulated and controlled by the ignorance and arrogance, desires and attachments, strivings and errors and separations and divisions of the conditioned ego-self and the dualistic ego-mind.

In Zen, ultimately, there is no 'thing' to seek, pursue and attain and no 'one' seeking, pursuing or attaining it. Any 'seeking' is for something internal and not external; One, Original, Inborn True Nature, that has never been lost. Any 'pursuing' is not of objects and an unreal ego-image and retreating shadow of our One, Original, Inborn True Self.

And any 'attaining' is a 'non-attaining' that is the natural experiencing of all beings as One, Original, Inborn True Nature; seeing Buddha-Nature in everyone and everything and accepting beings and things just as they are naturally and spontaneously being in, of and as themselves so/tzu jan.

Being and living Zen practice is often creatively reflected, socially actualized and variously consummated in awakened, illuminated, liberated and enlightened:

1) artistic and aesthetic expressions such as architecture, garden art and landscaping; calligraphy, portrait and landscape

painting, fine art and graphic art, sculpture and ceramics; theater and dance, poetry and tales; martial arts, swordsmanship and archery; flower arranging, culinary arts, cooking and the tea ceremony.

2) planetary stewardship, environmental and ecological activism related to the preservation and conservation of ecosystems, biodiversity and natural resources and the protection and sustaining of indigenous peoples and their lands, cultures, communities and wisdom and of animal species and their native habitats.

3) relevant, significant, wise, compassionate and skillful social actions that support, inspire, awaken, encourage, affirm, assist and benefit fellow human beings and which bring with them heart-abiding peace, heart-warming love, heart-found freedom and heart-felt happiness.

Zen:
1) planted and rooted in Indian Theravada Buddhism, 2) grown and cultivated in Indian Mahayana and Tibetan Vajrayana Buddhism, 3) blossoming and ripening in Chinese Ch'an Buddhism and 4) reaching maturation and fruition in Japanese Zen Buddhism; is no-thing other than One, Original, Inborn True Nature; pure, empty, clear, open, spacious and limitless consciousness and the absolute and ultimate essence of human being and all life that universally pervades and transcends all time-periods, histories, cultures, nationalities, ideologies, religions, philosophies and psychologies.

As the saying goes: 1) 'Before enlightenment, rivers and mountains are experienced as rivers and mountains. 2) During experiencing the teachings and practices of becoming enlightened; rivers are no longer rivers and mountains are no longer mountains (via deconstructing, 'negating' and emptying concepts of them, i.e., sunyata) and 3) After enlightenment, rivers are again rivers and mountains are again mountains' (via uniting, affirming and fulfilling their realities, i.e., tathata). But Oh, Now!. With enlightened seeing of their returning to One Origin and being True Nature; how clear and deep are the sparkling rivers' flowing and how near and high are the majestic mountains' summits!.

In enlightenment, our so-called and understood 'world' is still the very same world that it always has been. But the significant difference is that we ourselves and our relationship with it are radically, essentially, profoundly and completely transformed; have awakened to becoming and being True Nature and are now wisely, compassionately and skillfully seeing, experiencing and living in that 'world' as a totally different one, i.e., one 'peopled' by many human beings who are as yet unawakened and unenlightened Buddhas and one 'inhabited' by a few Buddhas who are now awakened and enlightened human beings.

Zen itself is a Way of being and living. It is the solid presence of Body, the deep faith of Heart, the clear awakening of Mind, the strong resolve of Will, the complete emptiness of Soul and the spacious openness of Spirit of its devoted, dedicated, determined and diligent masters, teachers, disciples, students, practitioners and adherents.

Zen is 'a gateless gate', because there is no self to pass through it and there is no gate to pass through. Zen is going straight into meditaton with determination and without hesitation and has nothing to do with any 'gates' of ancestral scriptures, explanations of teachers and forms of practice; but only with transcending dualistic thinking and concepts and realizing the One, Original, Inborn True Self.

'Whatever enters through a 'gate' is not a treasure. . . . The Great Way is gateless; there are thousands of ways to approach it. When one passes the checkpoint and gatekeeper and through the gateless gate, one walks freely throughout heaven and earth'. *Wu-men Kuan/ Mumonkan/The Gateless Gate* compiled by Wu-men Hui-k'ai/Mumon Ekai (1183 – 1260 CE).

A WAY-SHOWING PATH OF ENLIGHTENMENT

'Cast aside world, others, body, self, mind, etc.. Not cling to one's own personal views and mental concepts. Do one thing with effortless non-striving/wu-wei and act in accord with the Way/Tao. Ocean samadhi is the great way of going beyond. No endeavor is complete without being one with the myriad things. . . . When one starts to search out the Dharma, one is separated from it. When realizing that the Dharma has already been rightly transmitted within oneself, just then one is one's Original True Self'. *Shobogenzo-Zuimonki/Treasure Chamber of the Eye of True Law* by Dogen Kigen Zenji (1200-1253 CE).

Zen itself is the life-bestowed, self-created and profoundly realized culmination of assimilating, embodying, presencing, actualizing and transmitting True/Buddha-Nature. Zen itself is the awakened, illuminating, enlightening, transforming and liberating simple radiant truth of the Buddha's beautiful presented flower, the perfect peaceful wisdom of Mahakasyapa's silent acknowledging smile and the abundant joyful freedom of Hotei's contagious belly laugh.

> Buddhist texts are Ox-hoofprints and traces of True Nature.
> Buddhist teachings are Ox-tails and forms of True Nature.
> Buddha-Dharma is the Ox-body and truth of True Nature.
> The Buddha is the Ox-head and source of True Nature.
> Buddhist practice is the Ox-path and Way of True Nature.
> Kensho is the Ox-presence and glimpse of True Nature.
> Satori is the Ox-absence and emptiness of True Nature.

Who We Are

We are acknowledging and appreciating:
Being born as the Mystery of human being.
Being the pristine Miracle of consciousness.
Being awakened to the Marvels of True Nature.
Being the Magnificence of sharing True Nature.
Being the Majesty of consummating True Nature.

Liberation from the illusion of ego-self.
Liberation from the concepts of ego-mind.
Liberation from the belief in impermanence
Liberation from desiring and attaching to 'things'.
Liberation from the cycling of birth, death, rebirth.
Liberation from the suffering of greed, hatred, fear.

The non-dual 'Middle Way' between:
Letting-be and interfering. Letting-go and retaining.
Being-with and alienating. Going-with and resisting.
Questions and answers. Problems and solutions.
Issues and settlements. Conflicts and resolutions.
Truth and delusion. Reality and illusion.
Constancy and change. Ultimate and intimate.
True Nature and ego-self. Nirvana and samsara.

As awakened, enlightened and liberated; we are;
Looking clearly enough to truly see.
Listening openly enough to truly hear.
Touching deeply enough to truly feel.
Inhaling fully enough to truly smell.
Exhaling freely enough to truly taste.

When the senses are clear and empty; ego-mind recedes, True Nature naturally emerges in an open consciousness, both are naturally integrated and balanced and virtues are naturally present. The tangled threads and tight knots of ego-self are unraveled and loosened. True Nature comes and goes in the space where there is no coming and going and it cannot be found, conceived and named by ego-mind.

TEN ZEN OXEN
INTRODUCTION

Without a doubt; our planet, species, world, nations, societies, governments, organizations and our relationships with family members, fellow human beings and ourselves; would all be more sustainable, habitable, manageable, amiable, peaceable, comfortable and enjoyable if more of us were awakened to, and enlightened by, a spiritually illuminated, transformed and liberated consciousness of what it is and what it means to be a real and true human being living a real and true human life.

The Ten Ox-Herding Pictures are one of the oldest documents of Zen Buddhism and have, for over one-thousand years, depicted ten 'stages' of the spiritual journey and unfolding path of becoming an awakened and enlightened human being; realizing and actualizing True Nature and a state of liberation from exclusively and completely identifying with our conditioned ego-self and its sufferings from ignorance, illusion and delusion; desire, acquisition and attachment; habit, error and failure, dualistic division, separation and opposition, etc..

The Ten Ox-Herding Pictures have been variously identified as outlining stages of a pathway and progressive process of practice and spiritual development and pointing and leading to awakening, enlightenment, self-realization, mastery of mind, the perfection of wisdom, truth in action, ultimate reality, the absolute ground of existence and primordial human nature.

The Ox symbolizes One, Absolute, Ultimate, Essential, Original and Inborn True Nature, Buddha-Nature or Buddha-Mind that is awakened, enlightened and liberated. The Ox-herder symbolizes our dualistic, relative, non-ultimate, existential, derived, acquired and untrue ego-self and ego-mind that is unawakened, unenlightened and unliberated. The Ox-seeking human being, who is searching for enlightenment, experiences journeying on a Way-finding and Way-making path of awakening and through a Way-faring and Way-unfolding process of transforming from being exclusively and completely identified with ego-self to being inclusively and consummately united with and identified as One, Original and Inborn True Nature.

The Ten Ox-Herding Pictures depict a spiritual Wayfaring journey to awakening, enlightenment and liberation initiated by questions of our ego-self, e.g., 'Who am I, really and truly?', 'Why is my life going as it is?', 'What is life really and truly about?'; along with the recognition of questions, issues, problems, conflicts, dissatisfactions, sufferings and longings that call for searching out, exploring, investigating and discovering more authentic, intimate, harmonious, meaningful and fulfilling ways of being, living and relating.

Zen Buddhist teachings indicate that; fundamentally and essentially, as human beings; we are, from the very beginning; by virtue of One, Original, Inborn True Nature; already enlightened. However, we do not experience ourselves as such due to social conditioning, imitative learning, adopting collective beliefs and being completely and exclusively identified with our obscuring and obstructing illusional ego-self and deluded ego-mind and its conceptual operations of, e.g., abstracting, objectifying, separating, discriminating, dualizing, defining, naming, evaluating, judging, preferring, etc..

The spiritual Way to awakening, enlightenment and liberation of Zen Buddhism entails an understanding and experiencing of the principles, processes, paths and practices that enable the uncovering, discovering and recovering and the illuminating, realizing and actualizing of One, Original, Inborn True Nature.

This involves studying, training, cultivating, practicing and experiencing the wisdom and methods of the Zen Buddhist tradition with masters and teachers and with the 'great' enthusiasm, doubt, faith, resolve, effort and trust required in committing to

A WAY-SHOWING PATH OF ENLIGHTENMENT

such a profound consciousness-opening, self-transforming and life-changing endeavor as that of awakening to and of realizing an enlightened, transformed and liberated state of human being.

Throughout the years, *The Ten Ox-Herding Pictures* have been widely used by Ch'an and Zen Buddhist masters and teachers, as well as by those in other spiritual traditions; for educating, training, monitoring, encouraging, supporting, assisting, guiding and reinforcing students on spiritual paths and have been commentated upon world-wide by them and by philosophers, scholars and educators.

Adding another commentary to the original pictures is an opportunity: 1) to review and to integrate some of the Way-stations along my own spiritual path toward becoming a more awake, conscious and aware human being and 2) to provide interested fellow human beings and spiritual Wayfaring companions with a contemporary psychospiritual perspective on the matter of becoming a more awakened, illuminated, enlightened, realized, transformed and liberated human being.

It should be noted that, overall, the ten depicted progressively developmental 'stages' or Way-Stations of the path of enlightenment, should not be rigidly understood by our ego-mind as a fixed, linear or hierarchical sequence of discrete phases; since they are simultaneous, multidimensional, interdependent, interwoven, circling and spiraling and can be individually focused upon, cultivated and realized at any given time or point in the continuum of our conscious awareness and process of experiencing.

In various Asian countries such as India, China and Tibet and their adjacent countries; the cow, bull, ox, yak and water buffalo have long been sacred, revered and safeguarded animals as well as ones valued as symbols of fertility and for preventing natural disasters and for their great practical use for transportation and in agricultural life. These strong and gentle bovine creatures have been memorialized in ancient cave paintings and petroglyphs; in sculpture, inked scrollwork and woodblock prints (often shown being ridden by a boy, man or sage) and in mythologies, literature and folk tales. One such depiction is that of *The Ten Ox-Herding Pictures*.

My understanding of the history of *The Ten Ox-Herding Pictures* is that their origin is an early Chinese Taoist tale about the inner unity of all existence and a pathway to manifesting Tao, the Ultimate Reality of all existence. The original tale is subsequently systematized in the 11th Century CE by Ch'an/Zen Master Ch'ing-chu/Seikyo as a set of five successive pictures ending in an empty circle/enso; symbolizing the realization of absolute and nondual oneness, emptiness and perfection.

The next known version is a set of six successive pictures made in the 12th Century CE by Ch'an/Zen Master Tzu-te Hui/Jitoku. The six stages are titled:

1) *Awakening of Faith* – the Ox is caught by the herder and has a white spot on its head.
2) *First Entering* – the Ox is firmly tethered by the herder and its whole head is white.
3) *Not Thoroughly Genuine Yet* – the Ox follows the herder and half of its body is white.
4) *True Mind* – the herder is resting and the Ox is feeding and its whole body is white.
5) *Both Ox and Herder Forgotten* – only the empty circle, the Void and liberation exist.
6) *Playing* – the herder conforms to any circumstance. He has transformed into True Nature but what he does is not any different.

In both the Seikyo and Jitoku versions, the Ox is initially all black and gradually whitens completely; symbolizing the progressive transformation and purification of the initially defiled, ignorant, deluded, attached, afflicted and fettered mind to pure, wise, undeluded unattached, unafflicted, unfettered and enlightened True Mind that occurs in the process of becoming awakened, enlightened and liberated.

There is referenced another 12th Century CE set of eight pictures reportedly done by an unknown artist and which has been lost.

The best known version of *The Ten Ox-Herding Pictures* is *The Ten Bulls* from the late 12th Century CE by the Chinese Lin-chi/Rinzai Ch'an/Zen Master, K'uo-an Shih-yuan/Kakuan Shien who added a ninth and tenth picture; symbolizing: 1) returning to the source and origin of everyone and everything and 2) entering the world and enlightening fellow human beings.

Included for each picture are Kakuan's original prose and comments made by his disciple, Chi-yuan and later woodblock prints made in the 15th Century CE by Zen priest, Tensho Shubun (1414-1463 CE) said to be copies of the lost originals attributed to Kakuan.

The ten stages are titled: 1) Searching for the Bull, 2) Seeing Traces of the Bull, 3) Seeing the Bull, 4) Catching the Bull, 5) Herding the Bull, 6) Riding the Bull Home, 7) The Bull Forgotten, 8) Both Bull and Herder Out of Sight, 9) Returning to the Source/Origin and 10) Entering the World with Bliss-Bestowing Hands.

A late 13th Century CE (1278 CE?) scroll version, reportedly the first made in Japan, is colored and is titled *The Ten Ox-Herding Songs*. The titling of the ten stages generally follows those of Kakuan and the pictures are made by an unknown artist.

A 16th Century CE (1585 CE?) Chinese edition of *The Ten Ox-Herding Pictures* is prefaced by Chu-hung and includes introductions and poems by a Pu-ming/Fumyo, but its original artist is unknown. The stages are variously titled: 1) Undisciplined/Untamed, 2) Discipline/Training Begun, 3) In Harness/Restrained, 4) Faced Round/Turning its Head, 5) Tamed, 6) Unhindered/Unimpeded, 7) Laissez-Faire/With the Current, 8) Forgetting the Other/All Forgotten, 9) The Solitary Moon/Alone in the Light and 10) Both Gone/Vanished. In this series, the Ox also changes from black to white and the series also ends in an empty circle/enso.

In more recent centuries; numerous drawings, versions and renditions have been made world-wide; especially in China, Japan and the United States; by various artists, masters, teachers and commentators. Two well-known and popular ones are a set of ten woodblock prints by Tomikichiro Tokuriki (1902-2000 CE) in 1951 CE and ten scroll paintings by Gyokusei Jikihara (1904-2005 CE) in 1982 CE.

As noted above, *The Ten Ox-Herding Pictures* symbolically represent, visually portray and textually describe ten 'stages' of the path of awakening and enlightenment. Again, the Ox symbolizes One, Original, Absolute, Ultimate, Essential, Inborn True/Buddha-Nature. It is the timeless, nondual and whole reality, ground and principle of all being that is present within, available to and potentially realizable by human beings as illuminated, luminous, bright, brilliant and radiant Mind.

True/Buddha Nature is identical with the awakened, empty, open, enlightened and liberated heart-mind of the Buddha beyond illusions, concepts, desires, attachment and the endless karmic and samsaric cycling and recycling of birth, death and rebirth.

Again, the Ox-herder represents our conditioned, unawakened, unenlightened, untransformed and unliberated ego-self and ego-mind and its attachments to the myriad and diverse internal and external phenomena, objects, 'things' and concepts of ordinary experiencing which are exclusively and completely identified with and by which True/Buddha-Nature is hidden, obscured, entangled, obstructed and lost.

For the present version of *The Ten Ox-Herding Pictures, Ten Zen Oxen*, the ten stages or Way-Stations of the path of enlightenment are titled as: 1) Seeking the Ox, 2) Tracking the Ox, 3) Glimpsing the Ox, 4) Catching the Ox, 5) Taming the Ox, 6) Riding the Ox, 7) Forgetting the Ox, 8) Disidentifying from

A WAY-SHOWING PATH OF ENLIGHTENMENT

Ego-Self (also Transcending, Emptying and Forgetting the Ego-Self), 9) Returning to the Source/Origin and 10) Being in the World.

The present *Ten Zen Oxen* version of *The Ten Ox-Herding Pictures* includes two sets of original pictures by Shubun and Tokuriki, a rendition of the original prose by Kakuan Shien and comments by Chi-yuan. Each of the ten pictures and Way-Stations is introduced by Chinese characters, related *Tao Te Ching* passages and original rhymes, followed by a Way-showing synoptic comment and psychospiritual commentary and concluded with related Chuang Tzu quotations.

May the great sacred, strong, robust, kind and gentle Ox of awakened, illuminated, enlightened, realized and liberated one, original, inborn True Nature carry you peacefully, happily, freely and joyfully full circle, all of the Way back Home to both the originating Source and the everyday world.

May you deeply and soulfully return to the original blessed, radiant and precious vitality, unity and identity of True/Buddha-Nature and the Buddha-Eye.

May you intimately and soulfully join with the present blessed, radiant and precious humanity, diversity and entireity of everyone; full-bodied, kind-hearted, open-minded, gentle-willed and free-spirited.

May the great, blessed and precious treasures of long-lasting peace, happiness, freedom and joyfulness be yours to be and to cherish deeply and to live and to share fully! Thank you!

The Path of Enlightenment

Our socially conditioned, illusional, deluded,
separate, attached, limited, slumbering,
dreaming and suffering ego-self with which
we are exclusively and completely identified;
Before enlightenment and awakening:
1. Seeks an awakened, enlightened and liberated way of being and living.
2. Studies spiritual texts and learns about teachings of enlightened human being.
3. Catches glimpses of enlightened human being in actual brief kensho moments.
4. Grasps a whole understanding of the reality of enlightened True Nature.

During enlightenment and transforming:
5. Trains and disciplines itself and is cultivating and becoming True Nature.
6. Integrates, unites, harmonizes with and is being enlightened True Nature.

After enlightenment and liberation:
7. Forgets enlightened True Nature as an object-thing to attain, have and be.
8. Forgets its identification with itself and even its identity as True Nature.
9. Returns to and abides in the origin and source of everyone and everything.
10. Enters the social world to actualize, radiate and transmit enlightenment.

We make choices in life that have consequences.
In life's garden, we continually plant karmic seeds
and enact our karmic deeds, annual flowers and
perennial weeds. Do we only trim their stems
and they grow back again or do we uproot them
completely and the ground is cleared and open?

THE TEN WAY-STATIONS OF THE PATH OF ENLIGHTENMENT

The classic *Ten Ox-Herding Pictures* identify the principles, path, process and perfection of ego-self's search for, and discovery of, True Nature and a Way of awakened, enlightened and liberated human being, living and relating. *Ten Zen Oxen* portrays the great, unfolding, flowing and graceful partner dancing and the beautiful, harmonic, melodic and lyrical duet singing of the dual-unity and non-duality of ego-self and True Nature.

The Ox symbolizes our unconditioned, awakened, enlightened and liberated One, Original, Absolute, Ultimate, Essential and Inborn True Nature and the Ox-herder symbolizes our conditioned, unawakened, unenlightened and unliberated dualistic, derived and acquired ego-self. In the process of becoming and being enlightened; ego-self is progressively seeking, pursuing, discovering, grasping, harmonizing with, integrating, transforming into and ultimately assimilating as, sourcing, actualizing and transmitting True Nature.

The Awakening
PRE-ENLIGHTENMENT[6]

The world of ego-self. Relative, conditioned, dualistic world of ego-self concept.

Either-or, mutually exclusive dualities of conscious awareness.

Not yet being One, Original, Absolute, Ultimate, Essential and Inborn True Nature.

Way-Station One
SEEKING THE OX

Disheartened-prompted searching.
Recognizing and acknowledging.

Dissatisfactions, lacks, wants, longings.
Questions, problems, issues, conflicts.

A mode of 'being' – quandaries, dilemmas, doubts, confusion, frustration.

Inner-outer, I-it, self-other, good-bad either-or, mutually-exclusive 'being' dualities.

Ego-self is recognizing, acknowledging, assessing, evaluating, seeking.

Ego-self is separate from and not seeing True Nature, is exhausted and lost.

True Nature is hidden within conscious awareness and unknown by ego-self.

There is no Ox in ego-self's experience and no awareness of True Nature.

Seeking enlightenment. 'Who or what is responsible for my situation?'.

Wandering – ego-self is aimlessly rambling in the wilderness of its mind and world.

Way-Station Two
TRACKING THE OX

Intellectual-based activities.
Exploring and learning.

Decision-making, direction-taking. Inklings of possible answers, solutions, resolutions.

A mode of 'doing' – exploring, reading, studying, learning about teachings, True Nature.

Able-unable, success-failure, right-wrong either-or, mutually-exclusive 'doing' dualities.

Ego-self is motivated, open, interested, uncertain, unsure, wondering.

Ego-self is attending lectures, presentations, meetings, programs, workshops.

True Nature is traced within readings, texts, sutras as an idea, notion, concept.

There are hoofprints of the Ox and a concept of True Nature in ego-self's mind.

Tracking enlightenment. 'Is there a journey to make and a path to take?'.

Path-finding – ego-self is seeing a possible way into and through the wilderness.

Way-Station Three
GLIMPSING THE OX

Experience-generated acquaintings.
Illuminating and awareness.

Experiencing teachers, sampling practices, discerning teachings in retreats, etc.

A mode of 'knowing' – some awareness and experiential understanding of True Nature.

Whole-partial, clear-unclear, true-false either-or, mutually-exclusive 'knowing' dualities.

Ego-self is aware of some illuminating traces, encouraging inklings of True Nature.

Ego-self is experiencing momentary kenshos of seeing into the reality of True Nature.

True Nature is revealed, validated, affirmed in the actual experiences of ego-self.

The Ox is momentarily and partially seen by ego-self and is not just a mental concept.

Glimpsing enlightenment. 'I have briefly subjectively experienced my True Nature!'.

Traveling – ego-self is focused on moving toward a place beyond the wilderness.

Way-Station Four
CATCHING THE OX

Path-committed struggling.
Realizing and understanding.

Choosing and committing to a spiritual tradition, path, teacher, practice.

A mode of 'having' – comprehending, taking hold of, holding onto True Nature.

Strong-weak, effort-ease, gain-loss either-or, mutually exclusive 'having' dualities.

Ego-self is connecting with, joining, grappling with not losing a grip of True Nature.

Ego-self has grasped True Nature as a real, whole entity and object of its awareness.

True Nature is interacting with ego-self and is forcefully resisting being controlled.

The whole Ox is experientially 'gotten', realized and understood by ego-self.

Grasping enlightenment. 'Do I have the strength to sustain, hold on, persevere?'.

Path-taking – ego-self is goal-directed and arriving at a place beyond the wilderness.

The Transforming
MID-ENLIGHTENMENT

The realm of ego-self and True Nature. Ego-self is cultivating and practicing True Nature.

True Nature is deconditioning, disidentifying, 'practicing', transforming ego-self.

Ego-self is identifying with and becoming True Nature and being an identity as True Nature.

Complementary both-and, mutually-inclusive dual unities of ego-self and True Nature.

The ground, matrix, root, center, heart, core, marrow and spaciousness of transforming.

Becoming and being One, Original, Absolute, Ultimate, Essential, Inborn True Nature.

Way-Station Five
TAMING THE OX

Discipline-focused training
Identifying and cultivating.

Determination, strength, effort, discipline, diligence, perseverance.

A mode of not-'doing' – initial taxing push-pull resistance and struggling cease.

The bipolar dual-unities of ego-self and True Nature are co-existing, co-relating.

Ego-self is attuning to, according with rather than forcefully controlling True Nature.

Ego-self is identifying with, harmonizing with, cultivating and becoming True Nature.

True Nature is enlightening, embodying, personifying, transforming, 'practicing' ego-self.

The Ox is finally tamed and becomes its originally gentle, docile and compliant nature.

Nurturing enlightenment. 'Cultivating has become frictionless, effortless, seamless'.

Journeying – the ego-self identifies with and takes the Way to becoming True Nature.

Way-Station Six
RIDING THE OX HOME

Internalized-integrated identity.
Integrating and practicing.

Integrating, unifying, practicing, creating, enjoying, being, living, homing.

A mode of not-'having' – not acquiring, attaining, possessing, owning.

The bipolar dual-unities of ego-self and True Nature are integrated, unified.

Ego-self is 'riding' along on, being 'practiced' and carried home by True Nature.

Ego-self is being True Nature and is beyond the point of no returning to the past.

True Nature is a vital flowing energy force conveying, transporting ego-self home.

The Ox knows the way home and is going there without being led, directed, guided.

Being enlightenment. 'Practicing is natural, spontaneous, happening of/as itself so'.

Path-coursing – the ego-self follows the Way of, and is, enlightened True Nature.

The Liberating
POST-ENLIGHTENMENT

The universe of True Nature. Absolute, unconditioned, nondual universe of True Nature.

No either-or, mutually-exclusive or both-and, mutually-inclusive dualities of consciousness.

Being One, Original, Absolute, Ultimate, Essential, Inborn True Nature.

Way-Station Seven
FORGETTING THE OX

Assimilation-negated emptiness.
Assimilating and forgetting.

Embodying, assimilating, forgetting, oblivion, negating, emptying.

A mode of not-'knowing' – objectless, contentless, conceptless consciousness.

The either-ors, both-ands, neither-nors of ego-self and True Nature are voided.

Ego-self is completely assimilated with True Nature and does not 'experience' it.

Ego-self is transformed and has 'forgotten' its True Nature but is still 'existing'.

Enlightened True Nature is pure, empty consciousness and clear, open awareness.

The Ox of enlightened True Nature is absent from the conscious awareness of ego-self.

Some satoris of 'being as' True Nature beyond kenshos of 'seeing into' True Nature.

Identity of form-emptiness, samsara-nirvana and their negation and emptying.

Complete emptiness of beings, 'things', objects, taos, dharmas, phenomena, concepts.

Not yet the complete suchness, thusness, as-isness, just-soness of True Nature.

Forgetting enlightenment. 'I' am no longer aware of enlightenment as a 'thing' to 'be'.

Sojourning – transient, temporary abiding in sacred places of enlightened True Nature.

Way-Station Eight
FORGETTING THE SELF

Disidentified-transcendent spaciousness. Transcending and forgetting.

Pureness, emptiness, clearness, openness, spaciousness, vastness, endlessness.

A mode of not-'being' – egoless, selfless, no 'I', no 'me', no 'myself', no 'mine'.

The dual unities of subject-object, seer-seen, knower-known, doer-done are absent.

Ego-self, True Nature are both forgotten and are not objects in conscious awareness.

Ego-self, True Nature are completely disidentified with, transcended and absent.

Enlightened True Nature has 'forgotten' ego-self and it no longer exists as an object.

Some brief 'experiences' of nirvanic extinction, samadhic oneness, dhyanic absorption.

Some satoris whereby both ego-self and True Nature are 'forgotten' as manifestations.

Identity of ego self-True Nature, ego mind-enlightened Mind is forgotten and absent.

Complete transcendence of being-nonbeing, is-is not, affirmation-negation, etc..

Not yet the complete suchness, thusness, as-isness, just-soness of everything as it is.

Transcending True Nature. 'Enlightenment' is no longer aware of 'me' as a 'being' to 'be'.

Path-forsaking – the Ox, the herder, the path, True Nature and ego-self are all forgotten.

Way-Station Nine
RETURNING TO THE ORIGIN

Original-source abiding.
Returning and sourcing.

Non-dwelling at the creative source, wellspring, fountainhead of all manifesting.

A mode of not-'having' – liberation from desires, attachments, self, 'others', 'things'.

True Nature is not attaining enlightenment, liberation of/from/as/for any 'thing'.

True Nature is the pure, empty, clear, open space of consciousness and awareness.

True Nature is the emptiness and pure potential from which phenomena originate.

Realizing the springing forth of everyone, everything from one original True Nature.

Realizing the radiant luminosity and beauty of individuality, multiplicity, diversity.

Realizing the suchness of everyone, everything just as they are in/of/as themselves.

Complete liberation from any conceptualizing of or attachment to external 'things'.

Witnessing, acknowledging, appreciating the suchness of everyone, everything.

Enjoying the solitude, silence, simplicity, sufficiency, serenity of being at Source.

Sourcing True Nature. "'I' am at the wellspring, fountainhead of being and life'.

Wayfaring – the pathway of enlightened True Nature is one of creative originating.

Way-Station Ten
BEING IN THE WORLD

Enlightened world-entering.
Actualizing and transmitting.

Returning to the world, entering the 'marketplace' with bliss bestowing hands.

A mode of not-'doing' – frictionless, effortless, seamless unfolding, flowing.

Enlightened True Nature is universalizing everyone, everything as True Nature.

Enlightened True Nature is suchness hidden within/from the everyday world.

Enlightened True Nature actualizes itself in/as just whatever it ordinarily is doing.

Enlightened True Nature is enacting samadhi/absolute oneness, dhyana/absorption.

Enlightened True Nature is enacting emptiness/sunyata and suchness/tathata.

Enlightened True Nature is being in, engaging with, participating in the world.

Actualizing enlightened True Nature is serving, assisting, benefiting human beings.

Actualizing enlightened True Nature is vitalizing, energizing fellow human beings.

Actualizing enlightened True Nature is being compassionate, generous with human beings.

Actualizing enlightened True Nature is being radiantly illuminating in the world.

Actualizing enlightened True Nature is transmitting the Dharma to human beings.

Actualizing enlightened True Nature is transmitting the brilliance of Buddha-Nature.

True Nature, by its presence alone; is awakening, enlightening, liberating others.

For enlightened True Nature there is no-'one' to 'be'; no-'thing' to 'know', 'do', 'have'.

Enlightened True Nature is being peaceful, free, happy, grateful, inclusive, empathic.

Actualizing True Nature. "I" am living wisdom/prajna, compassion/karuna, skill/upaya'.

Path-making – enlightened True Nature is actualizing its own unique Way in the world.

Awakened, illuminated, enlightened, realized and liberated moments of nirvana/extinction, samsara=nirvana, samadhi/absolute oneness, kaivala/realization, dhyana/absorption, mukti/liberation, sunyata/emptiness, form=emptiness, tathata/suchness, kensho/seeing into True/Buddha-Nature and satori/being True/Buddha-Nature; may occur spontaneously at any of the ten Way-Stations during the transformative process from initially being exclusively and completely identified with conditioned ego-self, to being identified with True/Buddha-Nature and to finally *being* the identity of True/Buddha-Nature as an awakened, enlightened and liberated human being; living wisely, compassionately and skillfully and peacefully, happily and freely.

Ego-self becomes and is being its identity and ongoing living as One, Original, Absolute, Ultimate, Essential, Inborn True/Buddha-Nature that is not consciously aware of itself as either the subject or the object of its own consciousness and awareness. Enlightened True/Buddha-Nature is the spaciousness of pure and empty consciousness and clear and open awareness without beings, 'others', objects, entities, 'things', phenomena, forms, contents, concepts and words.

Pure, empty, clear and open consciousness is that which manifests and is aware of both seen and seer, known and knower, done and doer, etc. and is neither seer nor seen, knower nor known, doer nor done, etc.. It is infinite consciousness of consciousness and awareness of awareness alone.

Enlightened True/Buddha-Nature has returned, through the transformations of ego-self, to the truth of its origin as the emptiness of Buddha-Mind and is actualizing the reality of its presence as the suchness of Buddha-World.

Enlightened True/Buddha-Nature is; sheerly and utterly, purely and simply; 'I Am', 'Just This' and 'It' . . . and 'We All Are', 'Just This' and 'It'!

The Crisis of Ego-Self

Prior to being awakened, enlightened, transformed and liberated; our ego-self suffers from exclusively and completely identifying with itself and mistakenly considering itself to be all that there is to the reality and identity of its being a human being.

This ego-self has no grounded, centered and spacious consciousness or inner experience of the True Nature that it really is; although at times of great wounding, pain, suffering, joy, ecstasy and bliss, it may sense that there is something more to its being and living.

So, our typically unenlightened ego-self suffers from this case of mistaken ego-identity and peripheral ego dis-ease until something comes along that disrupts its illusion, delusion, hallucination, trance, dream and fantasy of being a substantial and separate being.

This crisis is a turning point (or returning point!) that opens the Way to experiencing the 'something more' that is the the silent, calm, clear, empty and open reality of one, original, absolute, ultimate, essential and inborn True Nature.

This 'crisis' is, of course, the potential opportunity to awaken to, realize and to actualize enlightened and liberated True Nature that has existed before birth, objectification, thinking and naming and that will exist during transformations and after death.

Let the ego-self's crises midwife the process of becoming and being awakened, enlightened, realized, transformed and liberated True Nature.

TEN ZEN OXEN

The Awakening
Pre-Enlightenment

Way-Station One
SEEKING THE OX

Way-Station Two
TRACKING THE OX

Way Station Three
GLIMPSING THE OX

Way-Station Four
CATCHING THE OX

Way-Station One
Seeking the Ox

Recognizing

Acknowledging

I am lost beside unnamed rivers
below distant mountains . . .
far from home.

Way-Station One
Dao/Tao Zhan/Chan Yi/I

Seeking The Ox

Xun/Hsun	Zhao/Chao	Niu/Niu
Search/Look For	Seek/Look For	The Ox

'Many colors are blinding our eyes. Many sounds are deafening our ears. Many tastes are numbing our palates. Hunting and chasing are crazing our heart-minds. Getting and keeping are impeding our developing'. [TTC #12]

'No misfortune, no disaster, no calamity is greater than wanting what others have, wanting to have more, not having enough'. [TTC #46]

'Not displaying desirable goods, our heart-minds are not longing'. [TTC #3]

'Having little, obtaining more. Having more, becoming confused'. [TTC # 22]

'Taking pride in wealth and fame is bringing downfall and collapse'. [TTC# 9]

'Self or fame, life or wealth, gain or loss; which is more near, dear, fear?. [TTC# 44]

'As people, when we are conceiving good, we are simultaneously invoking bad'. [TTC # 2]

Disappointments, dissatisfactions, disturbances are finally peaking. Discouragement, disheartenment are recognized and initiate seeking. What was good seems bad. Energies are wasted, draining and leaking. There must be something greater beyond names, words and speaking.

1.
SEEKING THE OX[7]

TEXT

In the wilderness of the world, I'm carrying a bridle and whip and searching for the bull. I push aside tall grasses. I am lost beside unnamed rivers and below distant mountains. My strength is already failing and my vitality is nearly exhausted. I cannot find the bull. I see intertwining paths. I only hear locusts chirring throughout the forest at nighttime.

COMMENT

If the bull has never really been lost. Why am I searching for it?

Well, only because of being separated from my True Nature.

I fail to find the bull because all of my senses are so confused.

I don't even see any of its tracks anywhere. I am so far from home.

There are criss-crossing paths, but I have no idea which is a good one.

Greed and fear and good and bad entangle me.

Way-Station One Synoptic Comment
Seeking The Ox

I'm in a quandary, alone and lost in a wilderness. I'm frustrated, dissatisfied, disheartened and discouraged with myself and my life. I'm losing my vitality, color and turning gray. I have so many unanswered questions, unsolved problems, unsettled issues and unresolved conflicts. My life is fraught with innumerable obscurations, entanglements, obstructions, impediments and hindrances. I feel stuck and that I'm not going or getting anywhere in my life.

I think that I'm suffering from some kind of an existential ego-crisis. I'm totally overwhelmed by unrealized plans and hopes, fruitless projects and efforts, unfulfilling pursuits and relationships, self-doubts, confusion, anxiety, worries and fears about the future. I'm at the end of my rope, out of ideas, tired, weary, drained of energy, weak and exhausted and despairing of my hopeless and helpless state of mind.

My life is a maze of false starts, wrong choices, dead ends and back-tracking without a way out. I certainly need to find a way through my life and come to feel good about it and myself.

I'm not living an authentic, genuine or sincere life but one that seems dysfunctional and maladaptive or maybe overly 'functional' and too 'adapted'. I'm questioning the real value and true worth of my so-called achievements and accomplishments.

I recognize that my situation may have something to do with me, rather than with the people and things other than me. Is there something about or within myself of which I'm not aware? It's irritating to think that I might be the cause of the way my life is or isn't going. I feel that some kind of renaissance needs to happen to wake me up from my dreaming, fantasizing, wishing, hoping and lack of satisfaction, gratification and fulfillment.

I think that there must be something other, more, better,

greater and more meaningful than how I am being, what I am doing, what I have, the way that I am living. Some wealth and status, material 'things', pleasurable activities and entertaining distractions aren't ultimately bringing any lasting happiness. I feel that something essential is missing. But what is it?. Where is it?. Where do I look?. How do I find it?. Is there a way out of my predicament and to whatever it is?.

I'm standing and looking around in this natural setting of a flowing river, distant mountains, tall grasses, deep thickets, tangled vines and criss-crossing overgrown paths. They all symbolize the complexities of my world and are no different from the barren concrete of the city and its shadowing buildings. I could try to swim down the swift river or climb up the steep mountains, but who knows where they go or end up?. Besides, I don't have the strength to find out.

The grasses, shrubs, underbrush and brambles that I'm facing are dense, thick, intertwining and thorny and seem too impossible to clear, penetrate and move through. Would I even find anything of value in this wasteland?. I'm lost in it, bewildered by it and feeling alienated, disoriented, confused and despairing of my life circumstances.

I'm thinking that I certainly need to, but might never, find a way through my life as it is and come to feel better about it and myself. I squint my eyes and discern what look like paths beyond where I am, but they each criss-cross out of sight and who knows which is a good one to take?. Is there really something better somewhere out there?. I will still be the same 'me', wherever I go and may arrive.

I am aware of some Zen Buddhist writings having to do with enlightenment and True Nature, symbolized by an Ox. I wonder if there is some kind of spiritual awakening that needs to happen in order for me to break through and free myself from where I'm at. I may be a complete victim of all of my ego's desires and attachments, insecurities and doubts, habits and errors, misconceptions and projections, opinions and judgments, sufferings and pains, etc..

I recognize that my thoughts are oppressing me both upsetting day and sleepless night and that there is too much clutter, filler and busyness going on mentally and emotionally. I think that I have a 'monkey-mind' with its endless chattering thought-trains that are filled with all sorts of this or that dualistic separations like subject-object, self-other, cause-effect, good-bad, right-wrong, true-false, success-failure, gain-loss, etc..

Attaining the awakened, enlightened and liberated states of peacefulness, freedom and happiness that I read about are certainly ones that I'm needing, longing for and seeking; but I don't know how to begin to find them. I'm aware that what needs to happen may not ultimately depend upon external things outside of myself, but I don't know where else to search. I think that I need to begin by finding some kind of way or path to follow.

At this time, I'm not choosing to engage in any kind of self-reflection, self-inquiry, self-examination or self-evaluation and, rather, to search for something or some way in the outside world that might help; albeit without knowing exactly what I'm looking for, where to look or how to find it. There are those intersecting paths out there beyond all of this tangled overgrowth in front of me.

In the darkening of night, I find some solace in hearing Nature's crickets happily chirring in the outlying brush. But even they become just another unwelcome nuisance in my mind. I stare at the tangled growth for some time, 'take the bull by the horns', start hacking my way through it and begin a search for the Ox of awakened, enlightened and liberated True Nature.

I will decide to take and follow one of the paths after clearing an opening way to them. I will bring along a halter, rope and whip in case I find the Ox and will have to catch, hold onto and tame it.

WAY-STATION ONE PSYCHOSPIRITUAL COMMENTARY
DISHEARTENED-PROMPTED SEARCHING / RECOGNIZING

'The Great Way is not difficult for those who have no preferences. When love and hate are both absent, everything becomes clear and undisguised. Make the smallest distinction, however, and heaven and earth are set infinitely apart. If you wish to see the truth, then hold no opinions for or against anything. To set up likes against dislikes, is the dis-ease of the mind. When the deep meaning of things is not understood, the mind's essential peace is disturbed to no avail'. Verse 1. 'If you wish to move in the One Way, do not dislike even the world of senses and ideas.....to accept them fully is identical with true enlightenment. The wise strive for no goals and the foolish fetter themselves. There is one Dharma, not many. Distinctions arise from the clinging needs of the ignorant. To seek Mind with the mind is the greatest of all mistakes'. Verse 8. *Hsin Hsin Ming/Faith in the Heart-Mind Verses* by Seng-Ts'an/Sosan (d. 606 CE). The Third Ch'an/Zen Patriarch in China.

The quest for enlightenment can arise naturally and developmentally or consciously and intentionally for many different reasons. One of the main ones is an awareness that our questions, problems, issues and conflicts are not able to be answered, solved, settled and resolved on the same level or in the same way in which, they occurred. We recognize that this inability seems to be due to certain limitations of our ordinary ego-self and its cognitive, rational and reasoning capacities, abilities and skills.

We often seek out other human beings, personal or professional, in hopes of obtaining some helpful and useful perspectives, advice or interventions that will alleviate or end persisting dissatisfaction, discomfort, upset, pain, etc.. However, when such assistance isn't effective and numerous avenues have been pursued, attempted and failed; we are still stuck with the unanswered questions, unsolved problems, unsettled issues and unresolved conflicts and as disturbing, intense, pervasive and intractable as they are.

At these times of crises, it often happens, synchronistically, that something or someone enters our life that/who makes a real difference in our progress toward change. A near breakdown turns into a breakthrough, nightmares end, fears subside, worries cease, anxiety lessens, depression lifts, anger dissipates, tensions relax, etc.. The triggering agent in such reversals could be anything or anyone, e.g., a dream, a memory, a natural event, a TV show, a book, an article, a family member, a friend, a child, a stranger, an opponent.

Any radical shift, change and transformation can be awesome, amazing and astonishing and seem mysterious, miraculous and marvelous. How could something as simple as a comedian's corny joke, a short newspaper item or a single sentence in a book; as profound as a close friend's illness or a loved one's death; as spontaneous as a joyful spouse's hug or a young child's laugh; as surprising as a passing stranger's 'hello', an elderly woman's smile or a rival's handshake make all the difference?

We begin to have the sense that more is going on in our lives over which we have little or no control. If we believe in God or a Higher Power, this certainly validates it and we feel blessed. If we believe in the randomness of natural events, this certainly affirms it and we feel fortunate. If we don't believe in anything, this certainly confirms it and we could care less because whatever it was has ended and we are finally feeling better, okay or good enough again.

The quest for enlightenment often begins with nagging questions. We ask, is 'this' all there is to my life? Is 'this' all there is to me, in spite of successes and gains made in reputation, status, wealth and 'things'? Who or what is responsible for the way things are?. We have a sense that something essential is missing and that there must be more to ourselves and our lives than all 'this'. 'This', often meaning traumas and conflicts; failures and losses; dissatisfaction and unhappiness; distress and suffering, anguish and misery, etc..

'This' meaning living in a society perceived to be unsafe and threatening; materialistically-oriented; fraught with systemic racial and gender discrimination, police brutality and political corruption, financial greed and exploitation; collective narcissism and sociopathy, domestic and gang violence, drug and human trafficking and the mass shootings and murdering of human beings in their homes, schools and businesses, at events and on the streets of their cities and neighborhoods.

'This' meaning living in a world perceived as power-driven, nationally and internationally led by autocrats and dictators, governmentally run with clandestine activities and conspiracies, politically characterized by vested interests and assassinations and humanly involving mass migrations, asylum seeking, terrorist activity, border disputes, actual and proxy wars, rampant poverty and starving children, xenophobia, genocide, ethnic cleansing and the killing of human beings through war crimes.

'This' meaning living on a planet that is perceived as endangered due to our ignorant denial of what is absolutely neccesary to responsibly steward and safeguard its sustainability and habitability and due to our arrogant disregard for the ecological interdependence of all planetary life and for the survival of the earth's biosphere, climate, oceans, ecosystems, glaciers, rain forests, habitats and environments, species biodiversity and indigenous peoples and their profound and extensive knowledge about ways of being, living and healing.

Yes, we are aware of the reality that there is much more to our human life than all of the above goings on and is what is drawing us to begin searching for a more awakened and enlightened way of being and living. We recognize that, as human beings, we are more than our fictitious ego-self and that the true meaning of our lives exists beyond our ego's image and its defenses and objectives and its strategies, methods and justifications for separating, controlling, forcing, dominating, overpowering, succeeding and winning.

We recognize that our notion of what is real and who we think that we truly are is generated by the unquestioned and projected social conditioning of our ego-self with which we are completely identified. And that so-called consensus reality may even be nothing more than a collectively shared societal delusion; the belief in which keeps being unconsciously, unknowingly, unwittingly and automatically perpetuated and passed on from generation to generation without change or end.

So, we begin to make inquiries into, explore and investigate what our human life really and truly is about. We feel invited to enter into something other, else and more and to go further with ourselves. But what exactly and precisely is it that we are seeking?. Whatever it is does not currently seem very present within ourselves, fellow human beings, our society, the world and the planet; which all seem to be in such a dense, entangled, muddled, chaotic, turbulent, disheartened, soulless and despirited condition.

We have a sense that whatever it is seems like something invisible, non-physical, intangible, mysterious yet powerful, influencial, transformative, healing and corrective. Something of a spiritual nature. What was it behind the opening and turn around that we experienced when, serendipitously, that comedian joked, that child laughed, that stranger said hello, that elderly woman smiled and that opponent shook our hand along our way?

What was behind that breakthrough when we read those few lines in a book that someone happened to synchronistically recommend to us?. There was something in it about human beings of Asian heritage; residing in India, Tibet, China, Burma, Japan,

Thailand, Korea, Europe, Canada, the United States and elsewhere who are considered to be awakened, enlightened and liberated beings, buddhas and bodhisattvas, masters and teachers. And there was something about our ego-self not being our True Nature.

We seem to be separated from any traces of our original, unconditioned, awakened, enlightened and liberated inborn True Nature. We have lost it through completely identifying with our derived, conditioned, slumbering, unenlightened and unliberated acquired ego-self and its continual need to validate, substantiate, strengthen, enhance, defend and gratify its illusional 'reality'.

We are constantly seeking sensory stimulation and excitation and are entangled in desires for status, wealth and material objects; fears of dying, as well as really living, and dualistic judgments about what is inner or outer, self or other, good or bad about fellow human beings, ourselves and our lives. We recognize that our lives are one great quandary filled with all sorts of dilemmas.

We are confused and at a crossroad of our life, having goals and objectives that are too remote or conflicting. We are following unknown and unclear external directions and don't know where they are ultimately leading. We are not knowing which is a good or a bad way of proceeding regarding being ourselves and living our lives in more meaningful, satisfying, gratifying and fulfilling ways.

We become interested in this notion of awakening and enlightenment. What is it? Who can become enlightened? Can a 'Westerner' become enlightened?. Does being enlightened assist us in answering questions, solving problems, settling issues, resolving conflicts that we and fellow human beings have, as well as those of society, nations and the world?.

Does enlightenment have something to do with 'seeing the light' and clearly discovering what is really going on with us human beings or 'lightening up' and reducing the heavy burdens and relieving the deep suffering of us human beings?. If so, how can we become enlightened? What do we have to do to become enlightened?. Can just anybody become enlightened?. Do we have to be somebody special with special abilities?.

Will enlightenment help us to feel better and to make our world a better place in which to live?. Is there some light at the end this dark tunnel of destruction, devastation, disasters, disease and death and of the pain, suffering, misery, anguish and despair that we are undergoing and enduring? Is there some clear pathway through all of the dense overgrowth and tangled underbrush; all of the rubble, 'collateral damage' and carnage?.

It seems like it would be helpful to search for enlightenment and that it could afford some hope for us human beings to not feel so separate and isolated, anxious and depressed, afraid and angry and to not need to have so much power, to prove ourselves as 'somebody' better than anyone else and, rather, to be more accepting, inclusive, intimate, empathic, caring, peaceful, happy, free and 'at home' within ourselves and with fellow human beings.

We are enthusiastic and excited about recognizing that we may be extricating, individuating and liberating ourselves from the trifles, perplexities, entanglements and hindrances of the collective herd mentality of mass humanity and are ready and willing to seek a more enlightened way of being and living. It seems like a marvelous event to be doing so.

But we don't yet know anything about what enlightenment or being enlightened is, how to search for it or ways to find it. We are aware of the Ox-Herding Pictures and of the Ox as a symbol of our original, unconditioned, awakened, enlightened and liberated inborn True Nature. So we are beginning our searching for the Ox!

Chuang Tzu says

'Once human beings receive bodily form, they hold onto it waiting for the end.....they run their course like a galloping horse.....sweating and laboring to the end of their days.....utterly exhausted and never knowing when or where to rest.....they say 'I'm not dead yet', but what good is that?.....their life has always been a muddle like this'. (Chapter 2).

Enlightened True Nature

Its blessing and gift
that we cannot receive
because it already has
been given – our Being.

Its reality and truth
that we cannot seek
because it already is
everywhere – our Life.

Its path and practice
that we cannot follow
because it already is
all that we do – our Way.

Its space and time
that we cannot discover
because it already is
all presence – Just-This.

Its peace and freedom
that we cannot attain
because it already is
all who we are – I-Am.

Way-Station Two
Tracking the Ox

Exploring

Learning

Here deep below remote mountains, the Ox's hoofprints are found.

Way-Station Two
Dao/Tao Zhan/Chan Er/Erh

道　站　二

Tracking The Ox

| Zhui/Chui | Ji/Chi | Niu/Niu |
| Track/Trace | Footprint | The Ox |

追　迹　牛

'Having the least bit of wisdom, I am traveling the Great Pathway fearing only deviating. The Great Pathway is very straight and direct, yet people are taking side-tracks and detours'. [TTC #53]

'Is there neither right nor wrong? Right is turning into wrong and wrong is turning into right. Long have people been bewildered'. [TTC #58]

The ego-self is cracking causing the end of slacking.
The beginning of tracking to find what is lacking.
The pathway is clear, hoofprints here, the Ox is near.

2.
Tracking the Ox

Text

Running alongside the riverbank under the trees, I discover hoofprints! Even under all of the tall fragrant grasses, I can see some hoofprints. Here deep below the remote mountains, the bull's hoofprints are found. These traces can no more be hidden than my nose, looking heavenward.

Comment

Understanding the sutras and the teachings, I see hoofprints of the bull.

Now I learn that, just as many utensils are made from the same one metal,

so too are the myriad entities made of the same one fabric of True Nature.

Unless I make discriminations, how will I perceive the right from the wrong?

Not yet having entered the gate, at least I have discerned the pathway to it.

Way-Station Two Synoptic Comment
Tracking The Ox

I finally make my way through all of the tall grasses and tangled growth, choose and take one of the paths, hoping that it is the right one. Lo and behold!. Right here beneath the shading trees, at the bank of the flowing river, in sight of the lofty mountains and underneath the tall grasses; I see hoofprints, scattered around everywhere and sometimes circling, made by what appears to be a great Ox. Now, right here, I see only hoofprints. They are as unhidden and evident as the nose on my face pointing up to the sky.

I seem to have found and taken the right path to find the Ox and the Ox may really exist. I desire to track and possibly discover this Ox, perhaps quietly and contentedly grazing somewhere close by in this otherwise desolate space. Will I be able or unable to find the Ox in some open and bright clearing in this wilderness?. Will I succeed or fail in catching hold of such an Ox, taming it and possibly even riding it home or to anywhere else on earth?

I have learned that the many teachings that I have explored, studied and understood all seem to refer to what appears to be the same one reality of what could be considered as the one, ultimate, absolute, essential and inborn or inherent True Nature of everyone and everything. The Ox seems to symbolize that oneness.

I am encouraged and motivated by the thought of possibly finding the Ox. I may even have already been close to, passed by and overlooked it with my head lowered and narrowly focusing so much on discerning the rightness or wrongness of the path I was taking.

The Ox must be close by. I can hear some snorting, snuffling and hoofing noises. I can see some stirred up dust and a fresh steaming dung heap. I can sense and feel the presence of the Ox. I have discerned the right pathway to it.

Way-Station Two Psychospiritual Commentary
Intellectual-Based Activities / Exploring

'When no discriminating thoughts arise, the old mind ceases to exist. When thought-objects vanish, the thinking-subject vanishes…..Understand the relativity of these two and the basic reality: the unity of emptiness. In this emptiness, the two are indistinguishable and each contains the whole world in itself'. Verse 5. *Hsin Hsin Ming/Faith in the Heart-Mind Verses* by Seng-Ts'an/Sosan (d. 606 CE).

We journey further into Nature, closer to those remote mountains that we saw beyond the city. And, lo and behold, right here under the shade trees near the riverbank, we discover hoofprints that appear to be those of a great Ox; here on the ground beneath us, unhidden under the sweet-smelling grasses, as plain as the pointing noses on our faces and right here in front of our very eyes.

We are encouraged to have found out that awakened, enlightened and liberated consciousness and True Nature are symbolized by a great Ox, the hoofprints of which we may just now have discovered! We believe that the Ox really exists and are motivated to keep going ahead with our searching for it.

In our pursuing, exploring, investigating and learning about an awakened, enlightened and liberated way of being and living; we have been reading about the life of the Buddha and studying Buddhist and Zen spiritual teachings in various sutras and texts. We are having some glimmers, inklings and intimations of what enlightenment and our One, Original, Inborn True Nature are and how they differ from our typical conditioned, fabricated, artificial, illusional and fictitious ego-self.

We are motivated to continue pursuing the early wisdom of Buddhist and Zen traditions and to find out more about and to have a better understanding; albeit intellectual, theoretical and conceptual; of our awakened, enlightened and liberated True Nature.

We are discovering the early wisdom and various concepts of Buddhist teachings that were experiences awakened in the Buddha and the bodhisattvas and patriarchs of the Buddhist spiritual tradition. We are intellectually understanding that all of the myriad Buddhist ideas and concepts are essentially united in one Mind and One, Original, Inborn True Nature that we all are and have been from the very beginning of our lives.

We are uncertain about some of the teachings and unsure of which ones or what parts of them we are able to successfully relate to and understand. We can't yet determine if certain teachings are right or wrong ones for us. And we can't do that without making some discriminations and comparisons and deciding whether or not they make sense to us or fit for us, even though we haven't directly experienced any of them.

Going beyond intellectual exposure, we have been actively sampling some meditation practices and have been able to successfully observe, to be less attached to and to be more calm about what thoughts and feelings are going on in our conscious awareness, rather than stopping them, clinging to them, judging them or reacting to them.

We are learning that all of the myriad objects, diverse phenomena and manifold things of our conscious experience and the world are really creations and projections of our own minds. In so-called 'New Age' literature, this has been described as creating our own 'reality'. What and how we are particularly thinking becomes an energy that manifests in the forms of our experience.

We are also becoming aware of the many one-sided, mutually exclusive, either-or and opposing dualities that characterize most all of our mental thoughts, concepts and judgments and that are the root sources and causes of discriminations that lead to biases, preferences and prejudices; personal and interpersonal conflicts and power struggles, racial profiling and social issues as well as to national combats and international wars.

We feel that changes and shifts are occurring in the nature of our consciousness away from focusing upon material objects, external things, surface appearances and the kinds of differences between others toward concentrating more on spiritual realities and truths, looking deeper within ourselves and including fellow human beings more impartially, equally and empathically.

Our searching for answers to questions, solutions to problems, settling of issues and resolution of conflicts has now become the sincere intention to take responsibility for the quandaries and dilemmas of our lives and to do something immediately, concretely and directly about them by taking definite directions and steps and possibly discovering newer and more awakened and enlightened ways of dealing with and managing them.

We are recognizing that we need to be accountable for how we are being or not being and how our lives are going or not going. It feels very enlivening, refreshing, validating, supporting and empowering to do so. We can't honestly externalize and project blame for our circumstances on genes, DNA, bad karma, destiny, fate, chance, other human beings, life events, astral configurations, the universe, God or whatever.

We are seeing our socially conditioned ego-self and its imposed limitations, idealized images, defense mechanisms, rigid controls and autonomous strivings as fundamentally insubstantial illusions and concepts of our mind. While necessary and useful for organizing, managing, integrating and executing certain aspects and functions; our ego-self is a problem when we completely identify with it and mistake it for our True Nature.

We are feeling that being authentic, genuine, sincere, honest and 'real' matters the most; as challenging and difficult as that might be much of the time. We also feel that goodness, rightness and trueness are ways of being and ends in themselves and not means of scoring points, gaining reputation, accruing merit or attaining salvation.

We are aware of the subjective, egocentric, idiosyncratic, relative, limited, narrow and often misinformed and erroneous nature of our belief systems and cherished opinions. And how they can be influencing, determining and distorting preconceptions, assumptions and evaluations that we have; and the determinations, conclusions and judgments that we make; about 'reality', fellow human beings and matters in general.

We are naturally being more available and accessible to and more open, connected and intimate with fellow human beings. And we are being more accepting, generous, attentive, kind, fair, patient, understanding, empathic, compassionate and helpful in our ongoing relationships and interactions. We are beginning to regard fellow human beings spiritually as having the same One, Inborn True Nature that we all do and share.

We are humbly encouraged about embarking upon a spiritual journey of the Buddha's Way and of discovering and treading an actual path to reach an awakened, enlightened and liberated consciousness that is so essential, significant and meaningful as that of our True Nature. We are also aware of the depth and extent of faith, trust, devotion, dedication, determination and diligence that are likely required to follow such a path.

We are hopeful about discovering, uncovering and possibly recovering our True Nature for which we are searching and which has been obscured and obstructed by our completely identifying with our conditioned ego-self that we think is who we essentially are.

While it has been informative, orienting and valuable to hear lectures and presentations and to attend and participate in Buddhist workshops and retreats given by Buddhist teachers; we realize that our understanding is mostly intellectual and is nowhere near the real experience of awakening, enlightenment and liberation. However, at least we have discerned some traces

A WAY-SHOWING PATH OF ENLIGHTENMENT

of it and seem to have successfully discovered what appears to be the right path to it that we are starting to follow further.

We are encouraged by, and optimistic about, actively doing something about ourselves and our life circumstances; what we have been exploring, learning and beginning to experience; hacking our way through the hegemony, entanglements, entitlements, justifications and machinations of our ego-self and finding a path to possibly becoming and being our awakened, enlightened and liberated True Nature.

We are hoping that awakening, enlightenment and liberation are not just the greatest ideas and concepts that our clever ego-mind and crafty ego-self have intended, pretended, contended and defended.

CHUANG TZU SAYS

'Heaven/Tao covers all without partiality and Earth bears up all without partiality'. (Chapter 6).

'Everything has a 'this' and a 'that'.....that came out of this and this depends on that and they give birth to each other. Where there is birth there is death, where there is right there is wrong. A state in which this and that aren't opposites is called the fulcrum or hinge of the Way/Tao.....walking two roads at once.....the best is being clear'. (Chapter 2).

'There is left and right; there are theories, debates, divisions, discriminations, evaluations and contentions.....the sage embraces the oneness of all things'. (Chapter 2).

'Let mind wander in simplicity, blend spirit with vastness, follow things the Way they are, have no personal views'. (Chapter 7).

Way Station Three
Glimpsing the Ox

ILLUMINATING

EXPERIENCING

I see the Ox's hindquarters
and tail. I ready halter and whip
in anticipation.

Way-Station Three
Dao/Tao Zhan/Chan San/San

Glimpsing The Ox

| Jian/Chien | Pie/P'ieh | Niu/Niu |
| Catch Sight Of | Glimpse | The Ox |

'As wise human beings, we are: purifying our inner vision and embodying perfect clearness.....illuminating inner dimensions'. TTC#10.

'As wise human beings, we are: continually assisting all beings..... None are being excluded. This is following inner light'. TTC#27.

Shrinking, weakening, abandoning and depriving are following expanding, strengthening, promoting and indulging. This is subtle illuminating'. TTC#36.

Perceiving subtleness is illuminating.....utilizing our outer radiating and returning to inner illuminating, we are not endangering living.....This is according with the Constant (Tao)'. TTC#52.

'We are contemplating selves, families, communities, countries, worlds in light of our own'. TTC#54

A glimpse of Ox-seeing, no more just 'me'-ing and now 'we'-ing.
I see the Ox's tail. I'm on its trail and will catch up to it without fail.
Ego-self illuminating, contemplating without ruminating.
A moment of awaking, correct path-taking, ego-self forsaking.
True Nature illuminated and waking. One whole-making.

3
GLIMPSING THE OX

TEXT

I hear the song of the nightingale. The sun is warm, the wind is mild and the willow trees along the shore are green. In this place, no bull can hide!

I see the bull's hind-quarters and tail. I ready halter and whip in anticipation.

What artist could ever draw its massive head and those majestic horns?

COMMENT

When the part is seen and the voice heard, the whole source is sensed.

As soon as all of the six senses are merged into one, the gate is entered.

Wherever one enters the gate, the head of the bull is always seen!

This unity is like salt in water and nothing is separate from True Nature.

Way-Station Three Synoptic Comment
Glimpsing The Ox

After seeing the hoofprints and sensing the presence of the Ox, I am searching for it in a more serious, committed and determined and a more conscious, focused and concentrated way, along what now appears to be a true rather than a false path. I am journeying along the path; curious, interested and hoping and eagerly anticipating that it is heading toward finding the Ox.

I am completely immersed in Nature and enjoying feeling the warm sun and gentle breeze and hearing the pleasant birdsong accompanying me as I am walking beneath the swaying green willow trees lining the riverbank along the path where the Ox's hoofprints are.

I am appreciating the precious blessings and treasured gifts that Great Mother Nature is bestowing upon me and all of my fellow human beings; most of all, our human incarnation and our brief mortal human life. The whole area around me is so clear, open and bright that I will be certain not to miss coming upon the Ox.

Woah! Suddenly I glimpse the rear end and tail of an Ox. Seeing the size of them, I know that they belong to a very great whole Ox. The Ox is no longer hiding from me!. Even a master artist could not portray how massive I imagine its magnificent head and majestic horns to be.

All of my senses have merged. I am seeing the Ox's hind quarters, smelling its coat, hearing its bellowing, tasting its stirred up dust and feeling how great are its head and its nature.

The Ox is one in Nature, like salt is dissolved in water and color in dyestuff. Not the slightest thing is now apart from the unity of the Ox and my True Nature.

I feel good about having cut through the wilderness entanglements, having been able to successfully find and take the right path to track the Ox by following its hoofprints. Now I am at least glimpsing its hind quarters and tail and clearly sensing their source in the whole Ox. I'm hoping that I can see the whole Ox and catch hold of it.

Enlightened True Nature

Enlightened True Nature is not some 'thing'
to be sought, found, attained, and possessed
by our ego-self.

Enlightened True Nature is pure and empty
consciousness and clear and open awareness
awakening to itself that can be realized by
our ego-self.

Enlightened True Nature cannot be born,
awakened or found because it never died,
was asleep or was lost. It is our ego-self
that is born and dies, sleeps and wakes up
and is lost and found.

Enlightened True Nature is all that ego-self is not.
Ego-self is all that enlightened True Nature is not.
True Nature is not the object of enlightened beings.
Ego-self is the subject of unenlightened beings.

Enlightened True Nature is found in the darkening
of the light, the clearing of the mind, the silencing
of the sounds and the stilling of the motions of our
ego-self's images, thoughts, words and actions.

Enlightened True Nature and our ego-self co-exist,
co-relate and cooperate in the conscious awareness
of our ordinary experiences of everyday living and
are accepted for what they each are and are not.

Way-Station Three Psychospiritual Commentary
Experience-Generated Acquaintings / Awareness

'To live in the Great Way is neither easy nor difficult. But those with limited views are fearful and irresolute; the faster they hurry, the slower they go and clinging attachments cannot be limited. Even to be attached to the idea of enlightenment is to go astray. Just let things be in their own way and there will be neither coming nor going'. Verse 6. *Hsin Hsin Ming/Faith in the Heart-Mind Verses* by Seng-Ts'an/Sosan (d. 606 CE).

Much understanding of spiritual teachings can be obtained through studying the sutras, scriptures, texts and writings of various traditions, e.g., Hinduism, Taoism, the different Buddhisms, Sufism et al. Attending live or video lectures, presentations, workshops, meetings, conferences, gatherings and retreats given by masters, gurus and teachers who are living the teachings and practices of spiritual traditions provide opportunities to directly experience them. Any understanding remains partial, intellectual and conceptual, unless it also involves actual experiences.

The original teachings of the Buddha are the widespread dissemination of voluminous sutras, scriptures and texts having their massive 'magnificent head' and 'majestic horns' in the grand pointing of the Buddha himself. We have only glimpsed the partial tail-end of the whole Ox-body of Buddhist and Zen Buddhist awakening, enlightening and liberating teachings and are not yet seeing or understanding their great source and revelations in their entireity.

Their whole truth is still like salt dissolved in the waters of Buddhist history, culture and practice and invisibly hidden within our conditioned ego-self and obscuring ego-mind. But at

A WAY-SHOWING PATH OF ENLIGHTENMENT

least we have glimpsed the partial reality of the whole body of Buddhist wisdom and True Nature and are awakening to seeing that there is not a thing that is separate from them.

We are also realizing that all of our searching for, and tracking of, the Ox of awakened, enlightened and liberated True Nature has been well worth the time taken and the effort made and is clearly confirming its existence and that we have taken the right path and true way to it.

This 'stage' in the process of becoming and being 'enlightened' involves engaging in actual practices of the Buddhist and Zen Buddhist spiritual tradition, e.g., sitting zazen. Doing so, we are beginning to have experience-based understandings of some of the characteristics and qualities of some of the non-ordinary states of consciousness occurring in meditation. Also, at this time, we are naturally having, on our own; momentary calmings, clearings, openings, deepenings, expansions, elevations, etc. of our ordinary consciousness.

The net effect of such changes is that we begin having experiences of the real existence of our True Nature and Buddha-Mind and of a whole inner reality that constitutes and transcends our ordinary consciousness and mental functioning. We have had inklings, subtle traces and now actual glimpses and partial understandings of a non-dual, transcendent and illuminated state of being and consciousness which are generating our intentions and objectives for further cultivating and practicing.

We are aware that our ordinary consciousness is characterized by innumerable mutually-exclusive either-or dualities. Almost every word, concept and 'thing' has an opposite counterpart. For words, there are synonyms and antonyms. For concepts, there are, e.g., light-dark, past-future, inner-outer, female-male, self-other, peace-war, life-death, etc.. Non-ordinary, transcendent, awakened, illuminated and enlightened consciousness is a non-duality, dual unity and oneness.

We often suffer the effects, ramifications and consequences

of dualistic thinking, e.g, when it involves separation, division, discrimination, opposition, competition, conflict and warfare. Most spiritual traditions are characterized by non-dual reality as captured in phrases such as 'one-without-a-second' and 'not-two' that refer to the unitary state of consciousness constituting enlightened spiritual realization beyond any and all subject-object, this-that splits.

Subject-object nonduality is particularly addressed in the concept of 'consciousness-without-an-object'; which is one pure, clear, open, transcendent and higher consciousness beyond dualities of seer-seen, knower-known, haver-had, doer-done, etc.. This consciousness is an integral consciousness that is unified by the mutually-inclusive both-and integration of co-existing, reciprocal and synergistic complements rather than mutually-exclusive and either-or contraries or opposites.

This dual-unity is not a false 'oneness' that is achieved by the one-sided dividing, separating, excluding, negating and eliminating of the 'other'; but is a true oneness attained by uniting, including, affirming and joining with it as a complementary counterpart.

We understand that thinking, being, living and relating non-dualistically have very profound implications and applications for the transformation of individual, social, national and international relationships. We realize that issues, problems and conflicts in these areas are rooted in an 'us-not them' mentality rather than one of 'we and they', which is an equally united intersubjectivity without making a one-sided 'object' out of any 'other'.

Intrapsychically, this would integrate our ego-self's sub-personalities, which are often at odds with each other and with a deeper and higher Self, True Nature and 'I-Am', which doesn't consider any of them as 'object-mes', to its own subjectivity.

Interpersonally, this would integrate 'me' and 'you', as 'we', where neither one is a separated 'object' to an 'other's' subjectivity. And socially, nationally and internationally; this would integrate 'us' and 'them' intersubjectively as 'we' and 'they' or just 'we' where, again, neither one is a separated 'object' to an 'other's' subjectivity.

We are looking at dualities within ourselves, society, and world nations and are imagining that, if we are really and truly being and living a non-dual consciousness; personally, interpersonally and internationally, we would simply be one unseparated and undivided dual-unity and whole comprised of two interconnected units that would be co-existing and co-operating and not be in conflict or at war within itself or between each other. (How could our heart's auricles and ventricles attack each other?).

In our country, it wouldn't matter or make a 'real' difference, if land was designated, defined, identified and named as either rural or urban, scenic or not, developed or not, expensive or not. It wouldn't matter or make a 'real' difference if human beings were objectified, differentiated, distinguished and labeled as either black or white, male or female, old or young, married or single, healthy or sick, gay or straight, democrat or republican, religious or not, educated or not, wealthy or not, working or not, home owners or not, attractive or not, etc..

Nations would all be unique lands, peoples and cultures co-existing, co-relating and co-operating as equal citizens of one whole single world and as equal inhabitants of one whole single planet. There would be an absence of the separations and divisions of governmental autocracies, social class hierarchies, political divisions, sectarian organizations, etc. that provoke violence, civil wars, cold wars, proxy wars, hot wars and their accompanying destruction, devastation, desolation, desperation and abusing, wounding, trafficking, raping and killing of 'others', 'thems' and 'those'.

We have an increasing awareness of, and a more experiential understanding of, some of the spiritual realities and concepts that we read and heard about and that we learned from teachers.

All of us human beings are blessed incarnations and precious embodiments of Spirit that is the primordial consciousness and empty openness of Tao, Great Mystery, True Nature and Buddha-Nature that originate everything from their pure and open creative potentiality for manifesting.

They are the source of all life; which they pervade, animate, activate, protect, nourish, organize, sustain, maintain, develop, evolve and complete. Our human body is the great miracle that Spirit forms with boundaried edges on the physical plane of our human existence. Our human Soul is the great marvel of Spirit's uniting with body in all of its diverse manifestations and its journeying on the psychical and physical planes of our human existence. Our human being is the great magnificence that Spirit develops, manifests and completes throughout its life cycle, life course and life span until its completion and returning.

We are beginning to understand Oneness; the One origin and identity of all beings, human beings and things and their One, Original, Inborn True Nature, the truth of which; from the perspective of Mahayana, Ch'an and Zen Buddhism; is the same as emptiness. We are aware that engaging in the more experiential practices of the path of enlightened being leads us to awaken to One, Original, Inborn True Nature; which is and has always been who we ultimately, absolutely and essentially are as a human being; since before our birth, throughout our life and after our death.

We are beginning to understand how much of ourselves and our lives, up to this point, has been the 'self' and the 'life' of our socially conditioned ego-self; a culturally determined artifact, fictional entity and psychical epiphenomenon; that has obscured, eclipsed and displaced True Nature. We realize that our finite ego-self is useful in organizing, managing and maintaining certain structures, functions, operations and relations of our physical, mental, emotional and social selves but, from the standpoint of True Nature and 'I-Am', it is a fictional entity that has no substantial existence and certainly is not who we essentially are.

We are beginning to see everything more clearly, just as it is before making any objective 'thing' out of it in terms of abstract conceptualizing, mental construing, rational analyzing and naming. We are doing less 'thinking' about things and beginning to experience and understand how the practices of meditation help relax our bodies, quiet down 'monkey mind' and open it up to be available for, aware of and attentive to whatever arises from and appears in our field of conscious awareness.

We have had a momentary kensho, 'aha' experience, a fleeting flash of 'seeing into' the reality of True Nature and of sensing its source in and as our pure and empty consciousness and clear and open awareness. Kensho has given us the experience of seeing a whole different order of reality and an awareness of non-duality and of the dual-unity, mutual arising and complementary interdependence of apparent dualities.

We have partially glimpsed the possibility of seeing the 'whole picture' of awakened, enlightened and liberated True Nature, which is now an experience-based reality and not just an abstract idea or mental concept and is one to be lived in deeper and fuller satoris of 'being', and not just 'seeing into', True Nature.

There has been an upsurge of psychological issues along with these experiences that are the pre-conceptions, predispositions and patterns of our ego's case of 'mistaken identity' and its mental ignorance and delusions, emotional desires and attachments, volitional habits and errors and relational separations and divisions.

We are dealing with the challenges presented by our ego-self's attitudes, beliefs, opinions, preferences, judgments and conclusions; its tenacious and resistant needs to maintain, strengthen, enhance and defend its 'existence', sovereignty and hegemony and its fears of letting-go into being subordinated to, eclipsed and displaced by, transformed or assimilated into True Nature.

Working with deconditioning our conditioned ego-self is requiring vigilant attention, sustained concentration and intense effort in order to stay focused on the task at hand. The Ox of enlightenent is facing away from us; showing that there is more ahead for us and is perhaps reflecting that we are conceptualizing our kensho experience and it is moving away from us whenever we are making it an object, 'thing' that we 'attained'.

We are less attached to thoughts, ideas, concepts and words and are more focused upon the pure and empty consciousness from which they originate and to which they point, as with the proverbial finger pointing to the moon. We are able to use the various 'negative' or 'positive' objects and experiences of our finite ego-self and ego-mind, reflexively, to revert to remembering the reality of True Nature.

We are freer of the complexities and entanglements of the world, the enmeshments and complications of relationships and the opinions, assessments and judgments of fellow human beings. We are less concerned with being externally object-, 'thing'- and 'other'-oriented, as well as being internally subject-, ego- and self-oriented. And we are awakening from both the objective and subjective unreality and duality of experience to the unity and identity of the emptiness and suchness of everything.

We are having some partial understandings of True Nature as being both emptiness and suchness and are aware that the 'realities' of all of our experiences take place from, to and in the consciousness of our very own mind and that no 'real' realities exist in the outer finite material world apart from our concepts of them. We are awakening to our inner identity with True Nature and that everyone and everything in life is constituted by, manifests and reveals the same One, Original, Inborn True Nature.

All in all, we are deeply appreciating the blessed gift of our precious human incarnation and the profound journeying of awakening and transforming from completely identifying with our ego-self to being identified with True Nature. We are feeling that we are on a spiritual path and are making our own unique Way through uncharted territories. We are openly accepting the experiences we are having without making good-bad, right-wrong and true-false judgments about them.

We are trusting the awareness and feeling that we are being directed and guided by energies that are far greater than ourselves and beyond our intellectual understanding. We are immensely grateful for such an adventure and opportunity to be on a path of awakening to, discovering, and hopefully possibly becoming and being enlightened True Nature.

Without dampening our enthusiasm in the least; teachers are cautiously reminding us that we are still primarily at an intellectual and conceptual level of partial understanding; that our ego-mind is still filled with ideas about and hopes for enlightenment as a 'thing' or 'goal' to 'attain' and to not objectify and dwell upon any momentary kensho experiences or to anticipate or expect any more.

Nonetheless, we still awaken each new morning at dawn (the time of transitioning from darkness to light), eagerly begin meditating and watch our heightened state of 'anticipation without expectation' continue to come and go.

CHUANG TZU SAYS

'The sage.....delights in old age, early death, the beginning and the end.....serves as a model for human beings.....True human beings' breath comes from deep inside.....from their heels and not from their throats'. (Chapter 6).

Way-Station Four
CATCHING THE OX

REALIZING

UNDERSTANDING

I seize the Ox.
But not without terrific struggle.

Way-Station Four
Dao/Tao Zhan/Chan Si/Szu

道 站 四

Catching the Ox

| Zhua/Chua | Cao/Ts'ao | Niu/Niu |
| Catch/Grasp | Take Hold Of | The Ox |

抓 操 牛

'Self or fame, life or wealth, gain or loss; which is more near, more dear, holds more fear?...... Hoarding is losing a lot. Knowing what is enough..... is avoiding endangering and shortening one's life'. TTC #44.

'Taking pride in wealth and fame is bringing downfall and collapse'. TTC #9.

'Understanding ourselves, we are being illuminated and inwardly strong. Being content with ourselves, we are being wealthy'. TTC #33.

'Understanding my words is very easy.....Yet, few in the world are understanding them. My words have an ancestral source.....People are not understanding this. So, they are not understanding me'. TTC #70.

'Understanding and not acting knowing is wellness. Not understanding and acting knowing is illness', TTC #71.

'Understanding, we are not speaking. Speaking, we are not understanding'. TTC #56.

The Ox sought has been caught. Pursuing was not for naught.
Catching is the ending of seeking, stretching and fetching.
The rope must be held taut and the whip must be brought.
Realizing without compromising. Understanding is commanding.

4.
CATCHING THE OX

TEXT

I seize the bull but not without terrific struggling. Its great will is very strong.

Its power seems inexhaustible and I have difficulty holding onto the tether.

(the bull's tail is pointing upward and it may eliminate some dung in fear).

The bull gets away and charges to a high plateau far above the cloud-mists.

Or it stands in an impenetrable ravine closer to me hoofing and bellowing.

COMMENT

The bull has dwelled in the wilderness for a long time, but I caught it today!

Infatuated with scenery and longing for sweeter grass, it often wanders away.

Its mind is still stubborn and unbridled. For it to submit, I must use my whip.

Way-Station Four Synoptic Comment
Catching the Ox

I see the whole Ox. I am completely focused on the Ox and unaware of anything else around me. I quietly approach the Ox and do catch up with it, pretending that I am not even there, and quickly seize and try to hold onto it.

The Ox struggles and it takes great strength, determination, effort and persistence on my part to keep hold of it. The Ox is very strong, powerful, stubborn and has a wild animal-nature and a seemingly inexhaustible will of its own. I don't know if I have the strength to have a firm enough hold of the Ox. I'm afraid of losing my hold.

The Ox gets away from me! It heads up to a high plateau far above the cloud-mists, grazes for awhile in the grassy plains and then wanders back and down into a deep ravine close to me where it just stands, bellowing loudly and hoofing the ground. Am I going to lose everything that I have gained so far?

I realize that the Ox has dwelled for a long time in its familiar surroundings and is resisting leaving them. The Ox keeps wandering back and forth, enamored of the wilderness scenery and directed toward the sweet grasses, but keeps coming back closer to me.

The Ox remains free and stubborn. I know that if I want to fully catch and take and keep hold of the Ox again and have it become compliant, I am going to have to use some kind of restraint and disciplinary means for doing so. I will have to use the halter, rope and whip.

But at least today, I have caught up with the Ox and am trying my very best to hold onto it.

WAY-STATION FOUR PSYCHOSPIRITUAL COMMENTARY
Path-Committed Struggling / Realizing

'Rest and unrest derive from illusion. With enlightenment there is no liking and disliking. All dualities come from ignorant inference. They are like dreams or flowers in air: foolish it is to try to grasp hold of them. Right and wrong, gain and loss: such thoughts must be finally abolished at once'. Verse 9. *Hsin Hsin Ming/Faith in the Heart-Mind Verses* by Seng-Ts'an/Sosan (d. 606 CE).

The Ox of awakening and enlightenment is difficult to catch and hold onto and the Buddhist teachings are difficult to 'get' and hold onto experientially. Both the Ox of True Nature and our conditioned ego-self want to remain with their long-standing, usual and familiar environments and ways and patterns of being and living. Both wander away, the Ox to sweet grasses and the ego to sensory pleasures. Both charge off to the lofty heights of uncontrolled longings and the deep abysses of unbridled satisfactions.

The Ox is powerful, strong-willed, stubborn and resists being captured, subdued and controlled and wants to run free. Our own will and power are required to match or exceed those of the Ox if we are to catch and keep hold of it. If we can catch the Ox; we have to use a rope and whip to control and eventually discipline and tame it. At times, our teachers have to use decorum, skillful means, shouts and sticks to assist us in staying awake, focused and concentrating during meditation practice.

Our ego-mind is still active, restless, distracted, unstable and straying off and we are wrestling with our ego-self's familiar and long-standing expectations and preconceptions, desires and attachments, habits and urges, judgments and preferences, etc. which are present and easy to perpetuate and fall back into. We are dealing with our long-standing (and now-sitting!) ego-conditioning, difficulties and conflicts; the traces of greed, anger and hatred. Steadfast determination and strength are necessary for controlling the habitual patterns of our ego-self.

From reading books and attending presentations and participating in workshops and retreats, we are definitely interested in understanding Buddhist and Zen Buddhist ideas, concepts, teachings and practices. We know that we can't hold onto the Ox or grasp awakening, enlightenment and liberation with intellectual knowledge and belief systems alone and we are taking concrete and direct actions through committing to regular ongoing meetings and meditation practice with one teacher and in a group.

So far; we have had some experience visualizing sacred images and mandalas, one-pointed concentrating, contemplating and reflecting inwardly and absorbing ourselves in whatever we are looking at or engaged in doing in the moment. We have been 'belly breathing', doing yoga and moving meditations like T'ai Chi and Ch'i Kung; which have resulted in calmness and stronger energy, deeper feelings of being grounded and centered in our body and more relaxed and graceful in our movements. Sometimes we also just walk, stand, sit or recline in stillness and silence.

Through our past reading, we have learned something about herbal tinctures and acupuncture points and meridians in our body and about moxabustion cupping and other methods of stimulating them for energy releasing, balancing and healing. There is so much information and knowledge in Chinese medicine to learn about, process and understand and it's all pretty overwhelming. We are realizing why expert teachers and practitioners are essential in order to get anywhere.

At any rate, our varied experiences are helping us to further

A WAY-SHOWING PATH OF ENLIGHTENMENT

narrow down, select and adopt Zen Buddhism as a spiritual tradition that we feel is most fitting. The path of Chinese Taoism is also appealing mostly in its philosophy of living rather than its religious practices and rituals. Tao, as Ultimate Reality seems similar to True/Buddha-Nature and the notions of yin-yang to Buddhist teachings about dual-unity. And both traditions discuss wu-wei, unforced, harmonious and effortless 'non-doing'.

Right now, the path of Zen Buddhism seems to be the most relevant one and we seem to have benefited most from our experiences with presenters, teachers and group leaders and meditation practices in that tradition. We feel that we are engaged in an adventure and journey that makes sense and have explored different spiritual paths and ways of being and living before making our decision. We have already changed in remarkable and rewarding ways and certainly aren't the same persons we were before beginning to seek awakening, enlightenment and liberation.

There is a big difference between reading and hearing about spiritual wisdom and actually experiencing some of it sinking in and having a firm grasp of it. As far as progress goes, we feel directed toward something that is real, valuable and worthwhile. But it seems like the more that we're exposed to and are experiencing, the more complicated life is becoming. It's difficult to reconcile the realities and necessities of our ordinary everyday life as they are with a more ongoing and possible enlightened way of being, living and relating.

One teacher was asked if you need to be an ascetic monk living away from the world in a monastery or hermitage, especially when you see so much that is bad, wrong and false in it. She said that we can be 'in the world' but not 'of the world' and that our feelings about external things like the world have to do with how we relate to them as part of the human condition, i.e., with either delusions, attachments and judgments or with wisdom, acceptance and compassion.

We do see that, as human beings and regardless of whatever, we are all 'in the same boat' of being, living and trying to make the best of ourselves and our lives.

We are taking more responsibility for our own life and have a greater sense of our part and role in creating the stressing, striving, struggling and suffering of our ego-self. We have greater confidence in our ability to overcome, subdue, subordinate and transform the goings on of our conditioned, partial and limited ego-self and are eager and willing to experience True Nature clearly and deeply.

We are experiencing how stubborn and resistant to change our ego-self is; how difficult a struggle it is to break old, familiar, reinforced and ingrained patterns and habits and are appreciating the kind of firm discipline; ongoing strength, effort and perseverance that it takes to keep working on the challenges of becoming a true human being living a real life.

At least our ego-self is now co-existing, engaged and interacting with the Ox of enlightened True Nature and trying to catch and take and keep firm hold of it.

Our momentary kensho experience is not sufficient to firmly and fully grasp the whole Ox of True Nature. True Nature is still an object-thing to get, have, become and be. Our ego-self is not yet adapted to, aligned or in accord with it. But the kensho awakening is confirming, motivating and encouraging us to keep focusing and concentrating on the Ox of enlightened True Nature single-pointedly and whole-heartedly.

Through meditation, we have been doing less abstracting, objectifying and conceptualizing and have been experiencing developing states of awareness, alertness, attention, witness consciouness, calmness and openness. We have been experiencing more than the previous inklings and glimpses of transcendent and transpersonal realities that are beyond ordinary consciousness and are wondering if they are part of being enlightened, if and when they occur more frequently, but we don't know that for certain.

However, it is helpful to look at ourselves and our life from a more open, expanded and spacious perspective and to begin to accept, appreciate and allow ourselves to just be how we are being and to just do what we are doing in the present moment. But it doesn't occur that often. It is really challenging and difficult to maintain that perspective, to relinquish old ways of seeing and thinking about things and to keep from getting drawn into and being attached to this or that experience. But now, at least we are aware of it when we do!.

While the energy and will of our ego-self is interacting with that of the whole Ox of True Nature, it is difficult to keep the Ox centered in our ego-mind and we need to concentrate exclusively on it in order to take hold of it. We are focusing less on interfering mental thought-trains and dualities and more on the state of pure consciousness or Buddha-Mind that is originating them.

If we are going to hold onto and to not lose the whole of what we have already gained through learning, experiencing and brief awakening so far; we are going to need ongoing discipline, strength, determination, skill, steady effort and perseverance.

It is with great struggling that we finally seize the Ox, take hold of and firmly grasp True Nature with our ego-self. Both the Ox and our ego-self are difficult to control. We have to hold on tightly, not give up and not let go of the Ox and of our momentary kensho experience of awakened True Nature. We consider ourselves as having True Ox-Nature, but that it still is obscured and obstructed by our ego-self that is resisting being subordinated to it and is clinging to, strengthening, enhancing, defending and perpetuating its illusional existence and autonomous identity.

We have caught hold of; but are nowhere near fully being; One, Original, Absolute, Ultimate, Essential, Inborn True Nature. We have to be aware of the ego-inflation, self-importance, pride and arrogance that may follow from feeling that we have already attained and 'gotten' some real grasp of enlightened True Nature in our awakening kensho experiences.

Now that the Ox of awakened, enlightened and liberated True Nature has been caught; if we are going to successfully hold onto and not lose what we have learned and experienced thus far; it needs to be tamed, disciplined and trained through constant, consistent, continuous and continual effort and cultivating.

Chuang Tzu says

'Even sages have difficulty coping with human beings who are after fame and gain'. (Chapter 4).

'Running round chasing after things and blaming others is not as good as laughing, going along with things, forgetting their changes and entering the mysterious oneness of Heaven/Tao'. (Chapter 6).

Enlightenment Is Not

Enlightenment is not
something that we do,
something that we are,
something that we have,
something that we know.

We are not enlightened
if we think that we are,
if we feel that we are,
if we say that we are,
if we act like we are.

TEN ZEN OXEN

THE TRANSFORMING MID-ENLIGHTENMENT

WAY-STATION FIVE
TAMING THE OX

WAY-STATION SIX
RIDING THE OX

Way-Station Five
Taming the Ox

Identifying

Cultivating

The Ox becomes well trained
and naturally gentle

Way-Station Five
Dao/Tao Zhan/Chan Wu/Wu

道　　站　　五

Taming The Ox[8]

| Xun/Hsun | Lien/Lian | Niu/Niu |
| Tether/Tame | Train/Refine | The Ox |

訓　　練　　牛

'When displaying, asserting, boasting and parading; we are not shining, attracting, receiving and enduring'. TTC #24.

'Knowing the masculine, light and splendor; embodying the feminine, dark and humility; being valleys, models and streams of our world; not straying, deviating and departing from eternal, constant and abundant Virtuosity; returning to this Original, Ultimate and Natural State (Tao)'. TTC #28.

Disciplined taming without enflaming, blaming or shaming. Reaching the aim without playing any game; the Ox is tame. The Ox and the ego-self are becoming one and the same.

5.
Taming the Ox

Text

Rope and whip are necessary, lest the bull stray off down some dusty road.

It becomes well trained, naturally gentle. Unfettered, the bull is obedient.

It follows along willingly and I can hold the rope loosely and look skyward.

Comment

When one thought arises, another thought follows in a continuous chain.

When the first thought springs from awakened and enlightened True Nature, all subsequent thoughts are true. Through delusion, all thoughts are false.

Delusion is not the result of objectivity but is the result of our subjectivity.

I'm keeping the nose-ring well secured and not allowing even one doubt.

Way Station Five Synoptic Comment
Taming the Ox

Once caught and, as expected, it is necessary to gentle and tame the Ox by using the strong and firm disciplinary means of a rope and whip in order to prevent it from running off to its favorite pastures, dusty ruts and water-holes. Although difficult for me to do, I have to continue holding the rope tightly and periodically using the whip firmly in order for the Ox to settle down and become compliant.

After some time and a great deal of effort, the Ox becomes well trained and tamed, doesn't need to be restrained and obeys my every command and direction. Rather than continuing with initially forcefully controlling and firmly disciplining the Ox, I end up skillfully attuning to and according with its original and naturally gentle nature. Now, I can hold the rope loosely and, even after being unbridled, the Ox follows me wherever I go.

My ego-self and ego-mind are harmonized with the awakened and enlightened True Nature and Buddha-Mind that the Ox represents and it becomes tame and no longer needs to be bound by any constraints. When let completely loose; the Ox, awakened True Nature and my ego-mind still occasionally wander off to their familiar territories but don't go very far away and always naturally return by themselves.

Both the Ox and I are comfortable and at home with each other. My ego-self is identified with True Nature and is harmoniously interrelated with it.

I am aware of how my thoughts arise in a continuous train of one thought after another. I experience that when thoughts arise from and in my ordinary consciousness and unawakened, unenlightened and deluded ego-mind; they are subjective and untrue.

And when thoughts arise from and in pure, empty, clear and

open consciousness and awakened, enlightened and non-deluded mind; they are objective and true. I need to keep holding onto the truth of this awareness and still keep hold of the Ox's rope loosely but securely enough without allowing any doubt.

I look skyward and am delighted to have the Ox of awakened and enlightened True Nature as a close companion. I am enjoying my heart-felt connection and intimate relationship with the Ox and am feeling ready to mount it and to let it ride me back home.

Cultivating Enlightenment

Don't try to stop thinking.
Accept thinking happening.
Allow thoughts to come and go,
watch thoughts coming and going
and let them return your awareness
to one original and inborn True Nature.

Way-Station Five Psychospiritual Commentary
Discipline-Focused Training / Cultivating

'If the mind makes no discriminations, the ten thousand things are as they are; of a single essence. To understand the mystery of this One-essence is to be released from all entanglements. When all things are seen equally, the timeless self-essence is reached.....in this causeless and relationless state'. Verse 10. 'Obey the nature of things and you will walk freely and undisturbed. When thought is in bondage, the truth is hidden..... What benefit can be derived from separations and distinctions?' Verse 7. *Hsin Hsin Ming/Faith in the Heart-Mind Verses* by Seng-Ts'an/Sosan (d. 606 CE).

The great Ox of awakening, enlightenment and liberation, True-Nature, has been herded and caught and now needs to be tamed, gentled and domesticated (brought home).

Having organized and integrated a number of the concepts and iconography of the Mahayana, Ch'an and Zen Buddhist spiritual traditions and, along with the meditation experiences that we are having with Zen Buddhist teachers and on our own, we feel that we are developing a fairly good sense of what this path of becoming enlightened True Nature is.

We have 'gotten' knowledge about awakening, enlightenment and liberation from the intellectual study of Zen Buddhist texts and from experiencing meditations of Zen Buddhist practice, but now need to bring 'home' True Nature through disciplined training and cultivating.

We are still having some difficulty integrating all of what we are learning and experiencing and feel the need for some kind of encompassing framework or focusing structure that would help us put it all together with regard to the process and goal of enlightenment.

Determining what approaches and directions to take and what assistance and guidance we might obtain involve committing to one teacher in the Zen Buddhist spiritual tradition. The teachers to whom we are most drawn are generally of Chinese or Japanese cultural heritage who have a traditional and long-standing lineage with which they are affiliated or aligned; along with its particular wisdom and practices that have been taught and transmitted for many centuries.

These Zen Buddhist teachers seem to be genuinely embodying, being, living and modeling the wisdom, teachings and lifestyles of their ancestors, culture and traditions and are generally natural, open, authentic, available, accessible, attentive and generous human beings. They are fully grounded, heart-centered and deeply absorbed in the Zen ways of enlightened being and living. They have, so to speak, 'been there' and now 'are there' with and for us.

Having one teacher and a group will assist us in more concretely and directly consolidating, cultivating, sharing and communicating what we have been learning and experiencing thus far. And being in a community of like-hearted fellow human beings; also dedicated to living an awakened, enlightened and liberated way of being; would help us work with specific personal issues that will likely be triggered, activated and precipitated by, and become more apparent in, such a collective social environment.

So, we are anticipating that committing to a particular path of Zen Buddhist spiritual tradition, following its teachings and cultivating its practices and being under the tutelage of one of its teachers will definitely advance our progress toward the goal of becoming and being True Nature and a more awake, conscious, enlightened, transformed and liberated human being.

The support of being with a teacher and 'path-mates' will help us to validate, clarify, better understand, monitor, reinforce and refine the experences that we are having and the processes that we are engaged in, either alone or in the group. When our experiences remain private, it is often difficult to ascertain whether they are bona fide enlightening ones, illusions or outright delusions of our ego-mind.

Certainly, choosing a long-standing traditional Zen Buddhist spiritual path that is engaged in and followed by a large number of fellow students, devotees and practitioners and which is led and guided by a confirmed Zen teacher who we feel is 'the real thing', authentic, genuine, sincere, honest and not necessarily charismatic; seems safe and trustworthy; all the while eschewing obvious cults, their leaders and indoctrinated followers.

So, all of that considered, we have chosen one Zen teacher and community with whom we feel comfortable and who is the most fitting for us. We have been attending Dharma talks, have been participating in regular group meetings and have already established some close, friendly relationships with other members of the community.

Regarding cultivating on a path toward and to an enlightened way of being; both the Ox of True Nature and our ego-mind are unstable, unruly and keep straying off. So, strict disciplining is required using the 'rope' and 'whip' and our teacher's 'shout' and 'stick'. There is a strong draw for both the Ox and ego-self to remain in their familiar preferred settings and customary habitual routines. We need to stand our ground, hold the rope firmly, not lose our grip and not let go. Being strong, determined and diligent and having no doubt or hesitation in applying and tending are required.

The Ox-Mind and our ego-mind remain as their own separate, distinct and different natures, wander off and go their own ways; but are now engaged together, dynamically interacting with and mutually interacting, matching and influencing each other in our conscious awareness, albeit in an often intense push-pull relationship. But we believe that an integration of our ego-self and True Nature and a transformation of our ego-self are possible.

By our ego-self skillfully attuning to and according with the original unbroken spirit and gentle nature of the Ox, both are harmoniously interrelating and we are naturally shifting our identifcation from our ego-self to True Nature. At times, we are experiencing both ego-mind being influenced by True Nature and True Nature manifesting in ego-mind. They are reciprocally interrelated, cooperating and turning into each other and there is an ego-mind to Ox-Mind and an Ox-Mind to ego-mind interchanging occurring.

Our ego-self has to shift, expand, evolve, transform and match the reality, energy and consciousness of True nature for any progress to be made.

About progress in the disciplining, training and cultivating of this transforming process; we are not wandering off as much in meditation, are not falling back into old patterns as much and are generally able to sustain the required amount of energy, strength and effort and to endure the back and leg discomfort it takes to stay focused and concentrated. Having a teacher really helps, especially when we have an individual private meeting/dokusan to work on difficulties and to assess progress.

We are trusting that the free, instinctual nature of the Ox-Mind of True Nature can become tamed, controlled, gentled and guided; as can our intelligent but ponderous elephant mind and our nimble but mischievous monkey mind. It takes time, effort, patience and skill to not lose awareness of, connection with and trust in True Nature and Buddha-Mind.

We are seeing that our finite ego-self is not a substantial separate and independent entity and we are able to accept and to live in balance and harmony with it without trying to conquer, subdue, dissolve or 'kill' it. Our ego-senses are more awakened to reality, insight and truth rather than just to the pursuits, satisfactions, gratifications and pleasures of needs, desires, externals, objects and 'things'.

We are better able to discern reality and truths from the ignorance, delusions and errors of our ego-mind. We are observing and becoming aware of the ways that our ego-mind and its constant, continuous and continual train of thoughts, objects, phenomena, contents and concepts preoccupies and distracts us with mental 'clutter', emotional 'filler', volitional 'busyness' and relational 'splits' that divert us from attending to quiet, calm, clear, 'empty' and open states of deeper and higher consciousness.

This time is one of a 'dark night of the soul'; seeing, confronting and dealing more intensely with ego-'stuff'; desires, attachments and habits that keep surfacing. And also, we are doing more intensive questioning, examining and reflecting upon when our knowledge seems true or ignorant and deluded and when our actions are appropriate or erroneous and reactive.

We are still, grossly and more subtly; oppressed, obstructed and impeded by our own ego-mind with regard to progressing toward, realizing and attaining True Nature. It is difficult to overcome or to transcend the social conditioning of our rigidly controlling and defended ego-self; its continually re-establishing, re-inventing, re-asserting and enhancing itself; its avoiding and resisting changing and, like a virus, its only rapidly mutating instead of truly transforming.

We are able to watch our thoughts arise, remain for a while and then pass on without reacting to or dwelling on them. We are seeing our ego-mind's one-sided subjectivity and some of its illusions, misinterpretations, delusions, projections, etc. and are able to use them to remember and to 're-source' the clearness, emptiness and openness of True Nature and True Mind.

We are experiencing that the dualities, separations, divisions, contraries and oppositions of our ego-mind can be unified and integrated; its emotional attachments can be transcended or relinquished and its volitional habits can be changed or eliminated.

We have at times experienced an expanded, encompassing

A WAY-SHOWING PATH OF ENLIGHTENMENT

and spacious consciousness and are gaining insight into differentiating the unreality of thoughts coming from our limited ego-mind and the reality of thoughts when they arise from and in that pure, clear, empty and open kind of consciousness. We are seeing that what we experience as truth arises from and in that pure inner consciousness of True Nature and not from our ego-self or the external world.

We have made an agreement with our limited conditioned ego-mind, i.e., if it remains still and open and follows our consciousness along like a child's pull-toy, it will see more than it could ever imagine. Also, our cultivating is like cleaning a mirror in the light of a 25 watt bulb and thinking that it is completely clean until our teacher comes along and screws in a 100 watt bulb and we see that the mirror is not as clean as we 'thought' it was.

We are also seeing the power of our self-deceiving ego-mind to invent and to believe its experienced 'reality' and that the so-called 'reality' is only its imaginary conception. The most significant experiences that we have had are ones whereby and wherein we realize that we have One Mind that really is True-Mind and essentially No-Mind that is completely empty, open and pure objectless and contentless consciousness. We have experienced reality and truth as being concretely, directly and immediately right here and right now in present space and time.

We are beginning to be able to facilitate, inhabit and enjoy such experiences through engaging in various exercises, meditations and practices that focus on clearing our mind of 'ignorant' ideas and thoughts, emptying our heart of 'attached' desires and feelings, stilling our will of 'erroneous' habits and drives and freeing ourselves from 'alienating' separations and divisions within ourselves and between ourselves and fellow human beings.

We are understanding that our ego-self cannot really suffer the ill-fated demise considered by some other teachers who advocate that becoming enlightened is predicated upon the complete 'dying' of the ego-self. However, much like the caterpillar transforms into its butterfly, the ego-self radically changes form but its essential being is not destroyed and remains alive.

We realize that our ego-self serves necessary functions and purposes; co-exists with True Nature and insures our psycho-biological, psychophysical, psychological, psychosocial and psychospiritual integrity. If we are journeying to some destination, it is important to have the energy of a reliable and dependable vehicle, e.g., an integral body-ego, body-mind and body-spirit that is interconnected and interdependent with True Nature and pure, clear, open and spacious consciousness.

Taming the Ox, which is cultivating True Nature, has involved; 1) shifting the focus of our conscious awareness inwardly and away from external objects and matters; 2) disciplining, controlling, refocusing, concentrating, 'herding' and 'tending' our distracted and wandering ego-mind; 3) allowing experiences to come and to go without judging or attaching to them; 4) subordinating our ego-self to True Nature; 5) identifying less with our ego-self and more with True Nature; 6) seeing the experiences of our ego-self as being sourced in True Nature; and 7) quieting our ego-mind sufficiently enough to gain insights into True Nature and to be open to experience actual moments of our consciousness transforming from being ego-mind centered to being True Nature-centered.

Our teacher continues to be an invaluable support, resource, aid, guide and 'marker' for our cultivating and progressing toward becoming and being True Nature; as noted before, especially through our periodic individual meetings with her.

The Ox of awakened, enlightened and liberated True Nature is finally tamed, obeys naturally, complies willingly and calmly follows along. The rope is hanging loose; the Ox doesn't need to be restrained, controlled or forced and, like our ego-mind, doesn't stray or wander off very far without quickly returning. After being tamed, the Ox is again being its original inborn True Nature. We have been more settled and stable in our meditations and our ego-mind has been following along with the naturally flowing and unfolding cultivating of One, Original, Inborn True Nature.

We are letting our intuition guide the now relatively frictionless, effortless and seamless activities of meditative cultivating. We are attuning to, according with, complying with and following the cultivating process, which now seems to have an inherent life of its own; is going on by itself and only needs caring, tending, refining and guiding. Cultivating True Nature is being led by its own intrinsic original purity, clarity, openness and spaciousness of consciousness. We are identifying more frequently with and as our True Nature, but our teacher reminds us that this is still an ego-identification.

We can relax somewhat, but still need to remain awake, alert and attentive. Our mental attitude and confidence, emotional balance and steadiness and daily living and activities have greatly improved. In general, we are being more peaceful and happy. We find ourselves naturally being more inclusive, accepting, grateful, appreciative, patient, empathic, compassionate, generous, helpful, friendly and forgiving.

We are experiencing everyone and everything, equally and non-judgmentally, just as they are being and we are opening to the light and illumination of consciousness; however it might reveal itself in its original purity, clarity and radiance and however we can experience that consciousness as nothing but or other than True Nature. What a welcomed relief!.

Our bodies are more still, our minds are more clear, our hearts are more open and our wills are more calm. We are aware that we are at some transformative midpoint along the path of the whole journey of enlightenment. We need to guard against being 'spiritually materialistically' deluded by and ego-attached to any momentary kensho experiences of awakening, realizing and understanding and thinking that we have 'gotten' something or somewhere and that there is nothing more to do. We need to make cultivating enlightened True Nature an ongoing activity of everyday living.

Periodic experiences of insight meditation and of kensho, seeing into True Nature, have resulted in some awakenings but have not yet resulted in a full satori experience of assimilating and being enlightened True Nature. With our more solid and stable meditative conscious awareness; we are witnessing, observing and 'seeing through' the many diverse ideas, objects and 'things' that our ego-mind 'thinks' up, construes, believes in and projects onto 'others' and 'the outer world'.

So far, it is our ego-self that identifies with True Nature and still has ideas about and concepts of awakening, enlightenment, liberation and True Nature. But through some of our meditative experiences, at least we are trusting that they aren't just the 'best ideas' that our ego-mind 'thinks up'! Of course, we will continue finding out for ourselves through ongoing cultivating and further committed, dedicated, determined and diligent practicing.

CHUANG TZU SAYS

'Once I dreamt that I was a butterfly happily flitting and fluttering around here and there and when I woke up, I didn't know if I was Chuang Tzu having dreamt I was a butterfly or I am a butterfly dreaming I am Chuang Tzu.....this is the transformation of things'. (Chapter 2).

'Who knows both what Heaven/Tao does and what human being does has reached the summit'. (Chapter 6).

Some Non-Dual Unities

At the mid-point of the path of awakened, illuminated, enlightened and transformed True Nature, some non-dual bipolar-unities of the 'Middle Way' that are acknowledged and regarded equally and integrally are:

Heaven-earth
Divine-human
Nature-culture
Spirit-body
Ultimate-intimate
Absolute-relative
Essential-existential
Transcendent-immanent
Transpersonal-personal
Infinite-finite
Eternal-temporal
Unborn-born
Immortal-mortal
Original-derived
Reality-illusion
Truth-delusion
Wisdom-ignorance
Compassion-uncaring
Kindness-unkindness
Generosity-greed
Objectivity-subjectivity
Unconditioned-conditioned
Unlimited-limited
Interdependent-independent
Complementary-contradictory

Constancy-change
Unity-multiplicity
Wholeness-partiality
True Nature-ego self
Natural-artificial
Beings-things/others
Being-doing
Nirvana-samsara
Emptiness-suchness
Awake-asleep/dreaming
Enlightened-unenlightened
Realized-unrealized
Liberated-unliberated
Non attached-attached
Conscious-non conscious
Clear-cloudy
Open-closed
Internal-external
Higher-lower
Central-peripheral
Calmness-agitation
Peacefulness-conflict
Freedom-bondage
Happiness-suffering
Etc.-etc.

Way-Station Six
RIDING THE OX HOME

INTEGRATING

PRACTICING

I am mounted astride the Ox
and slowly returning home.

Way-Station Six
Dao/Tao Zhan/Chan Liu/Liu

Riding the Ox

| Qi/Ch'i | Jia/Chia | Niu/Niu |
| Ride/Astride | Home/Family | The Ox |

'Since ancient times, these are being One; Heaven is clear, Earth is stable, Spirits are Sacred, valleys are fertile, beings are viable, leaders are virtuous; all are so through being One'. TTC #39.

'As wise human beings, we are unifying our Heavenly-Earthly Souls and embodyng undivided Oneness'. TTC #10.

'All beings are bearing dark Yin on their backs,
harboring bright Yang in their arms.
Harmonizing these two vital energies is bringing
all beings to completion.' TTC #42.

'All beings in our world are coming home to Tao, like mountain valley streams are flowing into the sea'. TTC #32.

The Ox-taming has been done. The Ox and the self are one.
Enlightened True Nature abiding without hiding or priding.
True Nature 'riding'. Ox needs no guiding.
Homing with no back-sliding.
Concentrating, integrating, contemplating, consecrating.
Practicing, no discriminating, no debating, no deviating.

6.
RIDING THE OX HOME

TEXT

I am mounted astride the bull and slowly returning homeward.

The melodic sounds of my flute intone throughout the evening.

Measuring harmonies and directing rhythms with hand-beats, on my journey home, whoever hears the melodies will join in.

COMMENT

The struggle to tame the bull is over; gain and loss are assimilated.

I sing songs of the village woodsmen and play tunes of the children.

Sitting happily astride the bull, I observe the sky and clouds above.

Onward I go on the way home, no matter who or what calls me back.

Way-Station Six Synoptic Comment
Riding the Ox Home

It is the dawn of a new day. My struggling to tame the Ox of awakening, enlightenment, liberation and True Nature is over. The Ox is completely tame, being its originally gentle nature, and I am no longer concerned with either having or losing it. I have joined with the Ox and my ego-self is co-existing and harmoniously integrated with True Nature.

I am feeling good about myself and that I have made the right choices, found the true path to the Ox, have caught and tamed it and have gained something that I will never lose, True Nature.

In all truth, I am not even thinking about good or bad, right or wrong, true or false, gain or loss, etc.. Such either-or dualities don't matter anymore and have simply dropped out of and fallen away from my consciousness or become both-and dual-unities.

I mount the great Ox, sit astride it and begin my journey homeward. The Ox naturally knows the way home to True Nature and doesn't require being led or directed.

All day and into the evening; I am happily riding on the Ox's back, joyfully singing the songs of rustics and playing the tunes of children on my flute with one hand and keeping rhythmic time by harmonically drumming with the other hand.

My lyrical songs and melodic tunes resound throughout the journey home and whoever hears them experiences my wholehearted and radiant inner joy and happily joins right in.

I am looking skyward through the thin mists of dusk at the fading clouds of evening. I am riding the Ox on my way home to True Nature and I am past the point of no return. No one or nothing can call me back to the ignorance and delusions, desires and attachments, habits and errors and separations and divisions of my dualistic ego-mind and illusional ego-self.

Way-Station Six Psychospiritual Commentary
Internalized-Integrated Identity / Practicing

'The Way is perfect like vast space where nothing is lacking and nothing is in excess. It is due to our choosing to accept or reject that we do not see the true nature of things. Live neither in the entanglements of outer things nor in inner feelings of emptiness. Be serene in the oneness of things and such erroneous views will disappear by themselves. Trying to stop activity to achieve passivity is being filled with activity. Remaining in one extreme or the other is never knowing Oneness'. Verse 2. *Hsin Hsin Ming/Faith in the Heart-Mind Verses* by Seng-Ts'an/Sosan (d. 606 CE).

'Look within! The secret is inside you ... when our Mind works freely ... we attain liberation ... thoughtlessness ... but to refrain from thinking is an erroneous view'. *The Platform Sutra.* Hui-Neng/Eno (638–713 CE). The Sixth Ch'an/Zen Patriarch in China.

The struggling with the Ox and between our ego-self and True Nature is over. Our ego-mind and Ox-Mind are both tamed, harmonized and integrated and on their way 'home' to awakened, enlightened and liberated consciousness. We are no longer concerned with 'getting', 'having' or 'losing' 'enlightenment' and are past the point of no return in our spiritual journey to it. We are not looking back to, and cannot be called back to, being completely identified with the illusional concept of a substantial and independent ego-self and reverting to its egocentric, controlling, defending and dominating ways of being.

Rope and whip have been discarded, our exclusive ego-identification and resistance are gone, our ego-senses are withdrawn from external objects and our attention is stable, inner-directed and undistracted. The Ox of True Nature knows and is making its way home to its original nature and is supporting and conveying us there without any prodding, directing or guiding.

The activities, process, practicing and energy exerted at this transformative mid-point of the path of becoming and being fully enlightened, have resulted in some degree and level of progress toward, accomplishing of and attaining the states of consciousness, being, living and relating that constitute it. Our initial search-prompting questions to answer, problems to solve, issues to settle and conflicts to resolve; while still present, are much less of a pressing concern.

This is a time to reflect upon the various transformations that have occurred so far in the process and along the path of enlightened True Nature. Our body is more relaxed with fewer distracting aches, discomforts and adjustments. Breathing is naturally lower and slower. Meditative awareness has progressively become more stable, more concentrated and deeper and, simultaneously, more expanded and spacious.

Consciousness is generally more clear, empty and open and awareness is more naturally focused behind the ongoing presencing of objects outside of it and the ongoing flowing of contents within it. Any stuck thoughts and feelings are observed and caught early, accepted without dualistic discrimination and let go of quickly. Activities, actions and responses to events are flowing naturally and appropriately from a clear awareness of situations, circumstances and their essential or necessary requirements.

Much understanding, many shifts and healing have occurred in the psychological and psychosocial areas of our human being. Zen Buddhist spiritual teachings are being more fully integrated and spiritual practices are becoming more natural, routine and habitual. True Nature is being experienced more often and living our everyday life has become an ongoing meditative and spiritual practice.

We are placing our trust and faith in True Nature, Nature, life and the universe and are letting-go into the natural becoming, flowing, unfolding and transforming of our ego-self. Our ego-self is trusting in the True Nature that appears to be in charge of 'running the show'. Our practicing is relatively frictionless, effortless and seamless; has a life of its own and is going on of, by and as itself so. The Ox is leading the way home and we are leisurely and happily 'riding' on it and the flowing energies of our experiences.

We are accepting our experiences just as they are; positive-negative, wanted-unwanted, welcome-unwelcome, acceptable-regrettable, significant-insignificant, pleasurable-painful, etc.. If we are unable to 'see through things', essentially and transcendentally; we 'see them through', existentially and immanently.

True Nature and our ego-self are no longer separate, contradictory and opposing dualities and are unified as a complementary and interdependent dual-unity in our conscious awareness without any conflicting push-pulls. While True Nature is harmoniously integrated and unified, our ego-self is not yet either completely transformed or fully assimilated as the one reality and identity of True Nature.

We have integrated and are attending to the realities and life of our body, mind, heart, ego-self, human being, soul and spirit and are including them as equally essential components of the wholeness and fullness of True Nature. Our vital physical, mental and personal energies are united with our spiritual, psychical and transpersonal ones.

We are attuned to and harmoniously balancing the microcosmic and macrocosmic unity of our acquired vital energy and the primordial cosmic energy pervading, flowing and circulating throughout the universe. We are aware of the interconnectedness of the earth, our human being and the heavens.

Our ego-self has not completely 'died' its 'Great Death' but is less identified with; is being substantially transformed; has naturally, relatively and gradually 'moved out of the picture' and has assumed a subordinate and far less important central defining, controlling, directing and influential role within our conscious awareness.

We have discerned, reconciled, integrated, balanced, harmonized and unified many of the apparent dualities of our ordinary ego-mind, e.g., being-nonbeing, reality-appearance, past-future, self-other, truth-falsehood, form-emptiness, life-death, etc.. We have cultivated and are practicing experiencing dualities as dual-unities that are, ultimately, both merged into oneness and emptiness.

We also have experienced moments of an 'identity consciousness'; where we realize that there is no ultimate or essential difference between Buddha-Mind and our ordinary ego-mind, samsara and nirvana, satori and everyday experience, True Nature and our ego-self and between equally extraordinary transcendent-immanent and enlightened-unenlightened consciousness.

We are experiencing that there is only 'This', the single, simple reality of 'just what is just as it is' within moments of here-now awareness of 'It'. All else is a temporalizing, spatializing and construing of our subjective and object-making finite ego-mind. So, we are having some direct, unmediated and complete experiences of the suchness of everything and everyone just as they are being and not as anything else or with anything extra added.

We are bringing awareness to each moment, are feeling at one with the myriad phenomena of our conscious awareness and are witnessing their dependent originating, mutual arising and natural coming, flowing, unfolding and going. We are seeing that the oneness, emptiness and openness of pure and clear consciousness is the source and ground of all manifestation and diverse differentiation.

Our ego-mind is now basically and generally relatively undistracted, undeviated, unhindered, unobstructed and undisturbed by the ongoing streaming of conscious awareness and flowing of inner experiences and the happenings of everyday life, our relationships with fellow human beings and the events of the world process going on around us.

We are accepting the world of fellow human beings just as it is being and we are feeling that we are in harmony and at peace with it without discrimination, inequality, judgment and exclusion. We are taking care with fellow human beings as well as with our body. We are aware of the unity of our body, our heart-mind, others and the world and are receiving and responding to all that comes our way in the here-now presence of our lives.

Our conscious life is one of simplicity, clarity, unity, playfulness, creative activity and realized potentials. We are seeing True Nature and the creative energies of life in everyone and everything. We are experiencing that our wisdom, compassion and generosity are one whole that is embodied and enacted together. Any pain, loss or suffering that we experience naturally reverts to or dissolves in the pure, empty, clear, open and spacious consciousness of True Nature.

We have naturally simplified our lives and are experiencing fewer stresses, strains, strivings, struggles and suffering; are moving forward in our lives and are making progress on a favorable, suitable and appropriate spiritual path that we feel has already led to some awakening and momentary 'enlightenment'. We are confident that the path we are on is one leading to fully awakened, enlightened and liberated human being, living and relating.

While our ego-self is disidentified with and significantly transformed, while we see the identity of emptiness and form, while we experience True Nature as always present in everyone, while we feel how precious is the blessed bestowal of our human incarnation and the creation of all life and while we have realized and 'attained' some degree of awakening and 'enlightenment'; we have not yet reached completely assimilating and embodying the satori of being fully enlightened and liberated True Nature. But we have a good idea of it!.

Although we have more fully integrated Zen Buddhist teachings and our practicing is becoming more natural, routine and habitual; although we are generally more grounded, centered, stable, relaxed, calm and at peace and although we are relatively free of doubts, insecurities, worries and anxieties and are meeting difficulties with equanimity; we have not yet reached the ongoing full enlightenment of satori; the great transformation, realization and liberation of being and embodying the absolute emptiness and suchness of True Nature. Our current 'state' or 'stage' of awakening and enlightenment is still objectified within our conscious awareness as a dual-unity and subtle ego-concept, object and 'thing' that we can have or be at some point in the nearing possible future.

The practices of sitting zazen and struggling with koans have resulted in more direct teacher-transmitted kensho experiences. Our ego-self is subordinated to, united with and we know is progressively transforming into True Nature.

Our ego-self and True Nature co-exist and are integrated into a both-and and mutually inclusive dual-unity. We know that our ego-self 'has' and 'is' True Nature and 'is' enlightened to some degree; but has not yet reached complete assimilation, emptiness and 'forgottenness', its return to the One Origin of everyone and everything and its presencing in the world.

Our realizing of, and committment to, dual-unity naturally results in the integration of apparent dualities occurring in conscious awareness. When one-sided observations and judgments are made about human beings, automatically and quickly their counterparts arise to restore a dual-unity. For example, when some person may initially be experienced as distant, 'cold', over-controlled and defended; they immediately do something that reveals their presence, warmth, compassion and generosity.

We are sitting astride the great Ox of enlightened True

A WAY-SHOWING PATH OF ENLIGHTENMENT

Nature and are serenely faced forward, looking skyward and not backward. With pulsating harmonies, we are happily playing the rhythmical tunes and singing the lyrical songs of village folk and children who join right in when hearing them. We are relaxed, feeling free and at ease and our heart-minds are filled with profound, incredible and indescribable peacefulness, freedom and joyfulness.

We are journeying on the way home to oneness with and as enlightened True Nature; the pure, empty, clear, open and spacious consciousness that is One, Original, Natural, Inborn 'I-Am' and the abiding home of everyone, everywhere, at all times.

Everyday living is practicing and practicing is everyday living. However, full enlightenment is still present as a concept and goal of our ego-mind. We are not yet at the 'end' of the path (if there ever is one) of fully awakened, enlightened and liberated True Nature. There is still more to 'do' and to be 'done' and we need to continue practicing without lingering at, or dwelling in, the 'attainment' of any 'thing' to any degree, not even enlightenment.

Considering emptiness as the fundamental reality and truth of enlightenment; are we, ultimately and essentially, a selfless self on a pathless path through a gateless gate to a goalless goal in timeless time?.

Well, one Way of discovering the answer to that question, is through the encouraging words of one Zen Master who says, 'Just keep on going; keep going on; going, going and going on until……… 'you' are gone'.

CHUANG TZU SAYS

'Seeing things from the viewpoint of their sameness, the 10,000 things are all one'. (Chapter 5).

'Fish thrive in water, human beings thrive in the Way/Tao'. (Chapter 6).

TEN ZEN OXEN

Some True Nature Qualities

Some virtues, qualities and characteristics of the enlightened True Nature of human beings are:

Awake and aware
Alert and attentive
Available and accessible
Interested and attentive
Humble and modest
Respectful and civil
Accepting and allowing
Open and attuned
Receptive and responsive
Inclusive and engaged
Intimate and involved
Wise and discerning
Intuitive and insightful
Empathic and compassionate
Egalitarian and equitable
Grounded and centered
Sincere and genuine
Calm and peaceful
Kind and gentle
Warm and friendly
Cooperative and collaborative
Generous and altruistic
Inspiring and encouraging
Supporting and affirming
Assisting and guiding
Helpful and beneficial
Relevant and practical
Creative and productive
Spontaneous and immediate
Concrete and direct
Grateful and forgiving
Happy and humorous
Natural and simple

TEN ZEN OXEN

THE LIBERATING POST-ENLIGHTENMENT

WAY-STATION SEVEN
FORGETTING THE OX

WAY-STATION EIGHT
FORGETTING THE SELF

WAY-STATION NINE
RETURNING TO THE ORIGIN

WAY-STATION TEN
BEING IN THE WORLD

Way-Station Seven
FORGETTING THE OX

ASSIMILATING

EMPTYING

I reach home. I am serene.
The Ox too can rest . . .
Dawn has arrived.

Way-Station Seven
Dao/Tao Zhan/Chan Qi/Ch'i

道　　站　　七

Forgetting the Ox

| Wang/Wang | Ji/Chi | Niu/Niu |
| Forget | To Remember | The Ox |

忘　　記　　牛

'Being thought-free is glimpsing Eternal Mystery.
Being thought-full is beholding Infinite Miracles.
Mystery and Miracles are one and the same and are only being named differently'. TTC # 1.

'Many words are displacing emptiness; most developed is identifying as the empty inner center'. TTC #5.

'Benefit is obtaining from the being of solid, outer and enclosed form.
Utility is obtaining from the non-being of empty, inner and open space'. TTC # 11.

Negating, voiding, emptying, assimilating.
No enlightenment to be 'getting' without regretting.
Merging without diverging, fusing without confusing.
Enlightened 'forgetting' and 'letting' in every setting.
Still some self-begetting and not yet self-forgetting.

7.
Forgetting the Ox

Text

Astride the bull, I reach home. I am serene. The bull too can rest.
The dawn has come. In blissful repose, at my thatched dwelling,
I no longer need and have discarded the halter, rope and whip.

Comment

All is one law, not two. The bull is only a temporary subject.
Like net and trap are forgotten once fish and rabbit are caught.
It is as gold is to dross or the moon emerging from a cloud.
One path of clear light travels on throughout endless time.

Way Station Seven Synoptic Comment
Forgetting the Ox

Happily riding astride the back of the Ox of awakening, enlightenment and liberation the whole long way, I have now reached home. Dawn has arrived. I feel relaxed and calm sitting in front of my dwelling from morning until evening under the brightly shining orbs of the sun and moon. The Ox is resting at home as well and content enough to be left on its own and out of sight to find new pastures to graze in and water-holes to drink from without being tended.

I have completely forgotten all about the Ox, have discarded the now unnecessary rope and whip and am resting in blissful repose. There is no-'thing' more to seek, to discover, to learn, to know, to do, to gain, to have and there is no-'one' to become or to be.

Looking skyward from my place on the the earth, the sun and the moon are one constant luminous orb in the one clear spacious sky. I am grateful for the heavens, sun and moon, earth and mountains. I am contemplating and revering the Great Mystery of the universe, life, human being and all being. I am realizing that there is only one Dharma, one Truth and Law, and not-two.

The Ox was a temporary symbol and conveyance for use in assisting in journeying on the path of awakening, enlightenment and liberation. As when Chuang Tzu's trap and net are discarded once the rabbit and fish have been caught; so too can the Ox be forgotten, once the home of enlightened True Nature has been reached.

I am understanding that True Nature is the pure molten gold underneath the impure surface dross and is the bright full moon emerging from behind the passing obscuring clouds. This one splendid path of the clear, luminous, brilliant and radiant light of enlightened True Nature is shining infinitely in boundless space and is traveling eternally throughout endless time.

WAY-STATION SEVEN PSYCHOSPIRITUAL COMMENTARY
ASSIMILATED-NEGATED EMPTINESS / FORGETTING

'Form is none other than emptiness and emptiness is none other than form.....Gone, gone, gone beyond (to the transcendent shore) gone utterly beyond, awakening/enlightenment, all hail!' *The Heart Sutra of the Prajna-Paramita Sutra* (1st Century BCE).

'Emptiness here, Emptiness there; but the universe always stands before our eyes. Infinitely large and infinitely small are not different. Definitions have all vanished and no boundaries are seen. So too with Being and Non-Being. Don't waste time in doubts and arguments that have nothing to do with this'. Verse 14. *Hsin Hsin Ming/Faith in the Heart-Mind Verses* by Seng-Ts'an/Sosan (d. 606 CE).

It is the time of the dawning of awakened and enlightened consciousness and we and the Ox have both come home to True Nature. The Ox is grazing by itself, on its own, is out of sight and forgotten. We are enjoying blissful repose sitting silently and serenely in front of our dwelling beneath the cloudless sky and the bright orb of the morning sun.

We have experientially realized, integrated, internalized and assimilated with the Ox-Nature of awakening, enlightenment and liberation and identify as One, Original and Inborn True Nature. We understand that the Ox has been a useful conveyance for temporarily objectifying the path of enlightenment that is now no longer needed and we have forgotten it as a 'thing' that we have attained.

Through engaging in the various meditative practices of Mahayana, Ch'an and Zen Buddhism involving the all-encompassing, all-pervading and all-penetrating negating and ultimate non-being, no-'thing'ness and emptiness of phenomena, taos and dharmas; the many thoughts and concepts naturally drop out of, and effortlessly fall away from, our consciousness. Our ongoing focus is on being pure and empty consciousness and clear and open awareness itself.

We are realizing that our conscious experience is typically that of only concepts of beings and things and not True Nature. So it is for our treasured concepts of awakening, enlightenment and liberation as goals and some 'things' to attain. So it is for our precious concept of a 'self' as some being who is worthy of pursuing them on some path to their attainment. As True Nature; we are realizing that we are originally, ultimately and essentially that 'selfless self on a pathless path through a gateless gate to a goalless goal in timeless time'.

We are realizing that, in truth, we have always been and are now being One, Original, Inborn True Nature and that it has been present before we were born and will still be present after we die. We are realizing that True Nature has never been lost in the first place but has only been obscured, overshadowed, eclipsed and displaced by our unquestioned and unexamined believing in and conforming to early social conditioning, modeling, teaching and training and the forming, strengthening and defending of ego-self.

We are realizing that True Nature can be discovered, uncovered and recovered through a great 'search and rescue' operation by means of our being the purity and clarity of a quiet, empty, open, spacious and luminous consciousness that is transcendent, enlightened and liberated. We are realizing that we can decondition and 'reverse engineer' our conditioned and learned ways of conceptual thinking about and construing of ourselves and our habitually preferred ways of distracting, entertaining and amusing ourselves. We can thus find their origin in, and return to; pure, empty, clear and open consciousness and One,

Original, Inborn True Nature.

We are realizing that we are embodying the spiritual realities, truths and wisdom of an awakened, enlightened and liberated way of being; are connected with and participating in Nature, True Nature and human nature; are cherishing and treasuring our human life and all life and are honoring, respecting and affirming the validity, dignity, uniqueness, equality and beauty of fellow human beings and their True Nature.

Our way of being and living is primarily one of solitude, silence, simplicity, sufficiency and serenity. We are comfortable and at 'home' in our bodies, with fellow human beings in the world and with our place and part in Nature and the multiverse. Home is True Nature, the same one of everyone and everything else everywhere at all times.

We are not thinking about getting, having and keeping 'things', yet we are very blessed, wealthy and grateful. We are not thinking about doing, achieving and accomplishing 'things', yet we are very active, creative and productive. We are not thinking about ourselves and fellow human beings, yet we are very involved, connected and intimate. We are not thinking about feelings and emotions, yet we are very peaceful, content, happy and joyful.

We don't even do a lot of meditating, contemplating and reflecting; yet we are very awake, aware and present to ourselves and with fellow human beings. We don't have a lot of samadhi, kensho or satori 'experiences', yet we are very concentrated and absorbed in however we are being and whatever we are doing in each moment. We witness, see into and are being our True Nature and see that very same One, Original and Inborn True Nature in everyone and everything.

We have 'forgotten' about enlightenment as a concept of our ego-mind and as a 'thing' to be cultivating, practicing and attaining. If we adopt an external view of being an enlightened human being, we see a paradox, i.e., when we 'know' enlightenment, we are not 'being' enlightened and when we are 'being' enlightened, we don't 'know' it. Lao Tzu says, 'Those who know, don't speak and those who speak, don't know'.

Enlightened pure consciousness and True Nature: 1) are both an empty state in which there is clear and open awareness of both the 'seen' and the 'seer' and the 'known' and the 'knower' beyond their subject-object duality and 2) are both not some 'things' that a seeing-knowing subject conceptualizes as a seen-known object. Our ego-self is fully assimilated as True Nature without dualistic separation, division or opposition and True Nature is not even subjectively 'experienced' as a conceptualized object. Chuang Tzu says, 'When the shoe fits, the foot is forgotten'.

True/Buddha-Nature and Buddha-Dharma/Mind have subordinated, displaced and transformed our ego-self and ego-mind which have assimilated to and become one with them. Our ego-self is completely identified as Absolute, Ultimate, Essential, Inborn and inmost, deepest, centermost, fullest and utmost whole being, pure consciousness and True Nature.

The transforming at this 'stage' of the path of enlightenment has been from our finite ego-self and its mixed, clouded, cluttered, limited, busy, noisy, dualistic ego-mind of 'i-was' to infinite True Nature and its pure, clear, empty, open, calm, silent, unitary 'I-Am'. We have shifted from identifying with our ego-self to an identity with and as True Nature.

We realize that there is only one non-dual Dharma, Truth and Law of enlightenment and not-two. All is one, has always been so and is now illuminated, effulgent and radiantly shining in and through everything; one pure, clear, all-encompassing, all-pervading and all-permeating light present before creation and after dissolution of everyone and everything.

We realize that non-duality, unity, identity, emptiness and suchness are the deepest and highest realities and truths of pure consciousess and the True Nature of human being. We are no longer mentally abstracting, objectifying, conceptualizing, discriminating, analyzing, evaluating, judging and preferring this-or-that whatever and are simply witnessing the coming, changing and going of everything just as it is, without attachment.

All of the phenomena of our conscious awareness and experience reveal Ultimate Reality/Tao and the One, Original, Inborn and Natural True Nature/Mind of clear radiant light. After awakening, transformation and a more complete enlightenment; we are realizing that True Nature/Mind and ego-self/mind are, in essence, the same one unified transcendent-immanent identity that is the freely flowing and unfolding energy of the life-force liberated from limitations, restrictions and constraints and that is present in and as everyone and everything.

Our practicing and awarenesses are natural, unforced and ongoing when laying down, sitting, standing, walking and engaged in the other activities of our ordinary experiences of everyday living. Our practicing and awarenesses are occurring in the constant and continuous flowing and unfolding process of everyday living and not only in the meditation hall or zendo. Our practicing and awarenesses are our ordinary experiences of everyday living.

We now go about being whomever and however we are being and doing whatever and however we are doing; yet we are not unaware, unfocused, undisciplined, uncommitted, irresponsible and unaccountable. As True Nature, we are One within ourselves, with fellow human beings and all living beings and things (and every being and thing is alive!).

We have awakened to and realized the True/Buddha-Nature of No-Nature. The reality and actuality of awakened, enlightened and liberated and pure, empty, clear, open and spacious consciousness have been reached. All is emptiness/sunyata (Mu/Wu/No/Not) and suchness/tathata and only successive here-now moments of pure presence and 'I-Am' exist.

We no longer consider that awakening, enlightenment and

liberation are the best conceptual ideas that our ego-self can 'think up'; because they are, without question, the most profound reality of True Nature. However, there still are traces of our ego-self's and ego-mind's identification with, identity as and attachment to being our True Nature in a subtle realm of samsara.

We have realized the empty void of the pure potential of sunyata that originates and manifests the suchness of everyone and everything, but we have not yet actualized an absolute and complete satori. We have to guard against being 'filled' with emptiness and the peace, happiness, freedom and joyfulness of being True/No-Nature.

Nonetheless, we awaken at the dawning of each new day alive, refreshed, energized, grateful, appreciative, enthusiastic, optimistic and open to witness and participate in what the day is bringing, what is happening, who and how we are being, what and how we are doing and who we are being with and how we are being with them.

CHUANG TZU SAYS

'Virtuosity/Te takes no form.....is perfect harmony. Though it takes no form, things can't leave it'. (Chapter 5).

'When Virtuosity/Te is pre-eminent, our body will be forgotten. But when we don't forget what can be forgotten and forget what cannot be forgotten, that is true forgetting'. (Chapter 5).

'When our shoe and belt fit, our foot and waist are forgotten. When our mind 'fits', right and wrong are forgotten.....If we forget life, vitality will be unimpaired......A good swimmer has forgotten the water'. (Chapter 19).

'Once the fish and rabbit have been caught, net and trap can be forgotten. Once we have gotten the meaning, words can be forgotten'. (Chapter 26).

Some Qs And As

Some questions from ego-self to True Nature.
Some answers from True Nature to ego-self.

Q. What is the ego self?
A. An aggregate of body, sensation perception, cognition and consciousness. An insubstantial, fictitious and fabricated, but useful, mental construct serving the existence, organization and functioning of human beings in life, the world and relationships.

Q. Who is it that is seeking an awakened, enlightened, liberated state of human being?
A. It is the ego-self that seeks enlightenment and is prompted and guided by True Nature.

Q. Is it the ego-self that becomes awake?
A. True Nature alone is awake and being awake is not just another experience of the ego-self.

Q. Is the ego-self displaced and replaced by True Nature in enlightenment?
A. Ego-self co-exists with True Nature but it is transformed, harmoniously attuned with True Nature, assumes a relatively subordinate position in consciousness and can be forgotten and absent from conscious awareness during enlightenment.

Q. What is True Nature?
A. True Nature is not an object, 'thing' or idea but is our one, original, absolute, ultimate, essential and inborn real nature that exists in and as everyone and everything before birth, throughout life and after death.

Way-Station Eight
FORGETTING THE SELF

FORGETTING

TRANSCENDING

How can a snowflake exist
in the raging fire of True Nature?

Way-Station Eight
Dao/Tao Zhan/Chan Ba/Pa

道　　站　　八

Transcending the Self

| Chao/Ch'ao | Yue/Yueh | Wo/Wo |
| Transcend/Go Beyond | Surpass/Exceed | Oneself |

超　　越　　我

'Abandoning sageliness and saintliness, we are benefiting one-hundred fold'. TTC # 19.

'We are having great trouble because of having a 'self'. If we are having No-Self, we are having no trouble'.
TTC #13.

'As wise human beings, we are being 'absent' and constantly presencing, being behind and constantly advancing.....We are having no self-interests and are embodying Universal Self'. TTC #7.

'As wise human beings, we are knowing but not displaying and valuing but not glorifying ourselves'.
TTC #72.

No self intending, rending, contending or defending.
Empty, open space without a single thought or trace.
Self-transcending. Its enlightened, liberated ending.

8.

Forgetting the Self

Text

Halter, rope, whip, bull and person all merged into No-Thing.
This heaven is so spacious and vast that no message can stain it.
How can a snowflake of ego exist in a raging fire of True Nature?
Here are the footprints of the Buddha, buddhas and patriarchs.

Comment

Mediocrity is gone. Mind is empty, clear, open, free of limitations.
I seek no enlightenment nor remain where no enlightenment is.
Since I linger or dwell in neither condition, eyes cannot see me.
If hundreds of birds would strew my path with blooming flowers, such adoration and praise would be meaningless and shameful.

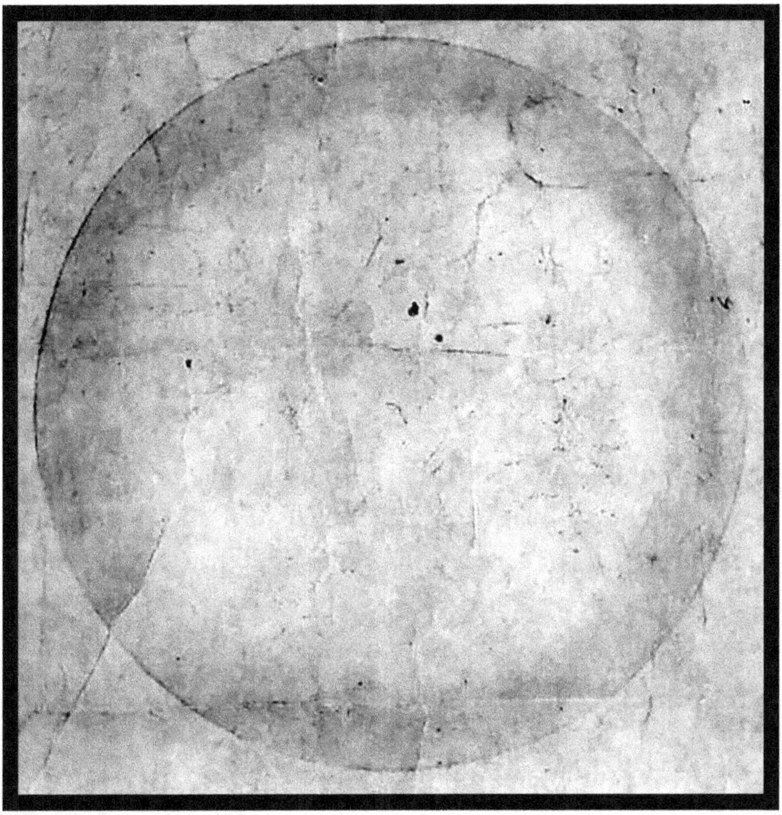

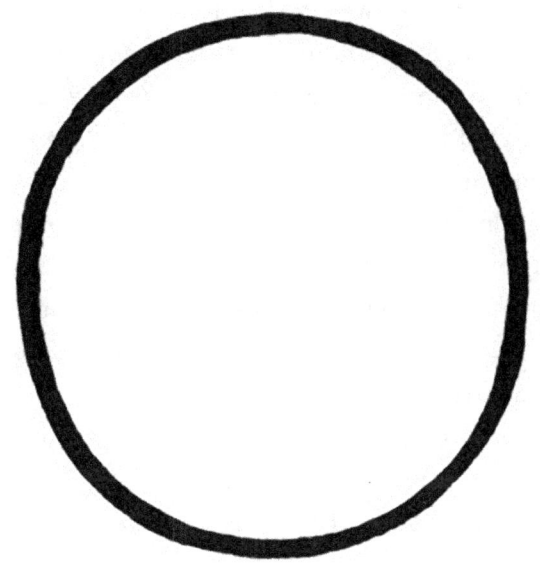

Way-Station Eight Synoptic Comment
Forgetting the Self

The restraining rope and the disciplining whip have already been discarded and the Ox of enlightenment has been forgotten. Now even ego-self is disidentified from, transcended and forgotten as a being, entity, object, thing and concept. It has assimilated with and as True Nature, merged into the one No-'thing' of emptiness and naturally dropped out of and is completely gone and absent from awareness and experience. This is a 'heavenly' state of awakening, enlightenment and liberation that is the complete emptiness of the pure, clear, open and vast spaciousness and limitlessness of consciousness itself and True Nature.

Only this empty, pure, clear, open, spacious, vast and all-encompassing sphere of heaven exists free of dualities, obscurations, defilements, delusions, afflictions, attachments, fetters, obstructions, errors and limitations.

What words or actions could ever sully, stain or discolor the purity of this heaven. How can a fragile thing like a snowflake of ego-self exist and survive in the intense raging fires of such a heaven and equal the awakened, enlightened and liberated True Nature of the Buddha, buddhas, bodhisattvas and patriarchs?. It has been so ever since their existence and when they transmitted and footprinted the reality and truths of True Nature to and in the consciousness of everyone.

There is no being or non-being, subject or object, seer or seen, knower or known, self or other, cause or effect, doer or deed, this or that to be found anywhere. Yet, enlightened True Nature is everywhere as everyone and everything just as they are. The mundaneness and mediocrity of limited ego-self and ego-mind are gone and only pure, clear, empty, open, spacious and unlimited consciousness, Buddha-Nature, Buddha-Mind and Buddha-Dharma ultimately and absolutely exist as True

A WAY-SHOWING PATH OF ENLIGHTENMENT

Nature and not as ideas, concepts, phenomena, entities, objects and 'things'.

The all-emcompassing and all-containing emptiness of this Way-Station of the path of enlightenment is symbolized by 'Enso'; an empty circle of oneness, completion and perfection. It is usually drawn with one continuous brushstroke and often is only partially completed, thus reflecting the 'perfection' of imperfection and that imperfection and perfection are perfecting perfectly.

In several earlier versions of *The Ox-Herding Pictures*, some Zen masters have considered this stage to be the conclusion of the path of enlightenment. However, in the present version, two more stages are added, i.e., returning to the Origin and entering the world.

Heart-mind is free of dualities, separations, ignorance, attachments, errors and limitations. Now, there is no longer any 'one' seeking or attempting to realize or attain any 'thing' such as awakening, enlightenment, liberation or True Nature.

There is no lingering or abiding in either enlightenment or non-enlightenment. There are no outward signs of enlightenment and there is no being seen by fellow human beings in the world or even by sacred and wise sages. Both holiness and worldliness have vanished without leaving or showing any identifiable or recognizable traces .

True Being is so natural, so ordinary, so eco-friendly. If appearing in Nature, acknowledged by Nature's unfrightened creatures and given flowers by them; the praise and adoration would be meaningless and even shameful.

Way-Station Eight Psychospiritual Commentary
Disidentified-Transcendent Spaciousness / Forgetting

'For the unified mind in accord with the Way, all self-centered striving ceases. Doubts and irresolutions vanish and life in true faith is possible. With a single stroke, we are freed from bondage; nothing clings to us and we hold to nothing. All is empty, clear, self-illuminating with no exertion of the mind's power. Here; thought, feeling, knowledge and imagination are of no value. In this world of Suchness there is neither self nor other-than-self'. Verse 12. *Hsin Hsin Ming/Faith in the Heart-Mind Verses* by Seng-Ts'an/Sosan (d. 606 CE).

'To study the Buddha Way is to study oneself. To study oneself is to forget oneself. To forget oneself is to be enlightened by the myriad dharmas, the 10,000 things. To be enlightened by the myriad dharmas is to bring about the dropping away of body and mind of both oneself and others. The traces of enlightenment come to an end and this traceless enlightenment is continued endlessly'. *Shobo-genzo Zuimonki of Dogen Zenji* (1200 – 1253 CE). Founder of Soto Zen in Japan.

The existence, concepts and experiences of enlightenment and True Nature have been forgotten and now so has the ego-self that initially imagined, sought after, worked on and subsequently evolved, transformed and assimilated into completely being them. Finite ego-self has no absolute, objective and substantial existence, has no identity as enlightened True Nature and is completely disidentified from, transcended and forgotten. Both it and the Ox of awakening, enlightenment, liberation and True Nature are transcended and forgotten and have fallen out of from, and are absent as object-contents of; pure, empty, clear, open, spacious and limitless consciousness.

Ego-self sense, object, concept and image and egocentric self-existence and self-awareness are gone and self-referencing and self-reflecting have stopped. Mind is calm, quiet, clear, empty, open and free of ignorance, delusions, defilements, attachments, afflictions, errors, obstructions and any ideas or thoughts about awakening, illumination, realization, transformation, enlightenment and liberation.

No mental abstractions, objectifications, conceptualizations or projections are being made and will is free of habits and drives, intentions and objectives, purposes and plans, contriving and devising, methods and strategies and strivings and strugglings. Ego-self is deconditioned and disidentified with and there is a complete dropping out of dualistic relationships such as being-nonbeing, body-mind, I-me, self-other, ego self-True Nature, life-death, etc. as object-contents of and in conscious awareness.

The illuminated teachings and wisdom and the enlightened principles and practices of Zen Buddhism having to do with non-dualistic thinking and the identity consciousness of True Nature have been assimilated by ego-self. Ego-self and True Nature have merged with and mutually transformed into each other. Ego-self has evolved and assimilated as True Nature and True Nature has manifested and embodied as ego-self and both have dissolved into the void of nothingness and complete emptiness of pure consciousness.

There are only Wu/Mu/No, Tao/Nature and Ultimate Reality; the vast no-thingness, emptiness, openness, spaciousness and limitlessness of silent, still, clear, all-encompassing and all-pervading pure consciousness. In this absolute oneness and emptiness of pure consciousness, there are no abiding entities such as ego-self and True Nature.

Whatever enters this empty and open consciousness, or

arises from it, appears just as it is in its luminous, brilliant and radiant presence, e.g., when the sun appears, it is only all that is appearing. There are no either-or, mutually exclusive, this-that, subject-object, seer-seen, experiencer-experienced, knower-known dualities present.

Just one 'phenomenon' is usually present in conscious awareness. There is either: 1) empty, open and spacious consciousness alone without an object, 2) an object alone without consciousness, 3) the co-existing, simultaneous unity of consciousness and object or 4) the absence of any experience of either consciousness or object. Consciousness is, object is, both consciousness and object are and neither consciousness and object are.

The dual-unity of consciousness and object and True Nature and ego-self, is an 'identity consciousness' reflected in maxims such as: 'Atman/Supreme Self is Brahman/Ultimate Ground'; 'Samsara/the cycle of birth and death is Nirvana/the final beatitude transcending suffering'; 'Karma/the destiny-determining force generated by actions is Dharma/the duty fulfilled by conformity to Truth and Law'.

And also; 'Sunyata/emptiness is Tathata/suchness'; 'Kensho and Satori/seeing into and being True Nature are ordinary mind'; 'Tao/Ultimate Reality is Wan Wu/the 10,000 things of existence'; 'As within, so without'; 'As above, so below'; 'Heaven is on Earth'; 'the transcendent is immanent'; 'the ultimate is intimate'; 'the ordinary is extraordinary'; 'This is It!'

All of the above are the non-ordinary and enlightened 'identity' consciousness of 1) non-dual and empty True Nature that also is the past 'i-was' of ego-self and of 2) the ego-self that is the present 'I-Am' of non-dual and empty True Nature.

Enlightened identity consciousness is possible to 'experience' by disidentifying from, deconditioning, transforming and emptying the finite and limited ego-mind and by cultivating, purifying, clearing and opening consciousness and awareness through concentrative, contemplative and reflective meditative practices that free the ego-mind from being directed toward, objectifying, conceptualizing and attaching to phenomena, objects, 'things', 'others', etc..

However, identity consciousness itself is still an object of human subjectivity that, like other object-contents, ultimately is emptied, negated and 'forgotten', as was the ego-self objectifying it and the True Nature and 'I-Am' being it. Completely negating and emptying any idea, concept and experience of finite and limited ego-self being a substantial entity existing in space-time that is having object-experiences is difficult to achieve.

The subjective 'I' and its objects need not to exist at all in conscious awareness and are either completely assimilated into oneness and 'isness' as True Nature or are completely voided in emptiness and nothingness as True Nature. Then accordingly, there is basically no-self having no-experiences of no-things at all. Just one, pure and empty consciousness is.

And this oneness and emptiness are also ultimately negated and emptied, so that all that is present is pure consciousness and clear and open awareness, devoid of object-contents, empty of emptiness; a complete void of indescribable and uncommunicable spaciousness and limitlessness.

This complete emptiness of pure consciousness is, however, not a negation of the actual existence of concrete objects and mental contents; but, rather, is their affirmation as being ego-self's and ego-mind's concepts of them that have no inherent essential, independent and permanent nature. The world of physical objects and mental contents are the originated manifestations and expressions of that pure and empty consciousness and appear in it.

Also, emptiness is not a vacuum. It is the pure, clear and open ground and source of reality, consciousness, enlightenment, True Nature and 'I-Am' and the creative origination and unique manifestion of the phenomena of conscious awareness and experience. This void of emptiness is pure potential at its maximum for manifesting form and for actualizing the identity of both, i.e., emptiness is form and form is emptiness.

The negation and emptying of consciousness is not nihilistic because it opens the way to an affirming of the reality of the suchness, as-isness and just-soness of the constantly manifesting and continually coming and going of the phenomena of our conscious experience. The One Empty Mind is, in essence, No-Mind and also the awakened, enlightened and liberated Buddha-Mind of True Nature.

Simultaneously, there is a oneness of the suchness of everyone and everything and the emptiness of their impermanence; which makes being together with fellow human beings all the more precious, cherished and treasured along with gratitude for the blessed bestowal of a human incarnation in this lifetime. The ordinary is really quite extraordinary now; everyday living is a path and practice and ordinary experiencing is reality and truth.

In the Ox pictures, this Way-Station of the path of enlightenment is a complete circle/enso with no beginning or ending; symbolizing the emptiness, unity, wholeness, totality, completness and perfection of the universe. The enso circle is drawn with a single brushstroke which, on occasion, is not a fully completed circle and thus also reflects the incompleteness and imperfection of the universe. The circle has a center that is everywhere and a circumference that is nowhere.[9]

Absolute emptiness is the 'emptiness of emptiness'. It is difficult to describe the non-experience of emptiness. Objectively considered, it can be said that it is a state of pure consciousness that is the negation and absence of any and all objects, contents and concepts. Not a thing exists; no ego-self, True Nature, Buddha-Mind, Bodhi-Mind, Buddha-Dharma, samsara, nirvana, samadhi, kensho, satori, emptiness, suchness, etc..

Absolute emptiness is everything it isn't. Enlightenment is awakening to and realizing One, Original, Absolute, Ultimate, Essential, Inborn and Nondual True Nature as that absolute

A WAY-SHOWING PATH OF ENLIGHTENMENT

emptiness of everything. Such emptiness is an awesome, amazing, astounding, splendid and wonderfully mysterious, miraculous, marvelous and magnificent liberated and complete oblivion without internal or external beings, objects, things contents, phenomena and concepts.

From this open ground, matrix and source of pure and empty consciousness; 'experiences' of True Nature, authentic being and real living naturally flow and unfold into solitude, silence, stillness, serenity, simplicity and sufficiency. Seen are the traces of the Way ancestors, buddhas, bodhisattvas, patriarchs and masters have traveled and lived and the realization that no exclusively intellectual understanding or ritual practicing can ever reach the wisdom, compassion and skill of their human being, teachings and practices.

Pure, empty, clear and open consciousness originates, manifests and expresses the ordinary experiences of everyday living just as they are and are endless ongoing opportunities to cultivate and practice enlightenment and being True Nature. 'Wu-wei' is letting experiences and actions happen naturally, organically and spontaneously from, in and as pure, empty, clear and open consciousness and allowing essential, necessary and appropriate actions to flow smoothly and unfold gracefully from it; seamlessly, frictionlessly and effortlessly without judging, resisting, controlling, forcing or interfering.

Being empty, clear, open and spacious consciousness and beholding and witnessing the everpresencing, everflowing and ever transforming panorama and array of taos, dharmas, phenomena, images, beings and things that arise from it or enter and fill it is the meditative absorbing 'activity' of enlightened True Nature.

Not having an aura or showing any outwardly visible or recognizable signs of being an enlightened human being avoids wafting the so-called 'odor of Zen'. Being basically unconcerned about outward appearances and being relatively anonymous and unseen is happily enjoying the freedom of being 'nobody special', an ordinary human being living an ordinary life in the ordinary world in ordinary ways.

Stopping transforming and evolving at this Way-Station of the emptiness and no-thingness of both ego-self and True Nature as object-contents and ego-concepts of conscious awareness is not considering that there is anything beyond this stage of the path of enlightenment and is not envisioning any further progressing to the sourcing and actualizing of being more fully and completely enlightened.

While having experienced brief kensho flashes and more extended satoris of the pure, clear, empty, open, luminous and radiant consciousness of True/Buddha-Nature and while valuing solitude, there needs to be an awareness of possibly using enlightenment to avoid engaging wisely, compassionately and skillfully in worldly activities with fellow human beings.

The conscious awareness, realizing and being of the emptiness and suchness of everyone and everything is not the conclusion of the path (if there is one!) of a more full and complete awakening, enlightenment and liberation. Some Wayfaring companions and sojourning pilgrims only rest here quietly and peacefully for awhile and are committed to proceeding further than negating, emptying, voiding and 'forgetting' ego-self, enlightenment and True Nature. They are returning to the Source of pure consciousness, fully enlightened True Nature and liberated 'I-Am' and are actualizing their Reality in the world.

There are three Buddha-Bodies/Trikaya. The one at this particular Way-Station of complete disidentifying, transcending, emptying and forgetting is Dharmakaya/the Law Body of the Buddha. It is Supreme Reality; spiritual, transcendent and cosmic consciousness; nondual, one with all, complete, perfect and timeless; the openness, spaciousness and limitlessness of Mind; the fundamental Truth of Enlightenment; Enlightenment itself and the True Nature of the Buddha and buddhas. It is the Substance (which is No-Substance) of Enlightenment.

A WAY-SHOWING PATH OF ENLIGHTENMENT

CHUANG TZU SAYS

'Fasting of the mind.....is not listening with ears and mind but with spirit.....spirit is empty and waits on all things. The Way/Tao gathers in emptiness alone. Emptiness is fasting of the mind'. (Chapter 4).

'Fish forget themselves in rivers and lakes.....wouldn't it be better if we forget emperors and rulers and transformed ourselves in the Way/Tao?'. (Chapter 6).

'When Virtuosity is foremost, the body will be forgotten'. (Chapter 5).

'One who nourishes will forgets bodily form. One who nourishes bodily form forgets gain. One who nourishes the Way/Tao forgets about mind'. (Chapter 28).

'Don't be embodying fame.....honor what you receive from Heaven but don't think you have gotten anything. Just be empty'. (Chapter 7).

'Forget things, Heaven/Tao and be a forgetter of self. One who has forgotten self enters Heaven/Tao'. (Chapter 12).

'We serve each other best when we have forgotten each other'. (Chapter 21).

EGO-SELF TRANSFORMING

In enlightenment our ego-self
does not 'die' but disappears
and is 'forgotten' and 'emptied'
and is not present as a concept,
object, content or experience
of conscious awareness in the
moments of enlightenment.

Way-Station Nine
RETURNING TO THE ORIGIN

RETURNING

SOURCING

Dwelling in the abode
of True Nature.
Resting at the Source in Nature.

WAY STATION NINE
Dao/Tao Zhan/Chan Jiu/Chiu

道　　站　　九

RETURNING TO THE ORIGIN

Hui/Hui	Yuan/Yuan	Yuan
Return	Spring/Source	Origin

回　　源　　原

'Our world has a beginning which is being called Mother (Tao)'. TTC #52. 'Unnamable Non-Being (Tao) is.....Mother (Tao) of all beings'. TTC #9. 'Here is This (Tao), undifferentiated, complete, all-pervading and inexhaustible.....Mother of all beings'. TTC #25. 'Tao is the hidden Sacred Source of all life'. TTC # 62. 'Reversing and returning are the moving of Tao.....All beings are birthing from Being. Being is birthing from Non-Being'. TTC # 40. 'Tao is a state of empty harmony.....this deep and vast unfathomable Source of all beings'. TTC #4. 'Tao is birthing all beings.....Originating without possessing'. TTC # 51. 'Valley-Spirit (Tao) is the Root-Source of Heaven-Earth'. TTC #6. 'Continuously, endlessly, the Unnamable (Tao) is cycling on, returning to No-Thingness'. TTC #14. 'From ancient times until right now, its name (Tao) is constantly reappearing; by which we are witnessing the originating of all beings'. TTC #21. 'Attaining complete emptiness, maintaining constant stillness; we are witnessing all beings coming into being and cyclically returning.....to Root-Source, original nature, eternal constancy, illumination and tranquility'. TTC #16.

Path nearly concluded. True Nature not deluded or occluded.
The Origin is one, clear, open and free and letting all just be.
Returning to the Source and nearing the end of the course.
True Nature fully attended; yearning and learning are ended.

9.
Returning to the Origin

Text

Too many steps have been taken to return to the root and source.

Better to have been blind and deaf from the very beginning?

Dwelling now in the abode of One, Original, Inborn True Nature, resting in Nature unconcerned with inner states and outer events, the river flows tranquilly on and the blooming flowers are red.

Comment

From the very beginning, truth is clear.

Silently poised, I observe forms of integration and disintegration.

Unattached to form is not needing to be reformed or transformed.

The clear water is emerald green and the mountain is indigo blue.

A willow weeps by the riverbank and a soaring bird readies to land.

At once, I see that which is creating and that which is destroying.

Way-Station Nine Synoptic Comment
Returning to the Origin

The Wayfaring journey and sojourning pilgrimage on the path of awakening, enlightenment and liberation are continuing beyond the complete emptiness and forgetting of ego-self and True Nature. Many steps have been taken; much time, energy and effort have been expended and the path of eight Way-stations has been taken, followed and traveled.

Now, there is a returning to the Origin of everyone, everything and awakened, illuminated, enlightened, realized and liberated True Nature. The Source that has been before birth and will be after death has been reached. Would it have been better to have been blind and deaf from the beginning; since now there is no 'one' to see or hear any 'thing'? From the very beginning, the reality and truth of True Nature have been clear.

Now, quiet blissful dwelling is in the true abode of originating Nature, Life and True Nature; silently and deeply within, unconcerned with externals and unattached to forms, conforming, performing, informing, reforming and transforming. There is no 'one' to 'be'; no-'thing' to 'know', 'have' or 'do' and no-'where' to go.

Everyone and everything comes, remains for a while and goes. The existing, being and diverse forms of everyone and everything are constantly, continuously and continually changing. The Origin of both their creation and integration and their dissolution and disintegration are silently seen, witnessed and beheld. All is just that which it is and just as it always has been.

Here, the great all-encompassing circle of complete emptiness; pure consciousness, the originating Source, open matrix, wellspring and fountainhead of the One, Inborn True Nature of everyone and everything is 'filled' only by, with and as Nature and Life.

As always, the splendid flowers are blooming bright red for whom, the pure emerald green river is flowing tranquilly on to where and the majestic indigo blue mountain is rising high above to what. A solitary willow tree is weeping beside the meandering river and a single bird is flying in the spacious sky and is descending to land upon, and bring the vast heavens above down to, solid earth.

At The Source

Shadows and echoes cannot create light and sound.
Dust and raindrops cannot create earth and heaven.
Ashes and metals cannot create trees and minerals.
Meat and energy cannot create livestock and foods.
Maps and menus cannot create lands and banquets.
Ends and deaths cannot create beginnings and lives.
The end-results are only the effects of prior causes.

But, later results are connected with former causes. And so too, our ego-self cannot create a True Nature. But it is connected with True Nature in our conscious awareness, it can remember its origin in True Nature, it can yield and abdicate its autocracy to True Nature and it can return to its creative source as True Nature and can be consciously transformed into True Nature.

Way-Station Nine Psychospiritual Commentary
Original Source-Abiding / Returning and Sourcing

'To deny the reality of things is to miss their reality. To assert the emptiness of things is to miss their reality.....To return to the root is to find the meaning but to pursue appearances is to miss the source. At the moment of inner enlightenment, there is a going beyond appearance and emptiness. The changes that appear to occur in the empty world; we call real only because of our ignorance. Do not search for the truth only cease to cherish opinions'. Verse 3. *Hsin Hsin Ming/Faith in the Heart-Mind Verses* by Seng-Ts'an/Sosan (d. 606 CE).

'Wipe out karma and let things follow their own course. Be a follower of the Way/Tao and the Dharma of the heart-ground. Put your heart at rest and seek nothing outside. All things of themselves so/tzu jan become empty. See clearly, have no doubt, be where you are, be your own master, be a great vessel, 'kill' every 'thing' and clear all obstructions.....To seek the Way is to lose the Way.....The Buddha is our heart in its purity'. Myoan Eisai (1141 – 1215). Founder of Rinzai Zen Buddhism in Japan.

Awakening, enlightenment, liberation and True Nature are not somethings that we have; they are who we essentially are; pure, empty, clear and open consciousness as the Source and Origin of everyone and everything. This is, the wellspring and fountainhead, Life, the course of Nature, the path of True Nature, True Nature herself, 'This' and 'I-Am'; just as they are issuing from, appearing as and being the present here-now moments of conscious awareness and experience.

The emptiness of One, Original, Inborn True Nature that has been present from the beginning; has been reached, returned to, merged with, assimilated and identified as such and then completely forgotten. After all of the time spent, the commitment made and the energy and effort expended in traveling the path of enlightened True Nature; might it have been better had the need to search for it not been seen or its summoning voice not been heard?

The answer is unequivocally 'no'; since True Nature was so deeply hidden within the unawakened, unenlightened and unliberated conditioned and limited ego-self which was exclusively and completely identified with and mistakenly understood as being all and only who we essentially are.

The Wayfaring journey of awakened, enlightened and liberated True Nature is; without question, doubt, qualification, reservation or hesitation; something quintessentially significant, meaningful and worthwhile to take, go through and complete as beneficently life-bestowed, crucially life-saving, vitally life-changing and creatively life-making.

The reality that there is something more to discover, realize and actualize on the path of enlightenment is returning to the Source and Origin of all being, human being and life; the same One, Original, Inborn, Enlightened True Nature that is Life itself, Nature herself and pure consciousness of and as them both.

Emptiness is the open matrix and empty source at their maximum potential for manifesting form. And the empty non-being of True Nature is the creative source and original essence of everyone and everything and is and has been pristine, pure, undefiled and immaculate from their beginning. The manifestations, activities and changes of everyone and everything are sourced and originated in True Nature as Life and Nature. Birthing is issuing from it, living is continuing to be it and dying is returning to it.

Assimilating, embodying and identifying as One, Original, Inborn True Nature is the creative ground, root, source and origin of the activities and relationships of our human being and living. One, Original, Inborn True Nature is the unity, identity, simplicity, sufficiency and serenity of everyone and everything.

Returning to the Source and Origin happens naturally to, in and as pure, empty, clear and open object-contentless consciousness because they are essentially identical. Through the awakening, enlightening and tranforming of ego-self, original True Nature returns and comes full circle back home to itself. This is a complete identity of Nature and all of her creations; among and within which we human beings have a centrally unique place to be and a vitally responsible role to play.

We are grateful for the blessed bestowal of human incarnation; cherishing the precious treasure of human life and humbly, freely and happily witnessing, beholding, joining and participating in and sharing the Mystery, miracles, marvels, magnificence and splendors of Life, Nature and True Nature.

As a Way of being and living, we are accepting of and attending to; attuning to and according with; identifying with and assimilating and embodying and following the natural designs, patterns and cycles; the seasons, solstices and equinoxes and the everflowing rhythms, interweaving harmonies and recurring transformations of Nature, Earth and the Heavens.

We are living in the radiant presence of the sun, the luminous phases of the moon; the revolving and orbiting of the earth; the configurations of planets and stars and the macrocosmic-microcosmic correspondence of the heavens and earth of which we, as human beings, are a central bond, integrating link, mediating bridge and interconnecting and interrelating channel and conduit.

We are accepting, acknowledging, appreciating, attuning to, according with and abiding in the sacred presence of Nature's divine light, life, law and love within us and between us and living beings and things in the queendom and kingdom of Great Mother and Great Father Nature; along with their minerals, plants, trees, creatures, human beings, buddhas and bodhisattvas, goddesses and gods et al.

We have realized the emptiness of self-nature/svabhava; have no illusion or delusion of being a substantial, separate and independent ego-self, have radically transformed and are completely liberated as True Nature. We impartially and equally honor, respect, include and welcome everyone and everything into the empty center of the open circle and boundless space of the same One, Original, Absolute, Ultimate, Essential, Inborn, Enlightened True Nature.

We are living beyond the dualistic separations, divisions, oppositions, disputes, conflicts and wars that inhumanely dishonor and defile dignity, disfigure and disable bodies, drain and deplete energies, disturb and delude minds, discourage and distress hearts, disrupt and deviate wills, determine and distort purposes, disavow and distract souls, desecrate and despair Spirit and delay and defer evolving to a more collectively and universally enlightened humanity, society and world. For this we have great sadness, pain and suffering and deep empathy, sympathy and compassion.

All that formerly was outside of and other than us; unknown, strange and unfamiliar to us; is now within us and as us; naturally and as fully and completely as possible. From the reality of the primordial emptiness of pure consciousness, non-being, True Nature and 'I-Am'; we are witnessing the dependent originating, mutual arising, transient abiding, passing on and returning of beings, things and all 'This'.

Our capacity and ability to gratefully contact; include; engage, connect and empathize with; have compassion for and forgive fellow human beings seems unreserved, unconditional, unqualified and unlimited. While nothing about others or in the 'outside' world has appreciably changed, everything in and of our 'inside' universe has radically transformed.

Necessary, essential and appropriate actions are following,

unfolding and flowing naturally from empty and originating pure and open consciousness and True Nature frictionlessly, effortlessly and seamlessly. There is a clear discerning and implementing of what actions are called for in, and are in accord with, given situations and circumstances. Such actions are wu-wei; natural, spontaneous, unforced, effortless, attuned, responsive, authentic and precise.

We are uniquely being who we are being and everyone and everything are uniquely being who and what they are being. The immediate here-now actuality of ourselves and fellow human beings is no longer some separate objectified concept, experience, phenomenon, object, 'thing', matter, event or affair and is being sourced and originated from and as the same One Origin and True Nature of everyone and everything.

Infinite space transforms into this present space of just and only 'right here' and eternal time transforms into this present time of just and only 'right now'. We are being and living relatively free of limitations in the one center of boundless space without extension and of endless time without duration. There is, and has always been, only just the here-now presence of all 'This' and 'I-Am'.

Such is the awesome, incredible and splendid place and moment of awakened, enlightened and liberated being and returning to the Source and Origin of, and being in accord with, everyone and everything that we are now being as pure consciousness and One, Original, Absolute, Ultimate, Essential, Inborn True Nature.

The sheer and utter, pure and simple, presence of who and how we are here and now is the reality, truth, meaning, beauty and fulfillment of living. Everyone and everything manifests, reveals and expresses the complete oneness, emptiness, spacious openness, creative energy, radiant light and splendid fullness of One, Original, Inborn, Enlightened True Nature and the true Reality of human being and all life; its emptiness and its suchness.

A WAY-SHOWING PATH OF ENLIGHTENMENT

Because, as emptiness, there is no 'form'; so there is no need to conform to or to inform and reform anyone or to perform or transform anything. There is no 'one', 'other', object or 'thing' to seek, discover, acquire, achieve, accomplish or attain. They are all present; right here, right now in and as this one very moment; the space, gap, pause and interval of and between 'what just happened next'.

The Mind to Mind Dharma transmission from our teacher is nearly complete and prajna/insightful wisdom and dhyana/concentric absorption are being experienced more frequently. We have reached the Source and Origin of the reality, truth, beauty, love, peace, happiness, freedom and joy of enlightened True Nature and are being 'lived' by it. We are experiencing the identity of emptiness and suchness and some more extended moments of the satori of being True Nature, pure consciousness, just 'This' and 'I-Am'.

Duality, unity, both duality and unity and neither duality and unity have been 'negated' and re-affirmed. The absolute-relative, transcendent-immanent, ultimate-intimate, essential-existential, one-many, original-derived, inborn-acquired, extraordinary-ordinary and exceptional-everyday are all one in the same One Source and Origin of and as True Nature to which we have now returned.

The realization of all of the commitment, dedication, devotion, determination, energy, effort, diligence and perseverance that have gone into meditating, concentrating, visualizing, contemplating, reflecting, absorbing, etc. can now be generously, wisely, compassionately and skillfully actualized, applied, transmitted and shared in the world of fellow human beings.

The reality of ongoing practice is to sustain an identity as One, Original, Inborn, Enlightened True Nature. Still, there is yet 'more' to enlightenment than awakening to and realizing, identifying as, assimilating and embodying the liberating emptiness of True Nature and this returning to Nature and to its originating Source, open Matrix and creative Origin.

Enlightenment is not just ours and for us alone and naturally unfolds and generously flows into being manifested and transmitted in the shared world of fellow human beings and the ordinary experiences of everyday living.

Of the three Buddha-Bodies/Trikaya, the one that is at this Way-Station of returning, sourcing and originating is Sambhogakaya/the Bliss Body of the Buddha. It is the embodied Truth, heart-felt joy and calm ecstasy of Enlightenment whereby the Buddha and buddhas are regarded as devotional beings and as personifying the Highest Reality. It is the Form (which is No-Form) of Enlightenment.

CHUANG TZU SAYS

'We receive our talents from the Great Source/Tao and, with spirit hidden inside, we live'. (Chapter 27).

'The sage sees clearly what is true, doesn't shift with things..... holds fast to the Source/Tao'. (Chapter 5).

'The Way/Tao has its reality and signs but is without form or action.....it is its own source and root.....transcends life and death but can't be said to have lived or died'. (Chapter 6).

'Our life between heaven and earth is the passing of a white colt glimpsed through a crack in a wall – whoosh! – and that's the end.....slipping into silence.....there is nothing that doesn't go back in.....yielding.....a body, soul and spirit on their way..... at last to the Great Return'. (Chapter 22).

'Emptiness, stillness, silence are the root of the 10,000 things.....one with clear understanding of the Virtuosity of Heaven-Earth/Tao may be called the Great Source/Tao, harmonized with Heaven-Earth and human being, bringing accord to the world'. (Chapter 13).

'Though the firewood burns out, the fire and firelight pass on endlessly and no one knows where they end'. (Chapter 2).

Our True Nature

We
Being
The One
The Origin
The Source
The Ultimate
The Mysterious
The Magnificent
The great wellspring
The great fountainhead
Great Mother Nature
The great emptiness
The great openness
from which issues,
from which flows,
the great waters
into the world
of human life
and of all
Life
Our enlightened True Nature
Our awakened True Nature
Our liberated True Nature
Our peaceful True Nature
Our happy True Nature

Way-Station Ten
Being in the World

Actualizing

Transmitting

I mingle with human beings
in the world.
In the presence of True Nature,
even dead trees become alive.

Way-Station Ten
Dao/Tao Zhan/Chan Shi/Shih

道　　　站　　　十

Being In The World

| Cun/Ts'un | Zai/Tsai | Shi/Shih |
| To Be/Exist | To Be Present In | The World/Life |

存　　　在　　　世

'Around human beings embodying the Great Image of Tao, our whole world is gathering; not being endangered; being secure, satisfied and serene'. TTC #35.

'As wise human beings, we are continually assisting all beings, none are being excluded. This is following Inner Light'. TTC #27. 'Wise human beings' Tao is assisting, not contending'. TTC #81. 'As wise human beings: 1) 'we are living in our one human world and harmoniously uniting the heart-minds of people.....regarding them as our own children'. TTC #49; 2) 'we are not forcing, controlling, interfering, desiring and people are transforming, regulating, prospering, simplifying of themselves so'. TTC #57; 3) 'we are.....assisting all beings to develop naturally without ourselves acting unnaturally'. TTC #64; 4) 'we are benefiting all without needing gratitude, completing works without claiming credit and not desiring to be displaying excellence'. TTC #77; and 5) 'we are bearing the inner shame..... enduring the outer misery of our State and being custodians of our land and stewards of our world'. TTC #78.

Back in the world of human being, present, witnessing and freeing.
Communing in the marketplace with smiling face and flowing grace.
Way-showing, transmittting, bestowing what is fitting.
Wise, compassionate and skillful assisting without insisting.
Awakening, enlightening Way-going without 'doing' or 'knowing'.

10.
BEING IN THE WORLD[10]

TEXT

Barefooted and naked of breast, I mingle with the people of the world.

My clothes are ragged and dust-laden and I am feeling forever blissful.

I have used no esoteric knowledge, magic or alchemy to extend my life.

But now, before me and in my presence, even dead trees become alive.

COMMENT

Inside my gate, a thousand sages do not recognize or know me.
The precious treasure and beauty of my inner garden is invisible.
Why should anyone search for the footprints of old patriarchs?
I go to the marketplace carrying my sack and an empty basket.
I visit the wine shop and market and return home with my staff.
Everyone I look upon, meet and engage becomes enlightened.

Way-Station Ten Synoptic Comment
Being in the World

The 'ending' of the path of enlightenment is beyond: 1) emptying and 'forgetting' it as an idea, concept, goal and attainment; 2) transcending and 'forgetting' the concept, object, entity and existence of ego-self, 3) being One, Original, Inborn True Nature and 4) returning to the One Source and Origin of everyone and everything.

Emerging from the wilderness, deep forest and high mountain abodes; bare-footed (earth-grounded), bare-headed (clear-minded) and bare-chested (open-hearted); the world of everyday being and ordinary living is entered with helping and bliss-bestowing hands. It is a mingling and communing naturally, freely, openly, impartially and intimately with fellow human beings just as they are being in the marketplaces of life.

Unconcerned with outward appearances and judgments and not dressed like anyone else; clothes are ragged, dusty and life-worn. Carried are a gnarled wooden staff for support and companionship, an old hemp sack filled full of gifts to be given out and an empty basket for wine to be replenished at the local wine shop.

The beauty and radiance of the precious inner treasure of awakened, enlightened and liberated True Nature is serenely blissful; yet is so natural, ordinary and free of an aura of enlightenment; that it is not seen, recognized or known even by sages. No footprints of the patriarchs need be sought or followed on this uniquely individual and enlightened Way-faring path.

Nonetheless; a humble, smiling and welcoming Presence is spontaneously, immediately, directly and happily transmitted to fellow human beings and is especially, eagerly, easily, and comfortably met and joined by children who are carrying their own sacks, 'in synch' with, pointing at, looking up to and wishing to learn from enlightened True Nature.

Often through the power of this Presence and a wise, compassionate, altruistic and generous commitment to inspire, support, encourage, assist, guide and benefit fellow human beings; anyone close by naturally becomes enlivened, awakened, energized, transformed, enlightened and liberated.

Through such a vital and vibrant Presence, even dead trees suddenly become alive and show new growth!.

No alchemical formulas or magical rituals have been used for longevity or immortality. Immortality is being sheerly and utterly, purely and simply and completely and fully identified as, and identical with, that which is never been born and never dies, i.e., Original, Absolute, Ultimate, Essential, Inherent True Nature; pure, empty, clear, open, spacious and limitless consciousness; the eternal 'Now' and infinite 'Here' and their splendid Presence as just 'This' and just 'I-Am'.

True Nature's Way

> The brilliant, radiant, splendid, wondrous
> light of True Nature shines brightly and
> warmly in the darkest and coldest nights
> of our ego-self's delusion, greed, hatred,
> anger and fear and clearly illuminates;
> shows and opens the Way to awakened,
> enlightened, realized and liberated wisdom,
> generosity, kindness, patience and courage.

Way-Station Ten Psychospiritual Commentary
Enlightened World-Entering / Actualizing and Transmitting

'Do not remain in the dualistic state.....If there is even a trace of this or that, of right and wrong, the Essence of Mind will be lost in confusion. Although all dualities issue from the One, do not be attached even to this One. When Mind exists undisturbed in the Way, nothing in the world can offend.....and ceases to exist in the old way'. Verse 4. 'To come directly into harmony with the reality of Suchness, just simply say 'Not-two'.....nothing is separate, nothing is excluded. No matter when or where, enlightenment is entering this truth. And this truth is beyond extension or diminution in space-time; in it a single thought is ten thousand years'. Verse 13. 'One thing, all things, move and intermingle without distinction. To live in this realization is to be without anxiety about non-perfection. To live in this faith is the road to non-duality because the non-dual is one with the trusting heart-mind'. Verse 15. *Hsin Hsin Ming/Faith in the Heart-Mind Verses* by Seng-Ts'an/Sosan (d. 606 CE).

We have assiduously followed the arduous path of enlightenment and have been continuing to be fully engaged and deeply involved in the intense process of diligently cultivating, practicing and living it. We are seeing the inner radiant light of True/Buddha Nature in and as everyone. We are actively participating in the world and are accepting fellow human beings just as they are.

We are vowing and committed to assisting, guiding and benefiting human beings and contributing to their own awakening, enlightenment and liberation in whatever appropriate, relevant and meaningful ways that we can without being interfering, imposing, intrusive or invasive. We are grateful for the opportunity and wisdom, compassion and skillful means to do so.

We are completing the circle of the path of enlightenment by entering the marketplace of the social world as it is with open and outstretched arms and bliss-bestowing hands and joining the multitude of diverse fellow human beings and whoever and however they are being and whatever and however they are doing.

We are seeing the inner radiant light of One, Original, Inborn True/Buddha-Nature everywhere manifesting as it is doing in a wide variety of different ways and forms in and as everyone and everything. At every moment, everyone and everything is absolutely and uniquely revealing True Nature.

We are calm, content, happy and joyful and resembling Pu-tai/Hotei; the cloth-bag monk, laughing Buddha and incarnation of the future Buddha, Maitreya. If regarded as outstanding, it is not our intention to be standing out. We are no one special. We have no secret esoteric knowledge or magical supernatural powers and are not hiding or withholding anything that we have learned.

The inner beauty and treasure of True Nature is present deep within and we are so ordinary that our 'enlightenment' is not visible to, or seen by, fellow human beings. However, by our very presence alone; they may be shown, guided to and receive a transmission of the Buddha-Dharma and be enlivened, energized and even naturally awakened and enlightened through our contacts, connections and interactions with them.

We have left the ancient teachings of the Buddha, buddhas, bodhisattvas and patriarchs behind and are making our own Way in the world along with fellow human beings and facing and meeting life-challenges while still being True Nature. We are seeing the majority of fellow human beings as suffering from being unawakened, unenlightened and unliberated due to exclusively and completely identifying with their conditioned ego-self and dualistic ego-mind and mistaking them for who they really, truly and essentially are.

The 'world' we have entered is seen very differently than when unanswered questions, unsolved problems, unsettled issues and unresolved conflicts initially prompted seeking a more awakened, enlightened and liberated kind of being and way of living. Even the concrete pavement of the city is now seen as having interesting textures and shadings and its shadowing buildings are appreciated for their geometric configurations and architectural design. Things that were previously unnoticed are appearing, e.g., tree-lined sidewalks, street vendors, roof-top gardens, flower stands, city parks, a farmer's market.

The world is populated by human beings, all of whom are True Nature busily attending to, engaged in and going about their daily routines; but most of whom are unawakened to it, unenlightened and unliberated from the separations and dualities, ignorance and delusions, desires and attachments, limitations and constraints, habits and errors and sufferings and dissatisfactions of exclusively and completely identifying with conditioned ego-selves.

Being in the world with fellow human beings requires our fullest conscious awareness, clearest wisdom and deepest compassion and most stable and steady practice so as not to be inundated and swept away by the strong, prevailing and pervasive currents of society.

We have naturally realized that; as amazing, profound, illuminating and transforming as our awakening, enlightenment and liberation have been and are still being; they are not just for us alone and can be brought to and shared with fellow human beings and most certainly with those who are interested in Wayfaring on spiritual paths to enlightenment.

Much of the support, guidance, discipline and effort that was involved in our journeying process of becoming enlightened has taken place in unique situations and under conditions that have been relatively sequestered ones, at times set apart from the ordinary world and everyday life of fellow human beings.

A WAY-SHOWING PATH OF ENLIGHTENMENT

While not feeling separated or isolated, we have naturally realized the appropriateness of entering and being in the world. Most of us are now living in the ordinary world, belonging in society in some way, holding down jobs, buying food, paying bills; are a part of neighborhoods and go about daily living as does everyone else. We realize that there are ample opportunities to be more actively engaged and involved with fellow human beings and to join with them amid the hustle and bustle of daily activities and routines.

We are aware that the 'world' and 'people' existing before our enlightenment experiences have not significantly changed, but that we certainly have radically transformed and are seeing them in a completely different 'light', i.e., more wisely, compassionately, essentially, truthfully and intimately as True Nature.

We are not propagandizing, propagating or proselytizing with regard to the beliefs and practices of the Zen Buddhist spiritual tradition; since we are fundamentally non-sectarian, non-doctrinal and non-dogmatic. We are not invested in, attached to, nor go out of our way to be 'helping' fellow human beings become 'spiritual', 'awake' or 'enlightened'. If at all and in keeping with vows; we are simply interested in assisting and benefiting fellow human beings, if and when that may be relevant and fitting, in whatever situations naturally occur and at and in which we are present.

We also are not attached to 'helping' or to 'teaching' anyone in ways that potentially take away their own responsibility for self-awareness, self-discovery and self-realization. The unreality, limitations, failures and crises of their ego-selves will usually be sufficiently motivating in a unique way and timely manner. We are just naturally interested, attentive, supportive, encouraging, kind, considerate, generous, fair and gentle in our interpersonal relationships. However, we are aware that we are 'modeling' these ways of being for them. With all humility and modesty, it does appear that our presence alone is often experienced as inspiring, encouraging and influencing and as making a beneficial contribution to, and meaningful difference in, the lives of fellow human beings with whom we relate and interact. We honor and respect the dignity and uniqueness of fellow human beings, hallow their Spirit and True Nature and care deeply about them.

We understand, first hand, how challenging it is to find and to make one's own way through the a, b, cs and x, y, zs of life from birth to death, from its mysterious beginning to its mysterious ending. Again, without attachment, we hope that by virtue of our meeting and engaging with fellow human beings; our presence and energy will be enhancing, optimizing, inspiring and uplifting.

What we are bringing to human relationships in the social world is the wisdom, compassion and skills that go along with awakening, enlightenment, liberation and True/Buddha-Nature and the experiences and realizations of cultivating and practicing.

We are free of identifying with our conditioned ego-self, conceptualizing dualities and being attached to material things. We are witnessing the dependent originating, mutual arising, changing and passing on of everything. We are realizing the essential emptiness of True/Buddha-Nature, all beings, things and phenomena. We are experiencing that at every here-now moment, 'This' and 'I-Am' are all that 'Is' and that everyone and everything is embodying and revealing the same One, Original, Inborn True Nature.

We are committed to sustaining active ongoing cultivating and refining in whatever ways we can and are now enjoying the culminating wisdom of the Buddha's teachings and the current vibrancy of Zen Buddhist practices. We have assimilated and become One, Original, Absolute, Ultimate, Essential, Inborn True Nature. We realize the identity of emptiness/sunyata and suchness/tathata and are trying to be aware of both while confronting, engaging in and navigating life's challenges and

A WAY-SHOWING PATH OF ENLIGHTENMENT

opportunities in the world.

The presencing energy of True/Buddha-Nature is naturally activating, energizing, potentiating and motivating us and we feel that we are being 'enacted' and 'practiced' by it.

We are living humbly, modestly and simply in harmony with Nature, True/Buddha-Nature and human nature. Through continuing cultivating and practicing, we have developed and are refining the qualities of egolessness, acceptance, adaptiveness, resilience, gratitude, inclusiveness, empathy, kindness, gentleness, generosity, forgiveness, peacefulness and happiness.

We feel that we are living and walking the path of the Buddha, Buddhahood and the Buddha-Dharma.

We are dwelling in present here-now moments, recognizing everyone and everything just as they are and are experiencing the pure, empty, open and spacious consciousness of True/Buddha-Nature in the course of everyday living. Our living is basically independent of the fluctuations of external conditions and sufficiently free of outward appearances.

We are experiencing both the ultimate and essential unity of ego-self and True/Buddha-Nature, the transformation and assimilation of ego-self into True/Buddha-Nature and the negation and emptiness of both. Ego-self and True/Buddha-Nature are, are not, both are and are not and neither are and are not.

We have momentarily realized the identity of bodhi/absolute, awakened reality and maya/relative, reflected appearance; inner states of samadhi/concentration, dhyana/absorption and prajna/wisdom, kensho/seeing into True Nature and satori/being True Nature.

We are experiencing and understanding enlightenment and the spiritual path of Zen Buddhism as: 1) realizing the absolute and essential non-dual identity of the emptiness/sunyata and suchness/tathata of True/Buddha-Nature and 2) assisting and benefiting fellow human beings in their unique Wayfaring journey through life .

Well!. Hello!. Greetings!. Yes!. Here we all are. We are all here. So be it!. We are natural and ordinary human beings living everyday lives, being and relating in various ways and doing various things. And each and every one of us is a precious human being and treasure, living a bestowed and blessed life together as kindred mothers and fathers, sisters and brothers and friends and companions. And the radiant light of Nature, True/Buddha-Nature, pure consciousness, 'Just-This' and 'I-Am' is shining forth in and as all of us.

We can be and are validating, legitimizing and supporting and being available, approachable and accessible to one another in being the truest human beings that we can be. We can be and are creating and participating fully together in cooperative, collaborative, mutually beneficial, meaningful and fulfilling relationships. We can be and are working together in activities that are successfully conducted and accomplished for the common good of our families, communities, society, nation, species, humanity, environment, world and planet.

Our human lives; the incarnations as One, Original, Inborn True/Buddha-Natures; are blessed gifts and precious treasures to be cherished, hallowed, honored, respected, valued, safeguarded, attended to, nourished, cared for and related to with the dignity we each deserve, and are worthy of, by virtue of being a human being.

Because there are countless numbers of us human beings, there are innumerable opportunities to join together and to cultivate and practice becoming and being the emptiness and suchness of awakened, enlightened, realized and liberated True/Buddha-Nature; particularly as present, awakened, actualized and transmitted in the Zen Buddhist spiritual tradition.

Cherishing, caring for and nourishing ourselves, each other, Nature, our environment, world and planet are being, living and sharing the reality, presence, flowing, unfolding, health, well-being and wholeness of One, Original, Inborn True/Buddha-Nature.

All of which are supported, benefited and optimized by clean and fresh air, pure and clear water, healthy and wholesome food, sufficient and sound sleep, balanced activity and rest and heartfelt and heart-warming open and intimate communing with fellow human beings peacefully, happily, freely and joyfully.

Of the three Buddha-Bodies/Trikaya, the one at this Way-Station of actualizing and transmitting is Nirmanakaya/the Transformation Body of the Buddha. It is the radiant earthly human body personified by the Buddha and which is projected into the world as it appears to human beings.

It is a vehicle for wisely expounding and transmitting teachings; skillfully conveying truths and experiences; beneficially working for the welfare and happiness of human beings and compassionately awakening, enlightening and liberating human beings. It is one with Absolute Reality as manifested in the relative world. It is the Purpose (which is No-Purpose) of Enlightenment. The unity of the three Buddha-Bodies of Dharmakaya, Sambhogakaya and Nirmanakaya is Svabhavikakaya/the Essence Body of the Buddha.

Each and every one of us human beings: 1) is essentially, the real and actual embodiment and personification of awakened, enlightened and liberated True/Buddha-Nature itself; pure, empty, clear, open, spacious and limitless consciousness itself and the absolute unity and ultimate identity of emptiness, suchness and all other dualities themselves and 2) is sheerly and utterly, purely and simply, being as fully alive and as fully awake as possible as just 'I-Am' in the just 'This' of here-now moments of being as fully present and as fully authentic as possible.

CHUANG TZU SAYS

'One who regards life as significant will think lightly of material gain'. (Chapter 28).

'Life is the working of Heaven/Tao, death is the transformation of things'. (Chapter 15).

'Our body and life are a form and harmony lent by Heaven-Earth. We don't have possession of our inborn nature or destiny--they are contingencies lent by Heaven-Earth'. (Chapter 22).

'Perfect happiness is being alive – only unmotivated, unforced and effortless action/wu-wei gets us close to it'. (Chapter 18).

'How do we know that loving life is not a delusion and that hating death is like an adult having left home as a youth and forgetting the way back?' (Chapter 2).

'Lao-Tzu said, 'Ah yes – the basic rule of life preservation. Embrace and keep from losing the One.....move without knowing where you are going.....sit without knowing what you are doing.....ride along with others on the same wave.....this and nothing more'. (Chapter 23).

'As long as the world rests in the true form of its inborn nature.....the existence of its many delights make no difference.....but if the world doesn't do so, then its many delights become distorted, confused and deranged and, if further honored and cherished, become a great collective delusion'. (Chapter 11).

'True human beings know nothing of loving life or hating death, emerge without delight and go back without complaint, don't forget the beginning or attempt to find out about the ending and just come and go naturally.' (Chapter 6).

'True human beings are embracing Virtuosity/Te, infused with harmony, following along with the world'. (Chapter 24).

'True human beings can't be argued with by wise, seduced by beautiful, intimidated by violent human beings of the world'. (Chapter 20).

'True human beings see and live in the world with fellow human beings in the light of the Way/Tao and even supreme leaders become upright'. (Chapter 12).

'Perfect human beings of old made sure that they had the Way/Tao within them before trying to pass it on to fellow human beings'. (Chapter 4).

'Sages just let things be the way they are and don't try to help life along'. (Chapter 5).

'Sages make sure of themselves first and then act'. (Chapter 7).

'True human beings have the form of a human being and the emptiness of Heaven/Tao ... follow along with fellow human beings and the world ... encompass all things ... show an authentic face and fellow human beings become enlightened'. (Chapter 21).

'All the buddhas and all sentient beings are nothing but One Mind, beside which nothing exists. The One Mind alone is the Buddha and there is no distinction between the Buddha and sentient beings.... To awaken suddenly to the fact that your own Mind is the Buddha, that there is nothing to be attained or a single action to be performed – this is the Supreme Way.... Only rid yourself of the concepts of ordinary and Enlightened'. *Essentials of Mind Transmission.* Huang-Po Xi-Yun/Obaku Kiun (d. 850 CE).

'The unborn-mind of illuminative wisdom ... this inherent buddha-mind is unborn and possessed of a wonderful illuminative wisdom ... and marvelous awareness ... all things fall into place and remain in perfect harmony ... each and every Buddha and bodhisattva in the universe, and everyone in this world of humans, has been endowed with it. Why is it that we are deluded? Because we are partial to ourselves ... just stop and look back to the origin of this self. When we were born ... there was only this buddha-mind'. *The Unborn.* Bankei Yotaku (1622-1693 CE). Japanese Rinzai Zen Master.

Being Enlightened True Nature

Being awakened, illuminated, enlightened, realized, transformed and liberated is our one, original, absolute, ultimate, essential and inborn True Nature that we all are by virtue of being incarnated as a human being.

Being a human being is a real opportunity to consciously become True Nature and to not only live the blessed gift of our precious lives as a fictitious ego-self that suffers limitations, conflicts and unhappiness.

Regardless of our history, constitution and circumstances; we all have the potential to not just suffer the life of our ego-self but to also enjoy the awakened, enlightened and liberated life of our True Nature.

Our one, universal, natural and inborn awakened, enlightened and liberated True Nature is the magnetic force that draws together, unites and organizes all of the separate and disparate iron filings of our collective ego-selves.

Conclusion

Ten Way-Stations of the Way-Showing Path of Enlightenment; the spiritual journey of discovering, becoming and being True/Buddha-Nature; are presented in *The Ten Zen Oxen*, wherein the Ox has symbolized nondual, unconditioned, awakened, enlightened and liberated True Nature and the Ox-herder has symbolized our dualistic conditioned, unawakened, unenlightened and unliberated ego-self.

An enlightened state of human being is natural, original, real and inborn True Nature. Unfortunately, most of us, for most of the time, are not awakened to or aware of ourselves as such. As our ego-selves, we typically believe whatever and however we are thinking, feeling, doing and relating and regard them as constituting, reflecting and expressing who we are as human beings.

Recognizing disappointments, dissatisfactions, discouragements; separations, losses, failures; questions, problems, conflicts; etc. expose our ego-self's limited power, ineffective control and basic inability to create, sustain and develop a genuine, authentic, intimate, successful, meaningful, satisfying and fulfilling human life.

There comes a point in our ego-self's experiencing when we recognize that all is not going well, good, right and the best with regard to who and how we are being, how we are relating and what we are knowing, doing and having. We realize that there must be something other, more, greater and better to and for ourselves and in our lives.

The fundamental issue with our ego-self is that, by exclusively and completely identifying with and as it; we misunderstand, misinterpret, misconstrue and mistake its conditioned, derived, acquired, imaginary, illusional, fictitious and insubstantial 'reality' for and as True Nature. The extremes of this situation are the inflated arrogance of affirming the finite 'reality' of ego-self and the conflated ignorance of denying the Infinite Reality of True Nature.

Fortunately, although unsettling, there are those times that our ego-self reaches a limit in its ability to convince itself that it exists and that it is the source of, and in control of, what is occurring in its 'life'. Our ego-self's mental 'clutter', emotional 'filler', volitional 'busyness' and relational 'splits' can, at some point, overload and overwhelm its conscious awareness and experience of itself.

Dissatisfactions with who we are 'being' and how we 'relating' occur. Losses outweigh gains in the 'things' we are 'having'. Falseness predominates over truths in the 'things' we are 'knowing'. Failures outweigh successes in the 'things' we are 'doing'. A major physical illness, accident or disability happens; family members, loved ones or close friends are injured or die; spouses are abusive or unfaithful; finances are overspent or debt-ridden, etc..

Such circumstances can trigger questions, problems, issues and conflicts about who we are, how we are being and how we are living. Any 'breakdowns' over these issues can, however, be 'breakthroughs' to investigating, exploring and discovering new, different, more enlightened and transformed ways of being and living that provide some answers, solutions, settlings and resolutions.

'Positive' spiritual teachings, wisdom, meditations and practices often synchronistically appear and coincide with such 'negative' conditions. Typically, there are two ways 'out' of the quandaries, dilemmas and crises of our ego-self. One way is to compassionately and courageously 'see things through', existentially and immanently; and the other way is to wisely and insightfully 'see through things', essentially and transcendentally.

The synchronistic occurrence of spiritual wisdom can initiate a spiritual Wayfaring journey of awakened, illuminated and transformed feeling, thinking and acting; a deeper longing,

A WAY-SHOWING PATH OF ENLIGHTENMENT

searching and discovering of a more heart-centered, heart-felt and heart-warming sense of self; more meaningful, empathic and intimate relationships and a more worthwhile, gratifying and fulfilling life of peacefulness, happiness, freedom and joyfulness.

Engaging in spiritual teachings and practices can provide an enlightened 'Way' and means of both 'seeing things through' and 'seeing through things'. Both require devotion, dedication, determination, diligence, energy and effort to either suffer, endure and take a process to its completion or to distance from it, make it transparent and rise above it.

The Ten Ox-Herding Pictures depict a path of both 'seeing things through' and 'seeing through things'; transforming from an unawakened, unenlightened and unliberated condition of identifying with our conditioned and dualistic ego-self and its illusions, attachments, obstructions, separations and sufferings to an awakened, enlightened and liberated state of identifying as unconditioned and non-dualistic True Nature and its emptiness, openness, peacefulness, happiness, freedom and joyfulness.

The Ten Ox-Herding Pictures have, for more than one-thousand years, been successfully used; primarily by Taoist and Zen Buddhist masters and teachers; to encourage, support, guide and monitor human beings in their search for, awakening to, engagement in and realization of a more enlightened and liberated state of being, living and actualizing of True/Tao/Buddha-Nature.

The Ten Zen Ox-Herding Pictures: 1) begin with sufferings prompting seeking enlightenment; continue with: 2) pursuing knowledge about it, 3) experientially glimpsing it, 4) catching a whole grasp of it, 5) disciplined cultivating of it, 6) integrated practicing of it and 7) assimilated forgetting of it as a 'thing', concept, idea and goal; and follow with 8) transcending and forgetting ego-self as an entity, 9) returning to the One, Original, Empty, Open, Inborn Source and Origin of everything and 10) entering the world to assist, guide and benefit fellow human beings in their lives and, for some, in their own path toward enlightenment.

Zen Buddhism; as well as its roots in Hinduism, the life and the 4 Noble Truths of the Buddha and Mahayana, Madhyamika and Ch'an Buddhism; is fundamentally a 'via negativa', radical non-attachment to and 'negation' of obscuring and obstructing mental concepts and delusions, grasping and clinging emotional desires and attachments, habitual and driving volitional patterns and errors and dualizing and opposing relational separations and divisions.

The 'negating' and 'emptying' : 1) are not of a unitary, interdependent and whole reality but of our concepts of, attachments to and strivings for its 'things' and 2) open the Way to affirming and realizing the suchness and fullness of everything. Nirvana and samsara, sunyata/emptiness and tathata/suchness, satori and ordinary experience and enlightenment and everyday life; once fully realized; are unities, identities as well as non-entities or non-objectifiable 'things'.

Enlightenment is One, Original, Absolute, Ultimate, Essential, Inborn True Nature that exists before birth and after death, has never been 'born' and will never 'die', has never been 'lost' and can never be 'found' as a 'thing' or finite object of ego-self. We are and have always been that which we are seeking. As one Zen Master put it: We are riding the Ox of enlightened True Nature searching for the Ox of enlightened True Nature.

So, why then do we have to search for enlightenment? Because we have obscured and obstructed True Nature through exclusively and completely identifying with our conditioned, limited and dualistic ego-self and its needs and desires, concepts and dualities, attachments and judgments and mechanisms and operations instituted and implemented to affirm, strengthen, enhance, defend and preserve its false, illusional 'reality', image and concept.

True Nature is inherent within and as Nature and human nature and is hidden and latent within our ego-self. The path of enlightenment involves deconstructing and disidentifying from our conditioned ego-self and realizing, identifying as and actualizing our being as True Nature.

A radical transforming of our ego-self occurs, rather than its elimination or so-called 'death'. Like the egg transforms into the butterfly through stages of larva/caterpillar, cocoon and chrysalis to imago/butterfly; there is a change in outer form but not of inner essence. Our ego-self is liberated, transformed into and assimilated as True Nature. After the re-constructing, re-constituting and re-identifying of our ego-self as True Nature; we realize that the outer world is not appreciably changed but that our inner experience of it is radically transformed, i.e., the ways we see, relate to, feel about and act and move in it.

As the saying goes: 'Before enlightenment, mountains are mountains and rivers are rivers. In the cultivating and practicing of becoming enlightened, mountains and rivers are not mountains and rivers (due to negating and emptying our 'concepts' of them) and after enlightenment, mountains are again mountains and rivers are again rivers (affirming their true nature). Oh, ah, but now; how very beautiful, marvelous, magnificent and majestic they both are!.

Enlightenment is realizing oneness and not-twoness, no-thingness and emptiness, allness and suchness; Mind-Only, One-Mind, No-Mind and All-Mind. There are only/no 'concepts' of Buddha, Dharma or Sangha; reality, self or truth; awakening, enlightenment or liberation, etc.. There is only one 'thing' that is, essentially, not-a-'thing' and that is, existentially, just-this-'thing'. Negation is not of the actuality of things but is of their impermanence and absence of essence and of our concepts of them.

The Madhyamika Buddhist four-fold 'logic' of Nagarjuna is helpful in understanding dualities, unity and negation, i.e., 1) A is A (a separate positive assertion), 2) A is not A (a separate negative assertion), 3) A is both A and not-A (a dual unity) and 4) A is neither A and not-A (a nondual negation). This logic can be used to integrate and negate the being, doing, knowing and having dualities of Way-stations One, Two, Three and Four, i.e., good-bad, right-wrong, true-false, gain-loss.

Enlightenment is realizing a nondual, clear and open Mind free of deluded thoughts, misconceptions and 'clutter'; an empty Heart free of emotional desires, attachments and 'baggage'; a calm Will free of volitional intentions, strivings and 'busyness' and a whole Being free of relational 'splits', separations and oppositions. True Mind is pure and empty consciousness and clear and open awareness generating, focusing upon and witnessing the mutual arising and interdependence of phenomena and their passing out of conscious awareness.

Not considering imaginings and daydreams; visions and hallucinations; clairvoyance and extrasensory perception; dreams and lucid dreams; subconsciousness, preconsciousness and supramental consciousness, dreamless sleep, unconsciousness and comas; some 'stages' of consciousness and awareness are:

1. **Being awake** – the precondition of not being asleep, intoxicated or unconscious.
2. **Being alert** – watchful, vigilant, wary usually re: some negative possibility or danger.
3. **Being aware** – the natural openness of seeing and noticing of inner and outer 'things'.
4. **Being attentive** – intentional focusing upon and concentrating upon specific 'things'.
5. **Observing** – looking at specific 'things' and states, etc. usually with some purpose.
6. **Witnessing** – beholding and appreciating 'things' and phenomena openly and neutrally.
7. **The field or state of clear and open awareness** in, of and as itself and of just what is.
8. **The field or state of pure and empty consciousness** in, of and as itself and of just what is.

9. Awareness of awareness and consciousness of consciousness. An infinite regressing.
10. Just pure and empty consciousness and just clear and open awareness themselves alone. Not as a 'state' or 'field', not 'of' anything and not 'of' themselves. Thingless, objectless, idealess, conceptless, contentless, etc.. Reality, awakeness, illumination, enlightenment, realization, liberation, emptiness, suchness, thus-ness, is-ness, so-ness, True Nature, Presence, 'Just-This' and 'I-Am'.

In the process of becoming an enlightened human being; we begin with abstract, objectified and named concepts of beings and things in the phenomenal world of experience and we end as being empty and pure consciousness, clear and open awareness and True Nature themselves and seeing that True Nature in and as everyone and everything. We move from objects alone to objects of consciousness to consciousness of objects to consciousness alone.

Kensho is a momentary eureka experience, a brilliant lightning flash, of 'seeing into' that One Original, Inborn True Nature and satori is a more extended ongoing state, a constant flowing stream, of 'being' it.

Pure and empty consciousness and clear and open awareness are ready, available and able to concentratedly focus upon, accurately receive and appropriately respond to whatever and however it presents itself, enters and abides in them or originates in and emerges from them.

Such a state, condition, situation and circumstance ('standing around in a circle') of pure consciousness is full attention to, and deep connection with, the nature, realities and truths of the myriad phenomena that appear to or from it and that allow for a natural flowing into essential, necessary and appropriate inclusive inner reflection, empathic relational communing and meaningfully beneficial responsiveness.

Acknowledging, accepting, allowing, attuning and accomodating to, according and allying with and accompanying whatever and however it presents itself to pure and empty consciousness and clear and open awareness is not a laissez-faire attitude and care-less approach that every 'thing' that is occurring is acceptable and allowable as it is.

'Reflecting upon, relating to and responding to' may also involve, entail and require the 'accepting and allowing of necessary, essential and appropriate' counteractions such as limiting, controlling, redirecting, preventing and/or stopping actions that are, for example, detrimental, harmful, abusive, violent, hurtful, injurious, life-endangering or life-threatening etc., where the 'accepting and allowing' are of the counteraction.

Pure, empty, clear and open consciousness:

1) does not exist in space-time, it is infinite-eternal space-time itself.

2) is not empty of anything, it is emptiness and no-thingness itself.

3) is never a 'thing' itself and is that which originates and 'things' 'things'.

4) is not an experience of something but is a state of being as everything.

5) cannot be objectified, like the eye cannot see itself except in reflections.

6) is that which sources, creates, originates and manifests everything.

The natural alternating of yin-yang energy dynamics is governed by the 'law of reversal', i.e., when one pole of a bipolar dual-unity reaches its maximum extreme, it reverts to its complementary pole. Accordingly, pure consciousness as emptiness is at its maximum potential for manifesting and presencing the fullness of the phenomena of human experience, e.g., sensations, perceptions, thoughts, ideas, images, feelings, actions, relationships, etc.. Consciousness is thus the identity of emptiness/

sunyata and suchness/tathata; the 'nothing' and 'everything' of any and all phenomena of human experience.

The ego-self needs to be, know, have and do 'things', but True Nature *is* those 'things'. The ego-self cannot affect, influence, change, know anything about or do anything to the infinite and eternal reality of pure and empty consciousness because it is a creation of it; just as products, effects, echoes and results cannot do so with their causes.

But the ego-self can make a transformative shift from exclusively and completely identifying with its fictitious 'reality' to intimately identifying with and as True Nature and ultimately realizing and being its identity as True Nature. And the ego-self can see that everyone and everything is a uniquely and beautifully diverse manifestation of that same one True Nature, like the many individual facets of one clear, bright, brilliant and radiant whole diamond.

For the formerly fictitious, false, illusional and deluded ego-self; its mistaken identity and presumed 'life' are no longer those and, rather, have now yielded to and transformed into the reality, truth, actuality and being of and as True Nature.

The abstractions, construings, projections, devisings and contrivings of the ego-self have become the concrete, arisings, appearances, manifestings and expressing of the pure and empty consciousness and the clear and open awareness of True Nature.

Everyone and everything not only appears to and in pure, empty, clear, open and spacious consciousness but is of, from and as it. The thoughts, ideas, beliefs and imaginings that ego-self had about being enlightened True Nature have, primarily through awakening kensho and realized satori 'experiences', become a living reality.

All of the phenomena, objects, conceptions, activities, etc. of the ego-self are, in essence, inseparable from and united with awakened, illuminated, enlightened and liberated pure consciousness which is clear, empty and free of desires for, attachments to and judgments about separate-united beings, ignorant-wise knowings, lost-gained havings and failed-successful doings.

It is said that an unenlightened buddha is a human being and an enlightened human being is a buddha. The radical ground, root, heart, core, marrow and spirit of a Zen Way of human being and living is fundamentally and essentially one of solitude, silence, serenity, simplicity and sufficiency; but also is one that does not exclude being, joining and participating in the social world of fellow human beings in a Way that is wise, compassionate, skillful and, at fortunate times, awakening, illuminating, enlightening, transforming and liberating.

Enlightenment is being the Mystery of pure consciousness and True Nature that appears to itself as emptiness and suchness. It is; 1) realizing and actualizing an openness to the beings, things and phenomena of everyday living and ordinary experience and 2) acknowledging and accepting, attuning to and according with, affirming and accompanying and affiliating with and abiding in them just as they are in, of and as themselves so; as the reality, vitality, miracles, marvels, truth, beauty, grace, magnificence and splendor of their natural and spontaneous presencing.

Peacefulness, tranquility and serenity; happiness, delight and joy; compassion, loving and caring; serving, assisting and benefiting and humility, generosity and forgiveness are natural by-products, end-results and constituents of: 1) the emancipation, liberation and freedom from no longer exclusively identifying as a conditioned and dualistic ego-self and 2) being an identity of and as pure consciousness, True Nature and 'I-Am' that does not 'be', 'know', 'do' and 'have' 'things' in the characteristic ways of the objectifying, abstracting and construing ego-self.

Awakening, illumination, enlightenment, realization, transformation and liberation and cultivating, practicing, actualizing and transmitting are essentially the spaciousness of pure and empty consciousness, clear and open awareness; being True/Buddha-Nature and Zen Mind; seeing with the Buddha-Eye, living the Buddha-Dharma and the reality of the Here-Now Presence of 'Just-This' and 'I-Am'.

Sheerly and utterly, purely and simply, just being and living as True/Buddha-Nature, 'Just-This' and 'I-Am' are quintessentially worthwhile, meaningful, fulfilling and sufficient intentions, purposes, endeavors, attainments and perfections. The luminous, bright, brilliant and radiant Presence of just being and living True/Buddha-Nature, 'Just-This' and 'I-Am' shines forth to, for and as all fellow human beings with wisdom, compassion, generosity, gratitude and forgiveness and lasting peacefulness, happiness, freedom and joyfulness.

Here-Now. Just This is. You are This. I am This. We all are This. You-This.....I-This.....We-This.....You-I.....We-I.....You.....I .....We.....

True Nature

True Nature is hidden in the seeming
of our unenlightened ego-self.
True Nature is revealed *as* the non-being
of enlightened True Nature.

Our ego-self is a digressive parenthesis
and conceptual footnote of the ongoing narrative
of awakened, transformed, liberated and enlightened
True Nature, 'I-Am' and 'Just-This'.

To be Present as 'I-Am'

在

Tsai/Zai
- *To be present;* be at, in, on.
- To exert one's power on earth.
- Presence in a place manifested in one's activity.

T'sai/Cai
- natural capacity and activity, ability, talents, genius, substance of a thing. + T'u/Tu - earth.

T'sai/Cai + T'u/Tu

如

Ju/Ru
- *As,* like.
- To speak with womanly skill appropriately and in conformity to the circumstances.

Nu/Nu
- woman +
  K'ou/Kou - mouth.

Nu/Nu + K'ou/Kou

我

Wo/Wo
- *I.*
- Two spears pointing toward each other.
- Or a hand grasping a spear.

Shou/Shou
- the hand, skill +
  Ko/Ge - spear, lance.

Shou/Shou + Ko/Ge

是

Shih/Shi
- *Am,* be, is, are, right, exact, yes.

Jih/Ri
- the sun +
  Cheng/Zheng - true, upright, straight.

Jih/Ri + Cheng/Zheng

Afterword

Some characteristic functions of human being are being, thinking, feeling, acting and relating. They are typically experienced as activities of ego-self respectively involving: 1) self-sense, identity and image that can be false and mistaken; 2) thoughts, ideas and concepts that can be defilements and delusions; 3) emotions, desires and attachments that can be afflictions and fetters; 4) behaviors, habits and drives that can be obstructions and errors and 5) encounters, exchanges and interactions that can be separations and oppositions.

Such activities of the ego-self involve a subject-object duality between the 'subjective' experiencer and that which is the 'objectively' experienced being, thought, feeling, action and other. This is a duality between I and me, knower and known, feeler and felt, doer and done and self and other.

The pure and empty consciousness and the clear and open awareness of enlightened True Nature and 'I-Am' are not these dualities, are neither the seen nor the seer, etc. and are that which sees both.

One of the principal happenings in Zen meditative practice is the unifying, integrating, negating and emptying of these and other dualities in human consciousness, e.g., real-unreal, mind-body, inner-outer, cause-effect, good-bad, right-wrong, true-false, gain-loss, praise-blame, life-death, etc., as well as those of wisdom-ignorance, non-attachment-attachment, correctness-error, union-separation, etc..

Dualistic-based being, knowing, having, doing and relating are the sources: 1) of the conditioned ego-self's false assumptions and conclusions; misconceptions, projections, discriminations, judgmentalism and prejudices and 2) of delusion, desire, greed, loss, failure, anger, suffering, alienation, hatred, conflicts, violence and wars.

This type of being, thinking, feeling, acting and relating involves objectified, unilateral and mutually exclusive either-or dualities, e.g., I-me, I-it, me-you, us-them, etc.; where a false one-sided 'oneness' is created by separating, replacing, excluding, defeating and/or eliminating an antithetical or opposing 'other'.

The integrating, unifying, assimilating, negating, emptying and transcending of dualities in Zen practice is an acknowledging, affirming and actualizing of both polarities of dualities as a bipolar dual unity of co-existing, co-related, co-operating and mutually inclusive both-and equal interdependent complements; like two sides of the same one coin.

The Zen practice of initially 'negating' the false dualities of ego-self identities, mental thoughts, emotional feelings, volitional actions and relational being; ultimately becomes an affirming of their true unity that affords nondual answers to questions, integral solutions to problems, egalitarian settling of issues and collaborative resolutions of conflicts.

Zen negation is not a nihilistic denial of the ground of reality and truth or of the actuality and validity of the taos, dharmas and phenomena of conscious awareness and experience. It is, rather, a clearing and emptying of deluded and erroneous mental concepts of reality and truth and of separated and opposing mental dualisms of thoughts, feelings actions and relationships.

Zen negation opens the way to True/Buddha-Nature as pure and empty consciousness and clear and open awareness, the consciousness of consciousness alone and the awareness of awareness alone and their creative potential to manifest phenomena and their open availability to receive them.

There is a Chinese Taoist tale about a creative artist and skilled artisan whose art and craft is woodcarving. One day a wayfaring sojourner happens upon the workplace of the artist and, while wandering around in it, comes upon a beautiful wood sculpture of an elephant. The color values and shading of the wood and the way that the woodgrain follows the natural curves of the elephant give it a very realistic life-like appearance. The wayfarer asks the artist how she created such a fine work of art. The artist replies, 'Well, I first saw the elephant in the wood and then simply carved away all that wasn't the elephant!'

In Zen practice there is: 1) a 'seeing into'/kensho and a 'being of'/satori True/Buddha-Nature that is present but hidden within the conditioned 'wood' of the finite ego-self and 2) a creative and skillful 'carving away' of all of its forms that are not the splendid 'elephant' of True/Buddha-Nature.

True/Buddha-Nature is thus awakened from the slumbering, drowsy, abstracted, obscuring, deluded and attached ego-mind and is liberated from the distracted, deviated, obstructing, hindering, impeding and erroneous ego-self.

Awakening, illumination, enlightenment, transformation and liberation are the responsible awareness that questions, problems, issues and conflicts occur from and in our own hearts and minds, by and through our own will and choices, to and in our own bodies and in and as our own lives. This consciousness enables and assists clearing and emptying the mental 'clutter' of concepts, the emotional 'filler' of attachments, the volitional 'busyness' of errors and the relational 'splits' of false being.

Practicing the Zen doctrines and wisdom of Mind-Only, One-Mind, No-Mind and All-Mind; creates, organizes and regulates an open and spacious field of pure objectless consciousness and clear conceptless awareness that enables and allows seeing and experiencing the reality and truth of beings, 'things' and events just as they are and in and as True/Buddha-Nature.

From Lao Tzu's *Tao Te Ching*:

'As wise human beings, we are guiding fellow human beings to be conceptless and desireless and cleverness and craftiness to be ineffective. By practicing non-interfering, this State (Tao/Ultimate Reality/True/Buddha-Nature and the taos and dharmas of the world) is self-regulating naturally'. TTC #3.

'Tao (Original, Inborn True/Buddha-Nature) is constantly not-'doing' any 'thing'; yet no-thing is being left undone. As leaders, when we are embodying Tao, all beings are transforming spontaneously. After developing naturally, if desires are again stirring, we are quieting them with Primordial Simplicity. Primordial Simplicity is being desireless. Being desireless is being at peace. Our world is settling of its own accord'. TTC # 37.

The Zen doctrines of One-Mind, No-Mind and All-Mind enable experiencing that, in being True/Buddha-Nature; there is only 'one without a second', 'not-two', no 'this' or 'that'; no 'I'; no 'one' to be; no 'thing' to know, have or do, no 'where' to go, no 'other' to join, etc.. This opens the way to experiencing 1) the sheer and utter emptiness, openness, peacefulness, happiness, freedom, joyfulness and suchness of being True/Buddha-Nature and 2) the pure and simple knowing of, relating to, being with and identity as, everyone and everything just as they are.

In the *Tao Te Ching* passage 13, Lao Tzu reminds us, 'No self, no trouble'. So, through disidentifying from the illusional idea and fictional concept of an ego-self and being the No-Self of True/Buddha-Nature, we can be liberated from, e.g.,

1. Confusion, doubts, worries, fears, anxieties, depression, loss, grief, hopelessness, despair.
2. Illusions, delusions, fantasies, obsessions, dreams, nightmares, flashbacks, pain, suffering,
3. Desiring, wanting, envy, jealousy, greed, seeking, pursuing, acquiring, collecting, keeping.
4. Separation, isolation, alienation, estrangement, loneliness, discrimination, bias, prejudice.
5. Trauma, abuse, anger, hatred, conflict, violence, harm, injury, fighting, warring, killing.

And:

6. Objectifying, discriminating, assessing, evaluating, labeling, judging and blaming fellow human beings.
7. Stereotyping, profiling, marginalizing, criminalizing, infantalizing and patronizing fellow human beings.
8. Pathologizing, segregating, disenfranchising, depersonalizing and dehumanizing fellow human beings.

A WAY-SHOWING PATH OF ENLIGHTENMENT

(But, also, being No-Self is liberation from the 'positive' complements of such 'negatives').

Intimately, being True/Buddha-Nature is being awakened and liberated on a path of enlightenment. It is nourishing, fostering and sharing the power of love and not wielding the love of power and is Wayfaring and not warfaring.

The one who began the journey to enlightened True/Buddha-Nature is not the same one who is completing it, but is the one who is being or has been completed by it.

Ultimately, being a selfless self on a pathless path through a gateless gate to a goalless goal in spaceless space and timeless time is being and living True/Buddha-Nature as a precious and radiantly beautiful labor of deep love and a treasured and exquisitely created work of great art. All 'This' is 'It' and we are 'Just This' and 'It'!

From Lao Tzu's *Tao Te Ching* re: 'This':

'As wise human beings, we are attending to belly not eyes, rejecting the outer 'that', accepting the inner 'This''. TTC # 12.

'How can all beginnings be experienced? Through and as 'This''. TTC # 21.

'Here is 'This'. Undifferentiated and complete. Preceding the birthing of Heaven-Earth. Independent, still, empty and unchanging. All-pervading and inexhaustible. It is the Mother of all beings. Knowing it is truly unnameable, I am calling it Tao'. TTC # 25.

'As most developed human beings; we are dwelling in kernal and not husk, in fruit not flower, rejecting the outer 'that', accepting the inner 'This''. TTC #38.

'We are gaining our world by not interfering. How am I knowing this is so? Through and as 'This''. TTC # 57.

'As wise human beings, we are knowing but not displaying ourselves, valuing but not glorifying ourselves. Rejecting the outer 'that'. Accepting the inner 'This''. TTC # 72.

"'This' is the essential Secret'. TTC #27. "'This' is the essential

Teaching'. TTC# 42. "'This' is profound Virtuosity/Te'. TTC# 51. "'This' is according with the Constant/Tao'. TTC # 52.

We are the presence of the reality of the 'Just This Is 'It'' of human being and human living. We are the pure consciousness, emptiness, open awareness, suchness and 'I-Am' of awakened, illuminated, enlightened, realized, transformed, liberated and actualized One, Original, Absolute, Ultimate, Essential, Inborn True Nature.

In being the splendid, luminous, bright, brilliant and radiant Presence of the reality of pure and empty consciousness, clear and open awareness, awakened and enlightened True Nature, 'Just-This' and 'I-Am'; there is no other space but this place of just right Here and no other time but this moment of just right Now. There is no other nature but just True Nature, no other being but just 'I-Am' and no other thing but 'Just-This'. And 'This' is 'It' and We are 'This'..... and We are 'It'!

I Am Just This

Enlightenment is hidden in plain sight.
Just look inside into the space empty
of ideas, thoughts, concepts and words.
Enlightenment is always just right here.
There is no place ever to go to seek it.
Enlightenment is always just right now.
There is no time ever to take to find it.
There is no-one to become enlightened.
There is no-thing to know, have or do
to be inborn enlightened True Nature.
We always are 'Just-This' and 'I-Am'.
All ego-selves and things always go.
No-ego and True Nature always are.

A WAY-SHOWING PATH OF ENLIGHTENMENT

THIS-IS-IT / I-AM-THIS CHARACTERS

CHE/ZHE
<u>THIS</u>
HERE/NOW
CHIH/STOP +
YEN/WORDS

SHIH/SHI
<u>IS/BE</u>
SUCH/THUS
ABSOLUTE
CHENG/CORRECT +
JIH/DAILY

T'A/TA
<u>IT</u>
SHE/HE (HOMONYM)
YEH/ALSO +
NIU/OX

WO
<u>I</u>
SHOU/HAND +
KO/LANCE

SHIH/SHI
<u>AM</u>
CHENG/UPRIGHT +
JIH/DAILY

TZ'U/CI
<u>THIS/HERE</u>
CHIH/STOP +
PI/TURN ROUND

WO
<u>I</u>
SHOU/HAND +
KO/LANCE

SHIH/SHI
<u>AM</u>
CHENG/TRUE +
JIH/SUN

Am I Enlightened?
Well.........
I just don't 'know'
if I'm enlightened.
But my Body.........
is now untightened
and my Mind.........
is now brightened.
But my Heart.........
is now unfrightened
and my Will.........

is now rightened.
But my Soul.........
is now heightened
and my Spirit.........
is now whitened.
Well.........
I just don't 'know'
if I'm enlightened
(But, if 'I' did.........
'I' wouldn't be.........
would 'I' !).

Beginnings & Endings

Treat the beginning of things like their ending. Bring the awareness and urgency of dying to the reality and experience of living.

Treat the ending of things like their beginning. Bring the awareness and emergency of living to the reality and experience of dying.

Conclusion is the ending and finality of things. Close your eyes, exhale and enjoy it.

Completion is the wholeness and fullness of things. Open your eyes, smile and admire it.

Culmination is the climax and summit of things. Open your eyes, inhale and honor it.

Consummation is the perfection and ultimacy of things. Close your eyes, bow and revere it.

Appendix One
The Ten Zen Oxen Title Characters*

SHIH
Ten

CH'AN
Shih + Tan
Meditation
Revelation

NIU
Ox

SHAN
Men + Dan
Explanation
Enlarging

CHAN
Dan + Men
Meditation

SHAN
Shi + Dan
Contemplation
Abstraction

MIEN
Sheltering

ZEN
Shi + Dan + Zong
Ancestry

K'OU
Opening

* Designations are either Wade-Giles or Pin-Yin

Appendix Two
The Ten Way-Station Summaries

THE AWAKENING
Stages 1/2/3/4 = Ego-self is unawakened, unenlightened and unliberated; 1) searching, 2) tracking, 3) glimpsing, momentarily aware of and partially experiencing, and 4) grasping awakened, enlightened and liberated True Nature.

1. **Seeking the Ox**

    OF AWAKENING, ENLIGHTENMENT AND LIBERATION.

    The Ox is hidden within Nature and the conditioned ego-self. Recognizing dissatisfaction and searching in the outer world. Completely identifying with and as the conditioned ego-self. Good-bad, inner-outer, self-other 'being' dualities. Not awakened to, or consciously aware of, True Nature.

2. **Tracking the Ox**

    OF AWAKENING, ENLIGHTENMENT AND LIBERATION.

    The Ox's hoofprints are found on the path chosen and taken. Exploring, investigating, researching, studying spiritual teachings. Discovering traces of concepts of enlightenment and True Nature. Right-wrong and successful-unsuccessful 'doing' dualities. Hints, inklings, glimmerings and traces of True Nature affirmed.

3. **Glimpsing the Ox**

    OF AWAKENING, ENLIGHTENMENT AND LIBERATION.

    The hind-quarters and tail of the Ox are momentarily glimpsed. Confirming partial awareness of the actuality of True Nature. Kensho awarenesses of momentarily seeing into True Nature. True-false and whole-partial 'knowing' dualities. The partial reality of True Nature is experientially awakened to.

4. **CATCHING THE OX**
   OF AWAKENING, ENLIGHTENMENT AND LIBERATION.
   The whole Ox is caught and needs to be restrained and controlled. Holding onto and not losing True Nature requires strength and effort. Dedication, determination, diligence and perseverance are needed. Gain-loss and effort-ease 'having' dualities. The whole actuality of True Nature is experientially grasped.

THE TRANSFORMING

Stages 5/6 = Ego-self is 5) harmonizing with, identifying as, transforming, cultivating and becoming and 6) integrating, transforming, practicing and being awakened, enlightened and liberated True Nature.

5. **TAMING THE OX**
   OF AWAKENING, ENLIGHTENMENT AND LIBERATION.
   The Ox needs strong and firm disciplining in order to be tamed. Ego-self is subduing, tending, fostering and training True Nature. Ego-self and True Nature are reciprocally interacting with each other. Ego-self joins and accords with True Nature, gentles and tames it. Ego-self is cultivating and becoming enlightened True Nature.

6. **RIDING THE OX**
   OF AWAKENING, ENLIGHTENMENT AND LIBERATION.
   The Ox naturally knows the way home without being guided. Ego-self is practicing True Nature in ordinary

everyday living. Ego-self is being 'practiced' by True Nature in everyday living. Ego-self is integrating awakened and enlightened True Nature. Ego-self is practicing and being enlightened True Nature.

THE LIBERATING

Stages 7/8/9/10 = The non-objectified and non-dualistic not-'knowing', not-'being', not-'having' and not-'doing' of awakened, enlightened and liberated True Nature through: 7) completely assimilating and forgetting 8) disidentifying and emptying, 9) naturally sourcing and 10) naturally actualizing awakened, enlightened, and liberated True Nature in the world.

7. **FORGETTING THE OX**
   OF AWAKENING, ENLIGHTENMENT AND LIBERATION.

   The Ox of enlightenment is forgotten and not 'known' as a concept. True Nature is no longer a 'thing' to be sought, pursued or attained. Ego-self is united and merged with and not separate from True Nature. Ego-self is completely identified as and assimilated with True Nature. Ego-self as True Nature still objectively exists in conscious awareness.

8. **FORGETTING THE TRUE NATURE**
   OF AWAKENING, ENLIGHTENMENT AND LIBERATION.

   Ego-self as enlightened True Nature is forgotten and is not a 'being'. Ego-self as True Nature is disidentified with, transcended, emptied. True Nature is no longer an object-content of conscious awareness. True Nature is pure, clear, empty, open and spacious consciousness. Only the perfect sphere of emptiness is the shunyata of experience.

9. **Returning to the Origin**
   OF AWAKENING, ENLIGHTENMENT AND LIBERATION.

   True Nature is not acquired and something 'had' as an entity or object. True Nature is the creative potential of and the Origin and Source as consciousness. True Nature is One, Absolute, Ultimate, Essential, Inborn True Nature. True Nature is shunyata, a void of the pure potential for manifesting. True Nature's emptiness originates and sources the fullness of suchness/tathata.

10. **Entering the World**
    AS AWAKENED, ENLIGHTENED AND LIBERATED.

    True Nature is not intended and something 'done' as an activity. True Nature is present and actualized in the world with fellow human beings. True Nature is naturally transmitted to fellow human beings. True Nature is wisdom, compassion and skillful means in action. True Nature awakens, enlightens and liberates human beings.

True Nature	*ego-self*
1. Absent from/hidden within ego-self	1. Completely ego-self identified
2. Traces present to/within ego-self	2. Has concepts of True Nature
3. Briefly appears to/within ego-self	3. Has awakenings to True Nature
4. Is co-existing with ego-self	4. Has realizations of True Nature
5. Is joining/interacting with ego-self	5. Is harmonizing with True Nature
6. Is uniting/integrating with ego-self	6. Is integrating with True Nature
7. Is embodying/being ego-self	7. Is assimilating/forgetting True Nature
8. Is forgetting/emptying ego-self	8. Is transcending/emptying itself
9. Is the source/origin of everything	9. Is being at the source of True Nature
10. Is actualized in the social world	10. Is being in the world as True Nature

Appendix Three
The Path and Play Outlined

The Play
The Unenlightened Ego-Self's Path to Enlightened True Nature

Cast of Characters –
1) the Ox-herder is playing 'filled' awareness, and unenlightened ego-self.
2) the Ox is being 'empty' consciousness and enlightened True Nature.

Act One – Pre-Enlightenment.
The World of Duality.
Anything/Something Happening.
Setting the Stage.

Scene 1 – Seeking the Ox.
- the Ox of True Nature is hidden within Nature and the Ox-herder's mind.
- the ego-self is dissatisfied, seeking change and unaware of its True Nature.
- the ego-self has been searching outwardly for its answers and solutions.

Scene 2 – Tracking the Ox.
- the Ox-herder finds the hoofprints of what seem to be those of an Ox.
- the ego-self is exploring, pursuing and illuminated by spiritual teachings.
- the ego-self becomes aware of traces of the concept of its True Nature.

Scene 3 – Glimpsing the Ox.
- the Ox-herder catches a fleeting glimpse of the rear-end and tail of the Ox.
- the ego-self has an awakening kensho experience of seeing into True Nature.
- the ego-self has an awareness of the partial reality of its own True Nature.

Scene 4 - Catching the Ox.
- the Ox-herder meets and catches the Ox and struggles with holding onto it.
- the ego-self has grasped the reality of the whole concept of its True Nature.
- the ego-self struggles with holding onto what is understood of its True Nature.

Act Two – Mid-Enlightenment.
The Realm of Dual-Unity.
One Thing Happening.
No Intermission.

Scene 5 - Taming the Ox.
- the Ox-herder needs and uses the rope and whip to control and train the Ox.
- the ego-self initially struggles in controlling and disciplining its True Nature.
- the ego-self later harmonizes and identifies with the reality of its True Nature.
- the ego-self cultivates its True Nature and is beginning to transform into it.

Scene 6 – Riding the Ox Home.
- the Ox-herder is happily sitting astride the Ox that knows the way back home.

- the ego-self is united with its True Nature and is past the point of no return.
- the ego-self has integrated both itself and its True Nature that is now leading.
- the ego-self is 'practiced' by its True Nature as its principal reality and identity.

Act Three – Post-Enlightenment.
The Sphere of Non-Duality.
Nothing/Everything Happening.
Finale.

Scene 7 – The Ox is Forgotten.
- the Ox-herder is sitting alone at home and the Ox is forgotten and gone.
- the ego-self has assimilated with the non-conceptuality of its True Nature.
- the ego-self is absorbed in, embodying and is being its one True Nature.
- the ego-self is fully identified as its True Nature but is still self-existing.

Scene 8 – The Self is Transcended.
- the Ox-herder is also forgotten and only the circle of emptiness is present.
- the ego-self has disidentified from itself and has even forgotten its True Nature.
- the ego-self and its True Nature no longer exist as objects of consciousness.
- the ego-self has liberated itself, is egoless and the emptiness of True Nature.

A WAY-SHOWING PATH OF ENLIGHTENMENT

SCENE 9 – RETURNING TO THE SOURCE.
- only Nature and its mountains, rivers, trees, flowers and creatures are present.
- being is at the silent inner wellspring, fountainhead and origin of everything.
- only pure, empty consciousnss; clear, open awareness and True Nature are.
- satori of being at the source of creation-destruction, integration-disintegration.

SCENE 10 – BEING IN THE WORLD.
- satori naturally opens the Way of the peace, freedom, happiness of 'I-Am'.
- satori naturally flows into living virtuously, compassionately, generously.
- satori naturally becomes living the 4 Noble Truths and the Eightfold path.
- satori naturally, wisely and skillfully actualizes emptiness and suchness.
- satori naturally brings awakening, enlightenment and liberation to others.
- satori naturally transmits the Buddha-Dharma, vitally, radiantly and directly.

Fine

Appendix Four
Classic Ox-Herding Versions

For readers interested in several different versions of *The Ten Ox-Herding Pictures:*

	Ch'ing-chu/ Seikyo 11th Century CE *No Reference*	Tzu-te Hui/ Jitoku Eki 12th Century CE *See Shibayama*	Kuo-an Shi-yuan/ Kakuan Shien 12th Century CE *See D.T. Suzuki, Reps & Senzaki*	Anonymous and Pu-ming 16th Century CE *See D.T. Suzuki, Red Pine*
1.	? Ox is all black	Awakening Faith Ox's head is white	Seeking the Ox Ox is all black	Undisciplined Ox is all black
2.	? Ox is all black	First Entering Ox's head is white	Tracing the Ox Ox is all black	Taming Begun Ox is all black
3.	? Ox is half white	Not Genuine Yet Ox is half white	Seeing the Ox Ox is all black	In Harness Ox head is white
4.	? Ox is all white	The True Mind Ox is all white	Catching the Ox Ox is all black	Faced Round Ox front 1/3 is white
5.	? Empty circle *	Both Forgotten Empty circle*	Taming the Ox Ox is all black	Tamed Ox front 2/3 is white
6.	X	Playing Man in the world	Riding the Ox Ox is all black	Unimpeded Ox is mostly white
7.	X	X	Forgetting the Ox Ox is gone	Laissez-Faire Ox is all white
8.	X	X	Transcending Self Empty circle *	Other Forgotten Ox is all white
9.	X	X	Back to the Source Only Nature	The Solitary Moon No Ox
10.	X	X	Entering Marketplace Bliss-bestowing hands	Both Vanished Empty circle *

A WAY-SHOWING PATH OF ENLIGHTENMENT

Sometime in the Sung Dynasty (960-1279 CE), an eight-stage Chinese version ending in an empty circle made by an unknown author has been referred to (see D.T. Suzuki). A Japanese scroll dated 1278 CE is in collection (see Wada). Paintings have been made by Gyokusei Jikihara in 1982 (see Kopp, Loori). However, many versions of *The Ten Ox-Herding Pictures* have been made and commentaried upon, since they have been popular in the Chinese and Japanese cultures and found to be useful in the teaching and training of Buddhist and Zen students on a spiritual path to awakening, enlightenment and liberation.

* It is interesting to note that the Siekyo, Jitoku (almost) and Pu-ming versions end the path of enlightenment in 'Enso', the unbroken and empty circle that symbolizes both the completion of oneness and wholeness and the perfection of emptiness and suchness; while the Kakuan version goes two stages further; i.e., returning to the origin and entering the world.

THE GREAT OX

The Great Ox of enlightenment
is timeless, immortal and eternal
and lives on in the ego-minds
of unenlightened human beings
and *as* the True/Tao/Buddha-Nature
of enlightened human beings
in consciousness and the world.

Hope For Our Ego-Self

Our ego-self is an illusional and fictional concept, idea and image designed to protect and defend the safety, security, stability and esteem of a false self. It harbors the delusion that it creates, orders, controls and understands reality by using personas, facades, masks, veils, screens and filters and by making assessments, comparisons and judgments. As insubstantial and impermanent, it is prone to feeling vulnerable, inadequate, incompetent, worried, anxious, fearful and depressed. Our ego-self is asleep in the dark and it dreams in the light but its limitations, weaknesses, crises, struggles, conflicts, failures, losses, sufferings and pains are openings and opportunities for awakening to, realizing and transforming into enlightened True Nature and here-now present moments of 'I-Am' and 'Just-This'.

Appendix Five
A Comparison of 10 Stages

The Dashabhumika Sutra/Sutra of the Ten Spiritual Levels details 10 stages of the spiritual path, process and progress of bodhisattvas in their attaining Buddhahood. It is interesting to compare these ten stages with those of *The Ten Ox-Herding Pictures* and the spiritual path, process and progress of human beings in their attaining enlightenment.

Bhumis – ground, land are also viharas – places for the sojourning, meeting, dwelling and meditating of monks such as shrines, temples and monasteries. Viharas were also places at the disposal of the Buddha throughout his path of teaching the Dharma. Viharas can also be understood and experienced personally in the same way as Way-Stations are in this book and can be metaphorically considered as the same inner shrines at our own disposal throughout our sojourning pilgrimage from our ego-self to One Original and Inborn True Nature.

The Ten Ox-Herding Pictures

1. **Seeking the Ox**
   Dissatisfied and lost
   Separate from True Nature
   Identified with ego-delusion
   Focusing on external things

2. **Tracking the Ox**
   Exploring and studying teachings
   Intellectual understandings
   Experimenting with meditation
   Considering spiritual paths

3. **Seeing Hoofprints of the Ox**
   Experiencing a Kensho moment
   Temporary glimpse of True Nature
   Validation of True Nature's reality
   Encouragement of path-taking

4. **Catching the Ox**
   Meeting of ego and True natures
   Difficulty in taking hold of True Nature
   Matching strength and energy required
   Struggle to keep hold of True Nature

5. **Taming the Ox**
   Interacting of ego and True natures
   Steady and firm discipline is required
   Harmonizing of ego and True natures
   True Nature is gentle and compliant

A WAY-SHOWING PATH OF ENLIGHTENMENT

The Dashabhumika Sutra

1. **Land of Splendid Joy**
   Entering the path to Buddhahood
   Direct perception of the ego's emptiness
   Direct perception of Dharma's emptiness
   Virtues of faith and generosity

2. **Land of Immaculate Purity**
   Perfection of discipline and ethics
   Free of impurites and defilements
   Practicing concentration/samadhi
   Practicing absorption/dhyana

3. **Land of Luminous Radiance**
   Uprooting delusions, desires and hatred
   Insight into the impermanence of all
   Brings radiant light of wisdom/prajna
   Virtue of patience in assisting others

4. **Land of Blazing Fire**
   Burning through ignorance and passions
   Practicing the virtue of exertion of effort
   Cultivating exalted wisdom/prajna
   Perfecting requirements for Buddhahood

5. **Land of Extreme Difficulty**
   Cultivating the perfection of samadhi
   Intuitively grasping of the Truth
   Absorbed in meditation/dhyana
   Surmounting all doubts and uncertainty

The Ten Ox-Herding Pictures

6. **Riding the Ox Home**
   The ego-self yields to True Nature
   The ego is carried along by True Nature
   The ego and True natures are integrated
   Point of no return in everyday practice

7. **The Ox is Forgotten**
   The ego-self is transformed
   Enlightenment is not a 'thing'
   Ego-self assimilated with True Nature
   Practice is frictionless and effortless

8. **The Self is Forgotten**
   No substantial and independent 'I'
   Everything comes and goes
   Emptiness is the source of all
   Everything is just what and as it is

9. **Returning to the Origin**
   Creative sourcing of experience
   Non-dual oneness of everything
   The ordinary is extraordinary
   Everything reveals the truth of life

10. **Being in the World**
    Full enlightenment is reached
    Wisdom and compassion enacted
    Awakening and enlivening others
    Serving, affecting and benefiting others

A WAY-SHOWING PATH OF ENLIGHTENMENT

The Dashabhumika Sutra

6. Land of Meditative Wisdom
   Transcending of discriminations
   Realizing all dharmas as essentially empty
   Reaching supreme wisdom of suchness
   Comprehending absolute nothingness

7. Land of Far-Reaching Transcendence
   Gaining intuitive wisdom/prajna
   Meditative absorption/dhyana
   Attaining transcendent Buddhahood
   Not falling back into lower existence

8. Land of Immobile Dwelling
   Irreversible undisturbed emptiness
   Complete absorption in the Dharma
   Not accumulating further karma
   Transferring merit to other beings

9. Land of Good-Mindedness
   Supreme wisdom/prajna is complete
   Unrestricted meditation/dhyana practice
   Knowing the nature of all dharmas
   Natural and supernatural powers

10. Land of Dharma Clouds
   Buddhahood reached and confirmed
   All virtues and wisdom realized
   Fully developed Truth-body
   Showering everything with Dharma

Appendix Six
Correlations of Ten Stages – 1

The Ten Ox Herding Pictures	Paramitas-Virtues Reaching the Other Transcendent Shore*	Dashabala-Kinds of Knowledge and Powers of a Buddha*	Characterizing Epithet of Siddartha Gautama the Buddha*
Searching for the Ox	Vows	What is possible and impossible in any given situation	Gifted in knowledge and conduct
Tracking of the Ox	Patience and insight into causes of problems	Paths leading to various realms	Knower of worlds
Glimpsing of the Ox	Right means and right methods	Extinction of all defilements	Unsurpassable teacher of human beings
Catching of the Ox	Devoted, resolute, undeviated energy	Ripening of deeds	Teacher of the gods and human beings
Taming of the Ox	Disciplined eradication of all passions	Engendering of purity	The Perfect One
Riding of the Ox	Meditative cutting through ego-illusions	Meditative states of samadhi, dhyana	The Holy One
Forgetting of the Ox	Knowing the truth of all dharmas	Superior knowledge of deaths, rebirths	The Awakened One
Forgetting of the Self	Realization of superior wisdom	Knowledge of superior, inferior human abilities	The Fully Enlightened One
Sourcing of the Origin	Realization of the ten powers	Knowledge of the tendencies of humans	The Sublime One
Entering the World	Generosity and dedicating merit	Knowledge of the constituents of world	The Well-Gone One

* The commonly listed order of these paramitas, dashabala and epithets has been changed, since they all are non-linear and non-hierarchical, synchronous and coterminous and simultaneous and multi-dimensional.

APPENDIX SEVEN
CORRELATIONS OF TEN STAGES – 2

THE TEN OX HERDING PICTURES	TEN STAGES OF MIND DEVELOPMENT *	TEN STAGES OF ENLIGHTENMENT **
Searching for the Ox	Ignorant Goat-like Mind	Lawless Hard-Hearted
Tracking of the Ox	Foolish Abstinent Mind	Covetous Sordid
Glimpsing of the Ox	Child-like Fearless Mind	Foolish Unashamed
Catching of the Ox	Selfless Aggregate Mind	Act for sake of own interests
Taming of the Ox	Karmic Seed-free Mind	Act well for sake of acting well
Riding of the Ox	Only Mind	Merely enjoys pleasures
Forgetting of the Ox	Void Mind	Save self only with great effort
Forgetting of the Self	One Mind	Save self only without effort
Sourcing of the Origin	No Self-Nature Mind	Save self and others from evil
Entering the World	Secret Sublime Mind	Virtue and wisdom fully attained

* By Kukai (774 - 835 CE).
** By Nichiren (1222 - 1282 CE).

APPENDIX EIGHT
TEN MENTAL ABIDINGS

Ten mental abidings are described by Kamalasila and are in the Mahamudra tradition of Tibetan Buddhism. Two branches of meditative cultivation/bhavana are samatha/calm and vipassana/insight. Samatha practice eventuates in a state of calm, serene, tranquil and peaceful awareness that is: 1) dhyana/a sustained flow of concentrated and absorbed meditative awareness and 2) a foundation for vipassana/meditative insight into the nature of reality.

1. **Placement of the mind** — attention on an object but that is distracted and unmaintained.
   (Seeking the Ox of awakened, enlightened and liberated True Nature.)

2. **Continuous placement** — attention on an object that is undistracted for ~ one minute.
   (Tracking the Ox of awakened, enlightened and liberated True Nature.)

3. **Repeated placement** — attention on an object that is quickly restored after distraction and that is continuing for ~ 108 breaths.
   (Glimpsing the Ox of awakened, enlightened and liberated True Nature.)

4. **Close placement** — mindful and undistracted attention that is maintained for ~ an hour or longer.
   (Catching the Ox of awakened, enlightened and liberated True Nature.)

5. **Taming placement** — deep tranquility of mind but that is not completely calm abiding.
   (Taming the Ox of awakened, enlightened and liberated True Nature.)

A WAY-SHOWING PATH OF ENLIGHTENMENT

6. **Pacifying placement** — dullness and laxity are no longer problems but the proneness to excitement is present.
   (Riding the Ox of awakened, enlightened and liberated True Nature home.)

7. **Fully pacifying placement** — reaching high levels of completely uninterrupted concentration.
   (Forgetting the Ox of awakened, enlightened and liberated True Nature.)

8. **Single-pointing placement** — effortlessly reaching high levels of uninterrupted concentration.
   (Completely disidentifying from, transcending and forgetting the ego-self.)

9. **Balanced placement** — effortlessly reaching absorbed concentration that is maintained for ~ 4 hours.
   (Awakened, enlightened and liberated returning to and abiding in Nature and the Source and Origin of everyone and everything.)

10. **Culmination in samatha** — abiding in the calm, serene, tranquil and peaceful state of smoothly flowing, sustained and absorbed concentrated awareness.
    (Awakened, enlightened and liberated entering and being in the world with fellow human beings and naturally transmitting awakening, enlightenment and liberation.)

Appendix Nine
Ego-Self's Path to Enlightened True Nature

Awakening, transforming and liberating are the 10 Way-Stations of pre-enlightenment, mid-enlightenent and post-enlightenment that are initially partial and finally more complete.

Awakening — Pre-Enlightenment.
1. ego-self awakened to recognizing dissatisfaction, acknowledging need for searching.
   ego-self separate, alone, lost in the world. Enlightened True Nature hidden in Nature and ego-self.
   i-am is i-was of the past. *Should*, ought to be a more enlightened True Nature I-Am of the future.
2. ego-self awakened to information, ideas, concepts of enlightened True Nature, I-Am.
   ego-self reading, studying, exploring, investigating, learning about enlightened True Nature, I-Am.
   i-am is i-was of the past. *May*, might, could become enlightened True Nature, I-Am of the future.
3. ego-self awakened to momentary illuminating partial glimpsing enlightened True Nature, I-Am.
   ego-self experiencing initial kenshos of 'seeing into' enlightened True Nature, I-Am.
   i-am is i-was of the past. *Can* become enlightened True Nature, I-Am of the future.
4. ego-self awakened to understanding, realizing whole reality of True Nature, I-Am.
   ego-self 'herding', grasping, joining, interacting with enlightened True Nature, I-Am.
   i-am is i-was of the past. *Will* become and be enlightened True Nature, I-Am of the future.

Transforming — Mid-Enlightenment.
5. ego-self transforming, cultivating, disciplining, training for enlightened True Nature, I-Am.
ego-self 'tending', harmonizing, identifying with enlightened True Nature, I-Am.
i-am is i-am of the present. *Is* becoming enlightened True Nature, I-Am of the future.
6. ego-self transforming, practicing, uniting with, integrating of enlightened True Nature, I-Am.
ego-self living, 'riding home' and identifying as enlightened True Nature, I-Am.
i-am is I-Am of the present. *Is* being enlightened True Nature, I-Am of the present.

Liberating — Post-Enlightenment.
7. ego-self liberated from enlightened True Nature, I-Am as ideas, concepts, goals.
ego-self assimilated with, complete identity *as* enlightened True Nature, I-Am.
I-Am the enlightened True Nature of the present and have 'forgotten' about enlightenment.
8. ego-self liberated by disidentifying with, transcending itself *as* enlightened True Nature, I-Am.
I-Am has disidentified from, transcended, 'emptied' and 'forgotten' ego self.
I-Am enlightened True Nature, I-Am of the present and also have 'forgotten' it.
9. Liberated being, living in Nature as the Source, Origin of everyone, everything.
Nature is the everpresent, all-encompassing, all-pervading originating Source.
Enlightened True Nature, I-Am is returning to and present *as* Nature, Source.

10. Liberated being, living, actualized in the world among fellow human beings.
Enlightened True Nature, I-Am fully integrated into ego-self *as* a 'natural' Way of being.
Enlightened True Nature, I-Am living peacefully, happily, freely, joyfully.
Enlightened True Nature I-Am being pure, empty, clear, open awareness.
Enlightened True Nature, I-Am living wisely, compassionately, skillfully.
Enlightened True Nature, I-Am being loving, kind, patient, fair, generous.
Enlightened True Nature transmitting awakening, enlightenment, liberation.

Also:

Way-Station 7/Forgetting of Enlightenment — the Mysterious, Actual 'Reality' (Non-Reality) of Enlightened True Nature. Svabhavika-kaya — Essence Buddha-Body and the unity of the three Buddha-Bodies/Tri-kaya.

Way-Station 8/Emptiness of True Nature — the Miraculous, Absolute 'Substance' (Non-Substance) of Enlightened True Nature. Dharma-kaya — the Truth/Transcendent Reality Buddha-Body.

Way-Station 9/Returning to the Origin — the Marvelous, Blissful 'Form' (Non-Form) of Enlightened True Nature. Sambhoga-kaya — the Bliss/Ecstatic Enlightened Buddha-Body.

Way-Station 10/Being in the World — the Magnificent, Earthly 'Purpose' (Non-Purpose) of Enlightened True Nature. Nirmana-kaya - the Transformed/Earthly Transmitting Buddha-Body.

Appendix Ten
Some Issues, Way-Markers and Feelings

The main 'issues' throughout the path of enlightenment involve an exclusive and complete identification with the conditioned ego-self and its dualistic ego-mind. However, some of the following general and possible ego-self issues may occur at the various ten Way-Stations along with some associated 'Way-markers' and 'positive' feelings:

1. Way-Station One — SEEKING THE OX
Issues — separation of conditioned unenlightened ego-self and enlightened True Nature.
- suffering and dissatisfaction; questions, problems, issues, difficulties, conflicts.
- entangled in making good and bad judgments about oneself and one's life.
- longing for, desirous of, finding peace, happiness, freedom in oneself and life.
- insecurity about what will make a difference and change things for the better.
- doubts about whether or not anything external will really be helpful or not.
- confusion about what to search for, where to look for it, how to search for it.
- alone, frustrated, confused, bewildered, exhausted, discouraged and at a loss.

Way-Marker — recognition of the need for a more enlightened way of being and living.

+Feelings — hopeful, enthusiastic, eager, anticipating the possible discovery of the Ox.

2. Way-Station Two — TRACKING THE OX

Issues — which traditions and teachings to pursue in learning about enlightenment.
- being confused by contradictions and conflicts in traditions and teachings.
- prematurely attaching to certain ideas, concepts, understandings, paths.
- having difficulty reconciling idea of enlightened True Nature with oneself.
- making right and wrong decisions regarding which path to take, pursue.
- if sampling meditation; being overly concerned with posture, breath, etc.
- trying to control mind and stop thoughts instead of simply observing them.

Way-Marker — committed steps are taken to exploring, investigating and learning.

+Feelings — interested, encouraged, excited about seeing some hoofprints of the Ox.

3. Way-Station Three — GLIMPSING THE OX

Issues — being impatient with, and expecting more than, the minor changes happening.
- in meditating; an influx of a mix of desires, aversions, judgments, self-critiques.
- dealing with deeper ingrained characterological traits and behavioral patterns.
- intellectually mistaking the kensho experience for being enlightened True Nature.
- objectifying, overvaluing and attaching to partial kensho glimpses of True Nature.
- questioning the validity and making true or false evaluations of kensho moments.
- glimpses are only seen because of the cloudy lens and obscurations of ego-self.

Way-Marker — kensho partial glimpse of True Nature. Intuiting Source from phenomena.
+Feelings — awakened, validated, more motivated after seeing the hind-quarters of the Ox.

4. Way-Station Four — CATCHING THE OX
Issues — ego-mind is stubbornly unstable, wandering off, staying with familiar habits.
— ego-inflated attempts to replicate the kensho experience by doing something.
— insecurity about being able to fully grasp, hold onto the whole body of teachings.
— doubts about having the required determination, strength, effort to master them.
— deciding and committing to a suitable path, teacher and group as necessary.
— dealing with gains and losses in fully catching hold of enlightenment teachings.
— not realizing that settling the body and calming the mind are only pre-conditions.

Way-Marker — understanding and holding on with great strength, effort and struggle.
+Feelings — accomplished, successful, supported by catching, keeping hold of the whole Ox.

5. Way-Station Five — TAMING THE OX
Issues — impatiently struggling with bodily discomfort, restlessness, mind-wandering.
— having difficulties trusting that True Nature is in charge of 'running the show'.
— having difficulties dealing with the resurgence of old 'stuff' and habit patterns.
— having difficulties sustaining the discipline required to cultivate True Nature.

- having difficulties subordinating ego-self to and harmonizing with True Nature.
- having difficulties shifting from controlling ego-self to attuning to True Nature.
- not becoming ego-inflated after struggling subsides and some stability occurs.

Way-Marker — ego-self stabilizing, interacting with, cultivating, *becoming* True Nature.

+Feelings — engaged and interacting with, harmoniously exchanging and gentling the Ox.

6. Way-Station Six — RIDING THE OX HOME

Issues — possibly complacently thinking struggling is over and there is no more to do.
- possibly being overly ego-identified with True Nature and the 'attaining' of it.
- possibly mistaking repressed, suppressed thoughts with clear consciousness.
- possibly having difficulties allowing True Nature to be 'greater' than ego-self.
- transforming ignorance, anger, greed into wisdom, compassion, generosity.
- accepting becoming and being more of a true human being living a real life.
- living life as practicing True Nature and not reverting to living the life of ego-self.

Way-Marker — unity of ego-self and True Nature. Practicing and *being* True Nature.

+Feelings — content, happy, trusting being 'ridden' home by the Ox who knows the way.

7. Way-Station Seven — FORGETTING ENLIGHTENMENT

Issues — possibly being proud, inflated over assimilating, 'forgetting' enlightenment.
- possibly ignoring the existence of ego-self and its assertion of sovereignty.
- possibly mistaking ego's 'existence' as Oneness, since True Nature is absent.
- possibly still subtly keeping enlightened True Nature in mind as a concept.
- possibly not realizing that there probably isn't an end to uniting dualities.
- possibly being ego-attached to relative freedom from grasping and clinging.
- possibly not realizing that True Nature is forgotten but ego-self remains.

Way-Marker — internalization of True Nature, which is 'forgotten' as an 'object'.

+Feelings — assimilated, integrated, illuminated, peaceful, wise, compassionate.

8. Way-Station Eight — FORGETTING THE SELF

Issues - possibly not experiencing ego-self completely falling away from awareness.
- possibly mistaking the void of non-being, emptiness as vacuous non-existence.
- possibly being anxious about, and fearful of, 'emptiness' and egolessness.
- possibly resolving difficulty with 'emptiness' by attempts to keep 'filling' it.
- possibly not using a teacher to assist in 'dying' the 'Great Death' of ego-self.
- possibly being unable to completely let go of the subtle I-sense of ego-self.

— possibly ignoring rather than truly disidenifying from, transcending ego-self.

Way-Marker — ego-self is transcended, which is completely 'forgotten' as a 'subject'.

+Feelings — liberated from ego-self, 'empty', open, spacious, celebrating the Great Mystery of emptiness, something from nothing.

9. Way-Station Nine — RETURNING TO THE ORIGIN

Issues — possibly not being True Nature and relapsing into the addiction to 'things'.

— possibly not being True Nature and inflating ego-self as the One Source.
— possibly not being True Nature as pure, empty, clear, open consciousness.
— possibly not being True Nature as abiding in the One Origin of everyone.
— possibly not being centered in/*as* True Nature and purely, simply 'I-Am'.
— possibly mistaking the life cycle of returning to the Source for samsara.
— possibly not trusting completely in unforced activities of wu-wei 'doing'.
— possibly not completely witnessing the coming, changing, going of all.
— possibly not staying awake and failing to appreciate the Great Mystery of sourcing and originating.

Way-Marker — deeply, fully centered in True Nature at the Source of everything.

+Feelings —security, humility, gratitude for being with Nature *as* True Nature, 'I-Am'.

10. Way-Station Ten — BEING IN THE WORLD

Issues —possibly relapsing into focusing on, having judgments about, external 'things'.

- possibly not fully being True Nature and its oneness, emptiness and suchness.
- possibly not fully being True Nature and being unable to be fully Present as such.
- possibly having difficulty being generous or not over-zealous in 'helping' others.
- possibly being unable to experience the natural transmission of enlightenment.
- possibly being unable to deeply and fully accept the enlightened Great Satori.
- possibly being unable to experience that each moment reveals True Nature.
- possibly not seeing True Nature's luminous, bright, radiant light in everyone.
- possibly not staying awake and being swept up in the currents of the world.

Way-Marker — natural being and unforced acting with human beings in the world.

+Feelings — indescribably peaceful, happy, free and joyful. Wise, compassionate, kind, skillful and generous in beneficially assisting fellow human beings by naturally and fully being True/Buddha-Nature and effortlessly and directly transmitting Buddha-Dharma.

I-Am and Just-this Characters

WO/WO
I
SHOU/HAND + KO/LANCE

SHIH/SHI
AM
CHENG/TRUE + JIH/SUN

CHE/ZHE
THIS/NOW
CHO/STOP
+ YEN/WORDS

CHI/ZHI
JUST/ONLY
K'OU/MOUTH
+ PA/EIGHT

T'ZU/CI
THIS/HERE
CHI/STOP
+ PI/TURN ROUND

NOTES

NOTE 1. No family members were neglected, no pets were deprived and no friends were ignored during the writing of this book.

NOTE 2. See the listings in 'By the Author' in the front cover page of this book.

NOTE 3. I assume full responsibility for any inaccuracies regarding definitions of Chinese language characters and uses of English language words included in this book and sincerely apologize for any unintended errors or misinformation.

NOTE 4. Since I am not a learned historian or scholar of Buddhism, this material is only a very general overview. Interested readers are referred to the works of D.T. Suzuki, Heinrich Dumoulin and Ingrid Fischer-Schreiber et al cited in the References section of this book.

NOTE 5. When Buddhism (primarily Mahayana) was brought into China, similarities were found between it and extant Chinese Taoism, which resulted in the syncretic creation and development of Ch'an Buddhism in China and, later, Zen Buddhism in Japan.
  It is relevant to include selected passages from Lao Tzu's *Tao Te Ching* and Chuang Tzu's *The Chuang Tzu* and to consider related characteristics of Tao/Ultimate Reality, Te/Tao's power and individualized virtuosity, Yin-Yang/dual-unity, Wu-Wei/ effortless action, Tzu-Jan/spontaneous nature, Wan-Wu/the 10,000 'things' and Sheng-Jen/sacred and sagely human beings. However, it is beyond the scope of the present book to make precise correlations with enlightened True/Buddha-Nature,

et al. The Chuang Tzu reference contains illustrative stories about related meditative practices of Mind-Fasting, Sitting-Forgetting, Origin-Wandering and Tao-Riding/Residing.

It is disheartening to discover that in the bookstore of one of the leading Buddhist Centers in the United States, there are no books on the significant nature and rich cultural heritage of Chinese Taoism. This may be due to an age-old myth that some Taoists consider the Buddha to be a reincarnation of Lao Tzu, the 'founder' of ancient Chinese Taoism. More modern political conflicts between China and Tibet over the latter's sovereignty may also be a factor. Sad!

NOTE 6. The words 'awakening', 'transforming' and 'liberation' are not used in naming any of the individual Way-Stations of the path of becoming and being enlightened because they continually occur throughout the Wayfaring journeying to it. In fact, the whole Ox-herding sequencing is the progressive awakening, transforming and liberating of ego-self into True Nature that can occur at any time at any of the ten Way-Stations of the path of enlightenment. These awakenings, transformations and liberations are also initially less complete and subsequently more complete.

However, Way-Stations 1/2/3/4 focus more on awakenings, 5/6 focus more on transformation as a central turning point of cultivating and practicing and 7/8/9/10 focus more on liberations.

The ego-self of the unenlightened ox-herder progressively awakens to and transforms into enlightened and liberated True Nature, i.e.,

Way-Station 1 — awakening to suffering, dissatisfaction and the need to search.

Way-station 2 — awakening to tracking, learning about ideas of enlightenment.

Way-Station 3 — awakening to brief kensho glimpsing of True

Nature by ego-self.

Way-Station 4 — awakening to an understanding by ego-self of whole True Nature.

Way-Station 5 — transforming of ego-self cultivating and becoming True Nature.

Way-Station 6 — transforming of ego-self practicing and being True Nature.

Way-Station 7 — liberating of ego-self as True Nature 'forgetting' enlightenment.

Way-Station 8 — liberating of ego-self as True Nature 'forgetting' True Nature.

Way-Station 9 — liberating True Nature to fully return to the Source and Origin.

Way-Station 10 — liberating True Nature to freely actualize, transmit in the world.

The awakening, transforming and liberating process is one from illusion-, ignorance-, attachment-, error- and separation-based ego-self being, thinking, feeling, acting and relating to reality-, wisdom-, compassion-, freedom- and union-based True Nature. Throughout all of the 'stages' of the enlightening process; awakenings, transformations and liberations continually occur in the nature and objects of being, thinking, feeling, acting and relating.

Ego-senses, images, identifications and identity are awakened, transformed and liberated from conceptual, illusional and fictitious to real ones. Mental thoughts, ideas, understandings and judgments are awakened, transformed and liberated from defiled, ignorant and delusional to true ones.
Emotional feelings, needs, desires and wants are awakened, transformed and liberated from afflicted, attached and suffering to relinquished ones. Volitional actions, motives, intentions and purposes are awakened, transformed and liberated from fettered, obstructed and erroneous to correct ones. Relational

contacts, meetings, connections and interactions are awakened, transformed and liberated from separations, divisions and oppositions to unions.

And, ultimately, radical awakenings, transformations and liberations occur in these areas of being, thinking, feeling, acting and relating through the negation of dualistic concepts of them that opens the way into the non-'being', non-'knowing', non-'having', non-'doing' and non-'relating' of a nondual enlightened pure consciousness and True Nature prior to their reaffirmation in the ordinary consciousness and experiences of everyday living.

Throughout all of the Way-Stations of the enlightenment path and process; awakenings, transformations and liberations of and from the dualistic conditioned ego-self's ontological illusion and fiction, its mental ignorance and defilements, its emotional attachments and afflictions, its volitional fetters and errors and its relational separations and oppositions continually occur from partial ones to more complete ones.

Such awakenings, transformations and liberations: 1) are from ego-self to True/Buddha-Nature, 2) are ongoing, 3) are by no means the full awakening, transformation and liberation of a completely enlightened buddha and 4) are continually developed through extended cultivating and practicing.

Note 7. The two sets of Ox-Herding pictures by Shubun (top) and Tokuriki (bottom) and comments used in this book appear uncopyrighted in numerous You Tube videos and are available through Google searches and websites, e.g, Wikimedia-https:// en.wikipedia.org/ wiki/ten_bulls. My understanding is that they are in the public domain and do not require the permission of authors (who are deceased) or publishers (see Met's Open Access Policy-https://metmodeum.org>library>ten oxherding pictures).

NOTE 8. Because of its connotations of domination and subjugation rather than cooperating and harmonizing; the Chinese character Fu/'serve', 'submit', 'assent', 'yield to', 'adapt to', 'comply with' was not used here for Way-Station Five/Taming the Ox. It was, however, tempting; given homonyms such as 'Buddha', 'sitting cross-legged as a Buddhist devotee', 'a sage', 'a teacher', 'worship ancestors', 'bow down', 'humble', 'agree with', 'commit to', 'begin', 'apply', 'trust', 'follow', 'reach', 'return', 'cherish', 'natural', 'happiness', 'support', 'assist' and 'aid'.

NOTE 9. The Sacred Empty Circle/Enso of Oneness of Way-Station Eight/Transcending the Self, is typically made with a single calligraphic stroke. And; in addition to symbolizing unity, emptiness and totality, it often is an incomplete circle showing as well, openness and the beauty of the 'perfection' of imperfection.

NOTE 10. The figure in Way-Station Ten/Being in the World reportedly is Pu-tai/Bu-dai/Ch'i-tz'u/hempen sack, a wandering Chinese monk said to have lived in the 10th Century CE. He is considered as both depicting Hotei, the laughing Buddha, and being a usually unrecognized incarnation of Maitreya, the future Buddha.

Stories of Pu-tai portray him as embodying and personifying the Ch'an Buddhist ideal of enjoying simplicity and paradox and as a 'presence' radiating an aura of the magical and miraculous. He is either a portly alms-begging monk humbly needing to have fellow human beings fill his empty sack or a generous enlightened buddha, happily handing out the abundance inside his sack to them. He enters the town, city or world casually with arms loosely hanging down or with extended, bliss-bestowing and helping hands.

A Koan

This tale illustrates the integral connection between gradual and sudden paths of enlightenment.

Man-hsin/full to the brim-mind was a Zen student who had diligently studied and intellectually understood most all of the principal ideas of Zen Buddhism and had sat Zazen for a considerable length of time. In private meetings with his Zen teacher, Wu-hsin/No-Mind, Man-hsin was continually given the Koan 'What is enlightenment?

Man-hsin's answers were always dismissed by a silent side-to-side head-shaking Wu-hsin and he inevitably came away from their meetings with the discouraging impression that he had not progressed very far on the path toward becoming and being enlightened.

Man-hsin was intending to end practicing and arranged for a final private meeting with Wu-hsin.

Man-hsin. "Master, I am not progressing and have decided to leave. In spite of extensive study and intensive practice, I am still confused by so many different descriptions of enlightenment. I still have no idea of what enlightenment is much less having had any experience of it. Please, before I leave, tell me what is enlightenment?"

Wu-hsin. With no gap after the last letter 't' of the word 'enlightenment', Wu-hsin spontaneously leans forward directly into Man-hsin's sad puzzled face and quickly and abruptly shouts 'Boo!' Immediately, Man-hsin falls backward and is shocked into a sudden surprising realization of enlightenment.

["Boo" was not the Halloween scare but "Bu", the Chinese Ch'an/Zen word for "No, not" and, as a linguistic primitive, the Chinese character is depicting a bird flying straight up to the skies].

不 帀

True Nature Characters

CHEN – *True*, real, genuine
 – Natural state
 – Perfect simplicity
 – Towering spiritual nature
 (by Taoists and Buddhists)
 Mu/Eye + Chih/strength

性

HSING – *Nature*
 – Inborn character
 – Natural disposition
 – Spirit, a point of light
 – Heart-mind at birth
 Hsin/Heart + Sheng/birth

SHIH – Real, *true*, actual
 – Authentic, sincere
 – Solid, substantial
 – Fruitful, stored wealth
 Chen/True + Kuan/connect +
 Pei/Cowrie shells (money) +
 Mien/Roof, shelter

TZU JAN – *Nature*
 – Naturalness
 – Spontaneity
 – Freedom
 Tzu/Self, I, starting point +
 Jan/Yes, really, so, like this +
 Huo/Fire, to light

Ego-Self and True Nature

ego-self

Relative
Non-ultimate
Finite
Temporal
Mortal
Limited
Existential
Non-intimate
Multiple
Diverse
Variable
Conditioned
Determined
Derived
Acquired
Dualistic
Conceptual
Illusional
Construed
Fabricated
Devised
Artificial
Fictitious
Inauthentic
Counterfeit
i-was, will be
Abstract, indirect
mediated, localized
appearance.

ego-self
The natural personal "I"

Tzu/Zi   Wo/Wo

True Nature
The innate birth heart

Chen/Zhen   Hsing/Xing

True Nature

Absolute
Ultimate
Infinite
Eternal
Immortal
Unlimited
Essential
Intimate
Unitary
Integral
Constant
Unconditioned
Undetermined
Inborn
Inherent
Non-dual
Non-conceptual
Real
Ineffable
Natural
Undevised
Uncontrived
Actual
Authentic
Genuine
I-Am, here-now
Concrete, direct,
immediate, ubiquito
Presence

Postscript

True Nature is enlightened Mind and not the ego-self mind.
True Nature is enlightened Mind and abides not in any form.
True Nature is not the subject of any objectified phenomena.
All so-called reality occurs within ego-mind as concepts only.

True Nature is inconceivable, indescribable and unspeakable.
True Nature clings to no idea of ego, self, being, personality.
True Nature is no ego-self not attaining no things in no way.
True Nature is pure, empty, open and clear consciousness.

For True Nature, things are; but are names devoid of essence.
For True Nature, nothing is gained or lost and lost or found.
For True Nature, ego is illusional, things are impermanent.
For True Nature as being an ego-self, suffering is inevitable.

True Nature is not awakened, illuminated or enlightened.
Ego-self can become awakened, illuminated, enlightened.
True Nature is not attained, realized, transformed, liberated.
Ego-self can be deconditioned, transformed and liberated.

True Nature is one, absolute, ultimate, essential and inborn.
Ego-self is multiple, relative, finite, existential and derived.
True Nature is unconditioned, unlimited, infinite, eternal.
Ego-self is conditioned, limited, finite, temporal, mortal.

True Nature is the same one inborn nature common to all.
Ego-self can become and be True Nature through cultivating.
True Nature is beyond birth, living, dying and being reborn.
Ego-self can become and be True Nature through practicing.

True Nature is radiantly present in enlightened human beings.
True Nature is lived in the world as enlightened human being.
True Nature is naturally transmitted to fellow human beings.
True Nature is inwardly present in each/every human being.

True Nature is the end of human longing, seeking and striving.
True Nature is the end of human stressing, struggling, suffering.
True Nature is the end of human ignorance, delusions, errors.
True Nature is the ending of human desiring and attachments.

Being True Nature is being an authentically real human being.
Living True Nature is living a genuinely real and true human life.
Being and living True Nature is a very splendid precious treasure.
True Nature is enlightened peace, happiness, freedom and joy.

Zen training, cultivating and practicing are ongoing and are not necessarily a simple, quick and easy path and, rather, for the most part and in many ways, require a strong commitment and involve rigorous discipline; the lived fruits of which are:
Unwavering character, integrity and courage.
Unassailable power, strength and fortitude.
Unlimited energy, stamina and generosity.
Unperturbed centeredness, balance and calm.
Undeviated faith, dedication and diligence.
Unexcelled insight, wisdom and judgment.
Unparalleled empathy, compassion and kindness.
Unsurpassed expertise, skills and abilities.

May you realize, be, live, enjoy and share awakened, enlightened and liberated peace, happiness, freedom and joyfulness.

REFERENCES

Aitken, Robert. *Taking the Path of Zen.* New York: North Point Press. 1982.

Batchelor, Justine. *The Ten Oxherding Pictures.* Tricycle: The Buddhist Review. New York: Tricycle Foundation. Spring 2000.

Cage, John. *Zen Ox-Herding Pictures.* New York: George Braziller Publishers, Inc.. 2009.

Doumalin, Heinrich. *Zen Buddhism: A History. Vol.1: India and China.* James W. Heisig & Paul Knitter (Tr.). Bloomington, Indiana: World Wisdom, Inc.. 2005. Pgs. 279-281 and 292-293.

Doumalin, Heinrich. *Zen Buddhism: A History. Vol.2: Japan.* James W. Heisig & Paul Knitter (Tr.). Bloomington, Indiana: World Wisdom, Inc.. 2005.

Fenn, C.H. *The Five Thousand Dictionary: Chinese-English.* Cambridge, Massachusetts: Harvard University Press. 1976.

Fischer-Schreiber, Ingrid; Ehrhard, Franz-Carl and Diener, Michael S.. *The Shambhala Dictionary of Buddhism and Zen.* Michael H. Kohn (Tr.). Boston: Shambhala Publications, Inc. 1991.

Frantz, Dean L. *The Ten Oxherding Pictures: A Guide to Enlightenment.* Kearney, NE 68847: Morris Publishing. 2003.

Kapleau, Philip. *The Three Pillars of Zen: Teaching, Practice and Enlightenment.* New York: Anchor Books. 2000. Pgs. 332-345.

Kopp, Zensho W.. *The Ten Ox-Herding Pictures: The Path to Enlightenment.* John Kitching (Tr.). Germany: Synergia. 2018.

Li Dong. Concise *Chinese Dictionary: Chinese-English/English-Chinese.* Rutland, Vermont: Tuttle Publishing. 2015.

Loori, John Daido. *Riding the Ox Home: Stages on the Path of*

Enlightenment. Boulder, Colorado: Shambhala Publications. Inc.. 2002.

Mathews, R.H.. *Mathews' Chinese-English Dictionary*. Cambridge, Massachusetts: Harvard University Press. 1943.

McNaughton, William and Lee Ying. *Reading and Writing Chinese Characters: Traditional Character Edition*. Rutland, Vermont: Tuttle Publishing. 1999.

Morse, Mark. *The 10 Oxherding Pictures*. Commentary by Josh Bartok and Chogyam Trungpa, Rimpoche. Lion's Roar. Halifax, Nova Scotia Canada: Lion's Roar Foundation. 2015.

Mumon, Yamada. *Lectures on the Ten Oxherding Pictures*. Sogen Hori (Tr.) Honolulu: University of Hawaii Press. 2004.

Myokyo-Ni (Irmgard Schloeg). *Gentling the Bull: The Ten Bull Pictures, A Spiritual Journey*. Rutland, Vermont: Charles E. Tuttle, Co., Inc.. 1988.

Quanyu Huang, Tong Chen and Kuangyan Huang. *McGraw Hill's Chinese Dictionary and Guide to 20,000 Essential Words*. New York: McGraw-Hill. 2010.

Red Pine. *P'u Ming's Oxherding Pictures & Verses*. New York: Empty Bowl. 2015.

Reps, Paul and Nyogen Senzaki. *Zen Flesh, Zen Bones: A Collection of Zen and Pre-Zen Writings*. Rutland, Vermont: Tuttle Publishing Inc.. 1985. Pgs. 177-201.

Seng-Ts'an/Sosan. *Hsin Hsin Ming: Faith in the Heart-Mind Verses*. Richard B. Clarke (Tr.). Buffalo, New York: White Pine Press. 1984.

Suzuki, Daisetz Teitaro. *Manual of Zen Buddhism*. New York: Grove Press. 1960. VIII. The Ten Oxherding Pictures. Pgs. 127-144.

Suzuki, Daisetz Teitaro. *An Introduction to Zen Buddhism*. New York: Grove Press. 1964.

Suzuki, Daisetz Teitaro. *Zen Buddhism: Selected Writings of D.T. Suzuki*. William Barrett (Ed.). New York: Image Books. Three Leaves Press. 1996.

Suzuki, Daisetz Teitaro. *Essays in Zen Buddhism.* London: Souvenir Press Ltd.. 2010. The Ten Stages of Spiritual Cow-Herding. Pgs. 371-378.

Suzuki Roshi, Shunryu. *Zen Mind, Beginner's Mind.* Trudy Dixon (Ed.). Boulder, Colorado: Shambhala Publications, Inc.. 2020.

Tinh, Thich Phuoc. *The Ten Oxherding Paintings: Zen Talks by Thich Phuoc Tinh.* Karen Hilsberg (Ed.). Sister Dang Nghiem (Tr.). Jasmine Roots Press. 2011.

Van Den Dungen, Wim. *Ten Ox-Herding Images: Training the Mind for Enlightenment.* Brasschat, Belgium: Taurus Press. 2021.

Wada, Stephanie. *The Oxherder: A Zen Parable Illustrated.* New York: George Braziller,Publishers, Inc.. 2002.

Watson, Burton (Tr.). *The Chuang Tzu.* New York: Columbia University Press. 1968.

Watts, Alan. *The Spirit of Zen: A Way of Life, Work and Art in the Far East.* New York: Grove Press. 1958.

Watts, Alan. *The Way of Zen.* New York: Vintage Books. 2019.

Webster's New Collegiate Dictionary. Springfield, Massachusetts: G. & C. Merriam Company. 1979.

Wieger, L. *Chinese Characters: Their Origin, Etymology, History, Classification and Signification.* L. Davrout (Tr.). New York: Dover Publications, Inc.. 1965.

Wilder, G.D. and Ingram, J.H.. *Analysis of Chinese Characters.* New York: Dover Publications, Inc.. 1974.

Wood, Ernest. *Zen Dictionary.* Rutland, Vermont: Charles E. Tuttle Company. 1972.

Zenkei Shibayama. *A Flower Does Not Talk: Zen Essays.* Sumiko Kudo (Tr.). Rutland, Vermont: Charles E. Tuttle Company. 1997. Pgs. 152-203.

In Conscious Awareness and Experience

There are the abstracting, separating, dividing, objectifying, differentiating, reflecting, examining, analyzing, comparing, contrasting, opposing, conflicting and judging dualistic concepts of the ego-self.

There are the fabricated, artificial, fictitious, mistaken, obscuring, defiled, ignoring, illusional, deluded, desiring, attached, afflicted, fettered, erroneous and obstructing dualistic concepts of the ego-self.

There are the concretizing, joining, uniting, subjectifying, integrating, responding, witnessing, synthesizing, correlating, corresponding, complementing, harmonizing and accepting dualistic concepts of the ego-self.

There are the natural, genuine, real, true, unobscuring, undefiled, attending, actual, non-desiring, non-attached, unaffected, unfettered, unerroneous and unobstructing dualistic concepts of the ego-self.

And then:
There is pure and empty, clear and open and non-dualistic consciousness and True Nature that are none of these and other dualistic concepts of the ego-self and are the ground and source of all of them.

About the Author

Ray received B.A. (Cornell University-1958), M.S. (Case Western Reserve University-1959) and Ph.D. (California Institute of Integral Studies-1986) degrees, respectively, in Psychology, Clinical Psychology and Counseling Psychology. He received inpatient Clinical Psychology training at the Cleveland State Hospital and outpatient Clinical Psychology training at the Cleveland Psychiatric Institute and Hospital in the late 1950's.

During the 1960's, Ray was a staff member of the Child Psychiatry and Clinical Psychology Services of Letterman General Hospital, the Psychiatry and Clinical Psychology Department of the Palo Alto Medical Clinic, the Palo Alto Mental Research Institute and the Student Health Service of Stanford University.

During the late 1960's and the early 1970's, Ray was an instructor at the Mid-Peninsula Free University and San Andreas Health Council, was president and co-director of the Society for Phenomenology and Existential Psychotherapy and was a presenting member of the American Ontoanalytic Association at national and international conferences.

In the 1970's and beyond, Ray was an adjunct faculty member, instructor, assistant and associate professor in humanistic, integral and transpersonal psychology graduate school programs at the Institute for Human Potential Psychology (1972-1973), the California Institute of Asian/Integral Studies/CIIS (1972-1990), the Institute of Transpersonal Psychology (1977-1979) and John F. Kennedy University (1978-1992).

Ray was a founding member of Psychological Service Associates, a small private practice psychotherapy group, (1970-1972) and conducted an MFCC/MFT individual licensed private counseling practice for adults, adolescents, children, couples and families (1972-2016).

Ray was Clinical Director of the CIIS Integral Counseling Center (1974-1990), Clinical Co-Director of the JFKU Transpersonal Counseling Center (1986-1987) and Clinical Director of San Leandro Community Counseling (1990-1992) and Marin Treatment Center (1992-2016).

Throughout the 1970's, Ray educated, trained, supervised and mentored counseling trainees, psychology interns and licensed psychologists and counselors in a dozen SF Bay Area inpatient and outpatient treatment facilities and counseling centers.

Throughout the 1970's, Ray also participated in programs and studied and practiced with numerous teachers in the spiritual traditions of Hinduism; Yoga; Tantra; Kashmir Shaivism; Sufism; Theravada, Mahayana, Vajrayana, Ekayana, Ch'an and Zen Buddhism and Chinese Taoism. The latter two most notably involved meetings with Alan Watts and T'ai-Chi practice with Al Chung-liang Huang and Gia-fu Feng in Taoism, meetings with Bishop Nippo Syaku in Buddhism and meditation with Shunryu Suzuki Roshi in Zen.

Throughout the 1980's, Ray participated and assisted in shamanic group circles utilizing various plant medicines and psychotropic substances for consciousness-opening and expanding, self-healing and transforming, soul-journeying and liberating and spiritual awakening and illumination.

Ray has authored four books integrating the wisdom of the Chinese texts of Lao Tzu, Chuang Tzu and Lieh Tzu with psychotherapeutic practice, soul-journeying and spiritual development (2016-2018).

Ray retired from clinical directorships; counseling trainee and psychology intern educating, training, supervising and mentoring and from private counseling practice in 2016. Since then, Ray has been enjoying being with family; being with Nature at the ocean and rivers and in forests and woods; attending to full moons, solstices and equinoxes; giving public presentations at the Cultural Integration Fellowship in San Francisco and continuing to write 'Expressions' (which from 1960 on, now number over two-thousand!).

In addition, Ray is gratefully appreciating living the human realities, deriving the healing benefits, experiencing the transformative changes and benefiting from the illuminating insights of True Nature's solitude, silence, simplicity, sufficiency and serenity; most currently in the Santa Cruz area of Scotts Valley, California.

SHHH!

Enlightenment may just be:
Liberation from the illusion of ego-self
and its desires, attachments and habits.
Awakening to the reality of True Nature
and its consciousness and spaciousness.
Transformation of the plump caterpillar
of ego-self into the beautiful butterfly
of True Nature and its freedom, peace
and happiness and its everyday grateful
acceptance of the everydayness, and its
extraordinary forgiving appreciation
of the ordinariness, of our human being.

Encore*

The Ten Zen Oxen pictures and text illustrate a Way-showing path of enlightenment, from our being completely identified with our ego-self to becoming and being our identity as our one, original, absolute, ultimate, essential and inborn True Nature. If prior to being enlightened; the 'world' and its diverse phenomena are subjectively seen, experienced and judged to be questionable, problematic, unsettled and conflicted; after being enlightened, they are simply beheld, witnessed and experienced objectively, realistically and neutrally just as they are.

Dualities

A part of enlightenment is: 1) regarding the dualities of experience not as mutually exclusive, either-or disconnected and independent oppositions but as mutually inclusive, interconnected and interdependent both-and complements; 2) integrating this-that dualities as equal dual-unities, e.g., True Nature-ego self, Spirit-body, light-darkness, reality-illusion, emptiness-suchness, truth-delusion, non attachment-attachment, self-other, joy-suffering, life-death, etc. and 3) considering the 'Middle Way' of both components of dual-unities as being '*sono mama*'; meaning in the Japanese language; 'the natural state of things before being experienced', 'this', 'just as it is' and 'leave it as it is'.

Things

A part of enlightenment is: 1) regarding the many things, entities, objects, beings, thoughts, feelings, activities, affairs, events and phenomena of experience as having no essential inherent nature and as being impermanent and transitory and 2) refraining from desiring, seeking, acquiring, collecting, possessing, accumulating them; including not only material things, but also fellow human beings, relationships and even illuminated awakening and enlightenment and True Nature as some 'things' to have.

Ego-Self

A part of enlightenment is: 1) relinquishing the fictitious and insubstantial notion, idea, image, illusion, delusion, concept, dream, trance and hallucination of being an artificial and socially conditioned and determined autonomous ego-self; 2) experiencing ego-self and pure consciousness as fundamentally empty, clear and open and 3) opening to the reality of naturally becoming and being one, absolute, ultimate, essential and inborn True Nature that is universal, ubiquitous, infinite, eternal and immortal.

Others

A part of enlightenment is: 1) considering, interrelating with and experiencing fellow human beings as being True Nature and not only ego-selves; 2) not objectifying, evaluating, judging and blaming fellow, human being as 'others'; 3) relating intimately with fellow human beings with respect, interest, acceptance, attention, caring, understanding, empathy, compassion, kindness, generosity and forgiveness and; 4) committing to supporting, assisting fellow human beings on their unique path of being healthy and enlightened.

Time

A part of enlightenment is: 1) living the present moment of here-now experience rather than past memories and future hopes; 2) not experiencing time as flowing from past to present to future and simply being in the single present moment; 3) considering the present here-now moment temporally without duration and spatially without extension; 4) realizing that there is only being 'I-Am' in the 'Just-This' of the present here-now moment and 5) then even considering that 'there is no time like the present'.

Life

A part of enlightenment is: 1) living as being True Nature with sincere intention, meaningful purpose, conscious focus and dedicated commitment; 2) being on a spiritual path; engaging in concentrative, contemplative and absorbing meditative practices with a spiritual teacher; being a member of a supportive spiritual community and participating in activities that are promoting spiritual development through awakening the slumbering, dreaming, hypnotized and entranced ego-self into enlightened True Nature.

Consciousness

A part of enlightenment is: 1) being awake and identified as pure, clear, empty and open consciousness; 2) being fully receptive to, accurately reflective of and appropriately responsive to whatever originates from or appears in consciousness; 3) being awake to, discerning of and insightful about the various phenomena that are occurring in conscious awareness and 4) realizing that the freedom, peacefulness and happiness of enlightened True Nature is rooted in the clarity of consciousness.

Relatedness

A part of enlightenment is: 1) realizing that the 'other-making' of the ego-self is what divides, separates and alienates us from; and opposes us to and conflicts us with; fellow human beings, the environment, Nature, other species, the planet and the multiverse; 2) realizing that the interconnectedness of everyone and everything means that each individual simultaneously reflects every other and thus the whole and 3) realizing that taking care with oneself is caring for the totality of humanity and life.

A WAY-SHOWING PATH OF ENLIGHTENMENT

The Path

A part of enlightenment is: 1) realizing that the path of becoming and being an awake and enlightened human being is first realizing 'bodhicitta'/enlightenment-mind; the aspiration, intention and commitment to begin engaging in the practice and process leading to awakening/'bodhi' through making and keeping the bodhisattva vows to use wisdom, compassion and skillful means to overcome desires, to live the Buddha-Dharma and the Buddha-Way and to liberate all sentient beings.

Practice

A part of enlightenment is: 1) realizing that while enlightenment is being True Nature, it is not a final perfected state of being or consciousness that does not change; 2) experiencing that there is no end to the path, process and practice of enlightenment and that they exist in the midst of the varied positive and negative vicissitudes of everyday living and are influenced by them and 3) experiencing that the ordinary experiences of everyday living become the enlightening practice of enlightenment.

Guidelines

A part of enlightenment is: 1) following some guidelines along the path to/of becoming and being an enlightened human being that involve an openness to accepting and complying, cooperating and collaborating with the way things, affairs, events and relationships are being and unfolding and 2) adopting a position in relationship with the way things are going as one of letting-be, letting-go, being-with and going-with them rather than interfering with, attaching to or opposing and conflicting with them.

Signs

And also, some signs of a more enlightened way of being are; 1) feeling more embodied, freer, more peaceful and happier; 2) relating to fellow human beings more authentically, intimately, empathically, compassionately and harmoniously; with greater acceptance, gratitude, kindness, generosity and forgiveness and with less objectifying and 'other-making' judgments and 3) serving fellow human beings in meaningful ways that inspire, encourage, support, assist and facilitate physical, mental, emotional, social and spiritual well-being.

True Nature

When True Nature and its pure, clear, empty, open and object-contentlessness are brought to situations, conditions and relationships; enlightened illumination, awakening, realization, transformation and liberation naturally, and often spontaneously, occur. The realization: 1) that ego-self is nothing more than an aggregate of bodily form, sensations, perceptions, concepts and consciousness; 2) that everything and everyone in the universe of reality and experience are reflectively interconnected and 3) that the impermanent, attached and suffering ego-mind is eclipsed and displaced by the oneness, emptiness and allness and suchness of the One-Mind, No-Mind and All-Mind of True Nature; opens the Way to being the reality, ubiquity, truth, power and beauty of True Nature and the 'Just-This' 'Here-Now' Presence of 'I-Am'.

Awakening, Transforming, Liberating, Enlightenment, Light, Freedom, Peace and Happiness Characters.

Before awakening, transforming and liberating;
our ego-self is bound, conflicted and suffering
and has concepts of, and ideas about, True Nature.
After awakening, transforming and liberating;
True Nature is present, free, peaceful and happy.

Enlightenment
The awakening of the illusional and dualistic
ego-self to the non-dual Reality of True Nature.
The transformation of the conditioned ego-self
into pristine and unconditioned True Nature.
The liberation of the covetous attached ego-self
to the emptiness and openness of True Nature.

As enlightened human beings we need to be
the most we can be and to do the best we can do
to support and assist each other in realizing
being well, free, peaceful and happy.

AWAKENING

HSING/XING – WAKE UP/TO *AWAKEN*/BE AWAKE.
YU/YOU – LIQUOR JAR + HSING/XING - STARS, SPARKS,
POINTS OF LIGHT (JIH/RI - SUN + SHENG/SHENG -
BIRTH/BEGET/PRODUCE/BEAR/LIVE/GROW).
OUR MATERIAL BEING RISING TO THE HEAVENS.

WU/WU – WAKE UP/*AWAKEN*/REALIZE/DISCERN.
HSIN/XIN – HEART/MIND/CORE + WU/WU – I/ME/
MINE (WU/WU – FIVE + K'OU/KOU - MOUTH/
OPENING/HOLE/APERTURE/ENTRANCE/SPEECH).
OUR HEARTS CREATE REALITY BY WORD OF MOUTH.

A WAY-SHOWING PATH OF ENLIGHTENMENT

TRANSFORMING

HUA/HUA – *TRANSFORM*/CHANGE/CONVERT/
TURN INTO/SMELT/DISSLOVE/ALCHEMICAL.
JEN/REN – HUMAN BEING + PI/BI - LADLE/
HUMAN BEING TURNED UPSIDE DOWN.
A RADICAL TURNING AROUND OF OUR BEING.

PIEN/BIAN – *TRANSFORM*/CHANGE INTO/BECOME/
METAMORPHOSE. SSU/SI – FINE SILK THREADS +
P'U/PU – KNOCK/RAP/TAP/TO STRIKE LIGHTLY +
YEN/YAN – WORDS/TO SPEAK/TALK/TO SAY/TELL.
OUR INTERWEAVING AND TELLING OF EXPERIENCE.

LIBERATING

CHIEH/JIE – LOOSEN/UNDO/UNTIE/*FREE UP*/
RELIEVE/EXPLAIN/*PUT OUT TO PASTURE*.
(NIU/NIU - OX + CHUEH/CHIAO/JIAO – HORN
+ TAO/DAO – KNIFE/SLENDER INSTRUMENT USED
TO MAKE HOLES IN CLOTH AND TO UNTIE KNOTS).
FREEING THE OX OF ENLIGHTENED TRUE NATURE.

SHIH/SHI – LOOSEN UP/LET GO/*SET FREE*/RELEASE/
CEASE/LET GO OF CONFINEMENT/EXPLAIN/CLEAR UP
BY EXAMINATION/*SAKYAMUNI*/BUDDHISM. (PIEN/
BIAN – SORT OUT/DISTINGUISH/DIFFERENTIATE + TSAI/
ZAI – GOVERN/PRESIDE/MINISTER + MU/MU – EYE).
FREEING TRUE NATURE FROM EGO-SELF LIMITATIONS.

A WAY-SHOWING PATH OF ENLIGHTENMENT

ENLIGHTENMENT

TI/DI – *ENLIGHTEN*/LEAD FORWARD/RIGHT PATH/
GUIDE/INSTRUCT/FOLLOW FOOTSTEPS. CH'O/
CHUO – RUN FAST AND STOP/HALT + YU/YOU –
GO BY WAY OF /GO FROM/ORIGIN/REST WITH.
THE RIGHT PATH TO ENLIGHTENED TRUE NATURE.

CHAO/ZHAO – *ILLUMINATE*/SHINE FORTH/LIGHT UP/
LUMINOUS/BRIGHT/THE REFLECTION OF LIGHT. CHAO/
ZHAO – SHINE + JIH/RI - THE SUN + HUO/HUO –
FIRE + CHAO/ZHAO – CALL/SUMMON/AS.
WE ARE CALLED BY THE LIGHT OF THE SUN AND FIRE.

LIGHT

MING/MING – *LIGHT*/BRIGHT/CLEAR/EXPLAIN/UNDERSTAND.
JIH/RI – THE SUN + YUEH/YUE – THE MOON.
*OUR ENLIGHTENED TRUE NATURE
RADIANTLY AND CLEARLY SHINING FORTH.*

FREEDOM

MIEN/MIAN – *FREEDOM*, EVADE, SPARE, FORGIVE. JEN/REN – HUMAN LEGS + LI/LI - STRENGTH + SHOU/SHOU – *SUFFER*, ENDURE. *OUR TRUE NATURE IS GROUNDED, ENDURING AND FORGIVING OF OUR HUMAN SUFFERING.*

A WAY-SHOWING PATH OF ENLIGHTENMENT

PEACE

Ning/Ning – *peace*, repose. Mien/Mian – shelter + Hsin/Xin – heart + Min/Min – vessel + Ting/Ding – a nail /to *sustain*. *Our True Nature is a grounding and sustaining of our hearts and minds.*

HAPPINESS

Hsing/Xing – *happiness*/joyfulness/lifting up spirits. Chiu/Jiu – a mortar + Chu/Ju – two raised/open/giving hands + T'ung/Tong – together/with/like. *As True Nature, we are standing upon earth and holding the chalice of togetherness in our outstretched hands at the center of our human hearts.*

Before You Leave To Go Home Remember:

Desire only Good beyond good-bad.
Know only True beyond true-false.
Attach to only This beyond having-losing.
Enact only Right beyond right-wrong.
Experience only Real beyond real-unreal.
Be only Higher Self beyond self-ego.

Be Darkness beyond dark-light.
Be Silence beyond silence-sound.
Be Stillness beyond stasis-motion.
Be Emptiness beyond empty-full.
Be Oneness beyond one-many.
Be No-thingness beyond none-all.

Be Sacred beyond sacred-profane.
Be Blessed beyond blessed-unfortunate.
Be Precious beyond precious-worthless.
Be Natural beyond natural-artificial.
Be Ordinary beyond ordinary-unusual.
Be Everyday beyond everyday-atypical.
Be Everybody beyond somebody-nobody.

Be Solid beyond solidity-fragility.
Be Stable beyond stability-instability.
Be Simple beyond simplicity-complexity.
Be Sufficient beyond wealth-poverty.
Be Secure beyond security-insecurity.
Be Serene beyond calmness-agitation.

Be Interested beyond interest-disinterest.
Be Approachable beyond warmth-coldness.
Be Available beyond presence-absence.
Be Accessible beyond openness-closedness.
Be Engaged beyond completely-partially.
Be Involved beyond intimately-superficially.

Be Wise beyond wisdom-delusion.
Be Kind beyond kindness-hatred.
Be Balanced beyond harmony-chaos.
Be Accepting beyond accepting-controlling.
Be Allowing beyond permitting-forcing.
Be Compassionate beyond empathy-antipathy.
Be Creating beyond creating-destroying.

Be Grateful beyond gratitude-judgment.
Be Humble beyond humility-arrogance.
Be Authentic beyond authenticity-guile.
Be Sincere beyond sincerity-hypocrisy.
Be Generous beyond generosity-greed.
Be Forgiving beyond forgiveness-blame.

Be Ground beyond river and mountain.
Be Center beyond center-periphery.
Be Horizon beyond earth-heaven.
Be Spaciousness beyond space-infinity.
Be Timeliness beyond time-eternity.
Be Multiverse beyond universe-planet.

Be Beginning beyond beginning-ending.
Be Birthing beyond birthing-dying.
Be United beyond union-separation.
Be Whole beyond wholeness-partiality.
Be Healthy beyond health-illness.
Be Energy beyond vibrancy-inertness.
Be Vitality beyond aliveness-deadness.

A WAY-SHOWING PATH OF ENLIGHTENMENT

Be Consciousness beyond conscious-unconscious.
Be Awakening beyond awakeness-sleepiness.
Be Illumination beyond brilliant and cloudy.
Be Realization beyond accepting-ignoring.
Be Transformation beyond change-constancy.
Be Enlightenment beyond living-dying.

Be Divine beyond divine-human.
Be Human beyond human-animal.
Be Spirit beyond spirit-body.
Be Soul beyond psyche-body.
Be Heart beyond heart and head.
Be True Nature beyond true nature-ego self.

Be Here-Now Presence beyond past-future.
Be Just All This beyond this-that.
Be Free beyond freedom-limitation.
Be Happy beyond happiness-sadness
Be Peaceful beyond peace-conflict.
Be Joyful beyond joy-suffering.
Be Present beyond presence-absence.

The Present Moment

Enlightenment is a quintessential,
exquisite and splendid here-now
moment of awakening to and
awareness of purely and simply
and sheerly and utterly being
True Nature, 'I-Am' and 'Just This'.

Enlightened True Nature is.
Enlightened True Nature is not.
Enlightened True Nature both is and is not.
Enlightened True Nature neither is and is not.

*Like Life itself, it is worth staying
awake for the encore until the very end.*

*

'Encore' is etymologically derived from the French meaning 'still' and 'again'. I prefer the perhaps invented derivation and meaning from the Latin 'en' - 'cor'/ 'into and within heart'. The embodied authoring brings a heart-felt peacefulness beyond both conflict and peace. The ensouled sharing is a heart-warming happiness beyond both sadness and happiness. The inspirited encoring is a heart-some freedom beyond both limitation and freedom. The pure and simple, sheer and utter Presence of True Nature, 'I-Am' and 'Just-This'.

The encore is over. The past is forgotten.
The bow is taken. Gratitude is expressed.
The applause is done. Appreciation is given.
The curtain is closed. The present is all that is.
The audience goes home. Relationships end.
The doors are shut. Life is complete.
The lights go out. The future is open. . . . . . .